THE WAY WE DO SCHOOL

THE WAY WE DO SCHOOL

The Making of Oakland's Full-Service Community School District

MILBREY MCLAUGHLIN
KENDRA FEHRER
JACOB LEOS-URBEL

Harvard Education Press
Cambridge, Massachusetts

Paperback ISBN 978-1-68253-484-7
Library Edition ISBN 978-1-68253-485-4

Library of Congress Cataloging-in-Publication Data is on file.

Published by Harvard Education Press,
an imprint of the Harvard Education Publishing Group

Harvard Education Press
8 Story Street
Cambridge, MA 02138

Cover Design: Ciano Design
Cover Image: Ciano Design

The typefaces used in this book are ITC Legacy Serif, ITC Legacy Sans, and Glober.

CONTENTS

PROLOGUE

Why This Book Now?

Districts across the country struggle with persistent student achievement gaps by race, income, and residence. Increasingly, educators and researchers recognize that factors outside the classroom—largely associated with social and economic disparities—account for much of the variation in learning and school outcomes. Many agree that students' successful learning and ability to achieve full and productive lives depend on a range of resources and opportunities in addition to quality classroom instruction: students can't learn if their basic needs are unmet. This perspective that schools need to serve the whole child must also acknowledge that they cannot do it alone. Schools need partners in providing comprehensive supports for students' personal and academic development.

This book is about the nearly decade-long effort by the community of Oakland, California, to reorganize its schools and school district, collaborate with community leaders, national philanthropists, and others to serve its children in a comprehensive way. In 2011, the Oakland Unified School District (OUSD) adopted the nation's first district-led full-service community school (FSCS) initiative. Today, Oakland's plan arguably stands as the nation's most ambitious community school initiative. It sought to transform an entire district system in serving its students with a whole-child approach rather than proceeding on a school-by-school model. Oakland operates as a community school district, not a district with some community schools.

Community schools represent a promising strategy for addressing the barriers to learning, especially those associated with poverty and inequitable resources. Twenty-five years ago, only a handful of community schools existed; today, more than seventy-five hundred community schools serve children and their families in the US, and the community school movement continues to grow. While community schools across the country differ in how they go about constructing a positive climate and supports for students' development, they all represent an expanded vision of schooling. Community schools move outside traditional school structures and routines to include attention to factors such as physical and mental health, safety, positive adult connections, expanded learning time, social supports, and family engagement.

Disparities in the resources and opportunities available to youth growing up in concentrated poverty represent structural problems—such as food insecurity, insufficient social and medical care, and homelessness in their lived contexts that are not amenable to quick-fix, adopt-a-program responses. These inequities require structural solutions to the patterns and underlying, reinforcing structures associated with the problem. It requires a system change to lead to significant, enduring change in students' school experiences and outcomes. System change calls for diagnoses in cause-and-effect terms, rather than just looking at a symptom such as enduring gaps in student achievement as "the problem to fix." Yet few community school initiatives approach their mission in terms of system change, instead focusing on transformation of individual schools. But without transformation in the underlying, reinforcing structures associated with the inequities students' experience, the long-term trajectory and sustainability of individual schools remain unpredictable, dependent on individual leadership and commitment. Further, while a community schools approach centered only on schools may successfully promote better outcomes for its students, students facing similar challenges elsewhere in the district miss out.

What does system change look like in an urban school district? What factors enable or constrain it? This book explores these questions, taking the OUSD full-service community schools initiative as a case of system change.

OAKLAND: A CASE OF SYSTEM CHANGE

From the outset, Oakland leaders focused on *system change* at both central office and school levels as necessary to disrupt inequities in the resources and opportunities available to students, and to establish a comprehensive, whole-child model as a way of "doing school." Oakland's strategic plan, *Community Schools, Thriving Students*, framed its warrant in terms of equity and invested in schools serving the most under-resourced neighborhoods.[1] From the start, OUSD's strategies integrated community schools' resources and academics, in contrast to a "co-location" model, in which external service providers operate more or less independently from the schools. OUSD reformers also pushed for central office supports to foster integrated site-level work.

More than nine years into *Community Schools, Thriving Students* implementation, Oakland shows significant change in systemic factors underlying inequities and positive implementation of a whole-child community school model. Several of Oakland's full service community schools components have been recognized as national best practice models: among them, tools for working with community-based partners; youth leadership and family-engagement policies; restorative justice programs; social-emotional learning trainings for educators and integration into academic work; and the African American Male Achievement (AAMA) program.

The FSCS initiative reports positive student outcomes, especially in behavioral domains. Oakland data indicate reduced suspensions and high-risk behaviors, improved school climate and culture, increased family and youth involvement in site-based decisions, and perhaps most notably, higher rates of high school graduation. OUSD's 2019 graduation rate increased by more than 13 percentage points over the past four years, giving the district its highest graduation rate (and lowest cohort dropout rate) since 2010. Oakland also counts positive student health and wellness outcomes associated with community schools' mental and physical health resources. The FSCS story is ongoing and shows that students need *both* academic and personal supports to address their school experiences and outcomes.

Since 2011–2012, the initiative has expanded in scope and scale. In the 2019–2020 school year, 42 of the 86 district-supported schools operate with a full-time community school manager, students made 36,000 visits to OUSD'S sixteen school-based health centers, the district's 75 afterschool programs involve 8,000 participants daily, and 215 community organizations partnered with Oakland schools. Furthermore, *all* of the district's schools incorporate core elements of a FSCS model such as social-emotional learning strategies and Coordination of Services Teams (COST). Moreover, remarkably, Oakland's FSCS initiative has persisted even in the face of significant leadership turnover and repeated budget crises.

This book draws on two related research projects focused on OUSD's *Community Schools, Thriving Students* initiative—one at the system level, and one at the site level. Milbrey McLaughlin's system-level research began in 2011 as OUSD rolled out its FSCS plan. She focused on understanding how the district went about organizing for and implementing the initiative, conducting more than ninety recorded and transcribed interviews with OUSD educators, administrators, and community partners and civic leaders several times annually, establishing a detailed longitudinal account of implementation issues, decisions, and outcomes.[2] Kendra Fehrer and Jacob Leos-Urbel began their school-level documentation and evaluation of FSCS in 2014, as researchers at Stanford University's John W. Gardner Center for Youth and Their Communities ("the Gardner Center"). Their research involved a multiyear collaboration between OUSD and the

Gardner Center to support efforts to assess, enhance, and scale their community schools work.[3] The research included extensive interviews with district leaders, site visits, conversations with a range of school stakeholders, and statistical analysis of longitudinal district data. Fehrer and Leos-Urbel conducted their site-level interviews and observations in nine schools—three elementary schools, four middle schools, one high school, and one "span" school serving both middle and high school students.

This book takes Oakland as a case of systems change and explores how OUSD successfully built a FSCS district despite an extremely challenging economic, political, and social context and constant leadership change. Evidence from Oakland's almost ten years of system- and site-level implementation provides a unique opportunity to consider how a community school model plays out in terms of whole-district system change, how a community school provides integrated academic and social services to enable a whole-child approach, and how a community school mindset becomes incorporated throughout a district system.

Introduction

The community school model, while not new, has gained momentum nationally as an education reform strategy with the potential to address the effects of poverty and other factors *beyond* instruction that contribute to disparities in student achievement.[1] Community schools have gained traction as a way to address these persistent inequalities. For instance, a 2017 *Phi Delta Kappan* poll found increased backing for schools' provision of wraparound services for children otherwise lacking access to them—most especially afterschool programs and mental health services.[2] Twenty-five years ago, only a handful of community schools existed; today, more than seventy-five hundred community schools serve children and their families across the country.

Community schools may be viewed as one strategy along the long and winding road of school reform efforts, from pushes for smaller schools to more centralized (or decentralized) authority to many other reforms.[3] For some, the community school approach reflects a fundamental conclusion that the traditional school model itself is insufficient to overcome the role of poverty in equitable access to learning opportunities and resources, and that improving student achievement requires addressing the needs of the whole child. Viewed this way, the community school model represents an expanded vision of what schools are, who they include, and what they are responsible for, by leveraging community resources both to address student barriers to learning and to shift relationships between schools, families, and community.[4]

Community schools operate in a public school building. They welcome students and their families before and after school, often seven days a week, all year long. A community school program reflects a partnership between the school and one or more community agencies and serves as a community center. All community schools take up three broad approaches:

- Provide expanded learning opportunities that are motivating and engaging during the school day, after school, and in the summer.
- Offer essential health and social supports and services.
- Engage families and communities as assets in the lives of their children and youth.[5]

Community school proponents see community partnerships as integral to an effective response to these wide-ranging, beyond-the-classroom issues. Proponents frequently stress that there is no cookie-cutter approach to creating a community school. Every community school should reflect the unique aspects of the neighborhood and families and youth it serves, and draw on the community resources available to it.

EARLY COMMUNITY SCHOOL CHAMPIONS

Early twentieth-century essayist Reverend Samuel Crowther underscored the continuing appeal of community schools: "The present movement for using the schoolhouse of a city for the promoting of neighborhood life is one that has a long history—as long as democracy."[6] Rooted in the ideas of education philosopher John Dewey and social reformer Jane Addams, community schools aim to be "the hub of the neighborhood, uniting educators, community partners, and families to provide all students with opportunities to succeed in school and life."[7] In Dewey's view, placing schools at the heart of the community and engaging community members in the operation of their schools advances democracy. Like Addams's Chicago Hull House, community schools provide expanded school-based services to students and their families through partnerships with community social and health providers. In 1934, in the heart of the Great Depression, Italian immigrant Leonard Covello established Benjamin Franklin High School in East Harlem. Covello's "community-centered" school represented one of the first attempts to make the public school the coordinator of social services and position the community as the starting point for learning.[8]

The Charles Stewart Mott foundation in Flint, Michigan, made one of the earliest, if not the first, investments in public community schools. In 1935, C.S. Mott and Flint educator Frank J. Manley, motivated like Covello by the Great Depression, initiated a "lighted schoolhouse" model that provided afterschool educational and recreational programs for youth, their families, and neighborhood residents. The foundation invested significantly in bringing the model to all thirty-six Flint schools by 1953. To publicize the community school model broadly, it launched the National Center for Community Education in 1962. NCCE provided training to thousands of Michigan educators, business and community members, and eventually to leaders throughout the country.[9]

The 1982 *A Nation at Risk* report provoked new interest in a community schools model, most especially in high-poverty urban areas.[10] One educator said, "With the publication of that report, people realized, 'Oh my god, it's a war zone out there [in poor neighborhoods]. Kids don't have the supports and services—they need nurses, social workers, things to do after school" . . . there was a lot of finger pointing when that report came out. Who is responsible for what? And at that time, schools were being stripped of non-academic services because of budget problems . . . "

Responding to these concerns, the Children's Aid Society (CAS) in New York City became an early champion of school-based non-academic services for low-income urban schools; in 1992, it opened the first of its "settlement house in the school" models in the Washington

Heights area.[11] CAS expanded beyond the usual "add-on" approach to health and social services found in many community schools at that time: "The CAS approach was aimed at school transformation and reform, the creation of a full-fledged community school."[12] To structure their work, CAS created a Developmental Triangle for Community Schools (figure I.1).[13]

Credit for the term *full-service community schools* goes to Joy Dryfoos. Her 1994 book, *Full-Service Schools*, elaborated the interrelationships of such problem behaviors as school failure and dropout, mental and physical health, drug use, and early pregnancy to argue that schools enrolling young people at risk needed to provide comprehensive, long-term, and full supports.[14] In contrast to schools that targeted specific needs such as vision, dental care, or early pregnancy, Dryfoos argued that they must be *full-service community schools* (FSCS) in order to engage the multiple challenges to poor students' school success and positive development.[15] The FSCS approach differs from a one-shot approach that focuses on a single factor—such as family supports, recreational opportunities, and nutrition—as opposed

Figure I.1 *Children's Aid Society's community schools developmental triangle*

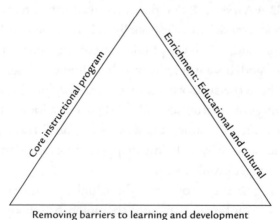

Removing barriers to learning and development

Source: Joy G. Dryfoos, Jane Quinn, and Carol Barkin, *Community Schools in Action: Lessons from a Decade of Practice* (New York: Oxford University Press, 2005), vii.

to multiple and cumulative elements that shape a child's life.[16] The community school model articulated by Dryfoos and others in the 1980s and 1990s also stood in stark contrast to the "no excuses" approach to school that dominated federal and many state education policies (and many funders' agendas) at that time. The "no excuses" position held that schools should be able to push students to academic success, no matter their background or life context.[17]

However, others disagreed with those taking this tough perspective and continued to explore strategies that addressed the needs of the child beyond academics. Former Boston Public School superintendent Thomas Payzant was not alone in pointing out the philosophical disagreement inherent in these two coexisting reform approaches.[18] Community school advocates argued that paying attention to the whole child and engaging the community did not mean deprioritizing instruction or students' school success. Not surprisingly, however, spikes of interest in community schools came and went, depending on urban crises, and many community school initiatives functioned more as add-ons rather than the cohesive full-service initiatives Dryfoos promoted.[19]

INSTITUTIONAL RESPONSIBILITY FOR COMMUNITY SCHOOLS

Contemporary community schools usually operate as single or multiple sites within a host district; many have little formal connection to the district system in which they reside. Instead, a non-school entity often takes the lead in supporting and overseeing the community school. For instance, Akron's *I Promise School* or *Strive Cincinnati* provide many new resources but function relatively disconnected from their host districts. Albuquerque's community school efforts are led by community-based organizations (CBOs). In instances such as these, the lead partners tend to be CBOs, health agencies, or universities.

Lead partners assume advocacy, brokering, and coordinating roles and responsibility as fiscal agent and resource developer; and they often employ or supervise on-site community school coordinators.

For example, CAS organized a technical assistance center in New York City to serve its twenty-one community schools. The United Way sponsors Indianapolis's Bridges to Success community school program and brings an array of services into schools through its agency consortium. In instances of district-led community school initiatives, often a community schools approach is not integrated into the district's policy system. In Tulsa and Nashville's community schools initiatives, for instance, the district operates more as a supportive intermediary.

Mayor Bill de Blasio launched New York City's ambitious community schools initiative in 2014.[20] City Hall plays the lead role in aligning city resources, partnerships, and policies in support of community schools. City collaborators include the Department of Education's new Office of Community Schools, the NYC Children's' Cabinet, and the Community Schools Advisory Board. New York's initiative now includes more than 215 schools (out of the fourteen hundred–plus schools served by the system) and continues to expand.

Funders play a role in these institutional arrangements because they have tended to focus on individual schools or a school-based model and shy away from district or system level proposals. In the last twenty years or so, in large urban areas, established community anchors such as the United Way or universities have sold "ideal" community school models to philanthropy, along with clear lines of support and oversight.[21]

WHAT DO WE KNOW ABOUT COMMUNITY SCHOOLS?

Broad agreement exists among community school advocates, policy makers, and researchers that evaluation of community schools has a long way to go. Evaluation and measurement issues are challenging because community school models are complex and multifaceted, heavily process dependent, and not "projects" or "programs" with clear and consistent parameters. The challenges to evaluation and research about community schools are challenging to conceptualize and carry out for many reasons. As long-time community schools promoter Jane Quinn, formerly of the Children's Aid Society, acknowledged with a sigh: "We are where we are." (See "Lessons for community school research and evaluation" in the book appendix.)

An expanding body of research examines the relationship between community schools (and integrated school-based services more broadly) and student outcomes.[22] Dryfoos and Maguire's 2002 review of community school evaluations throughout the country reports mixed outcomes, and finds generally positive results on one more or more outcome measures.[23] A 2014 review of existing research found that integrated student supports models could improve academic outcomes (although findings are mixed).[24] A recent study of community schools in Redwood City, California, found increases in attendance when students and their families accessed available services, as well as English proficiency gains for English language learners whose parents consistently participated in family engagement opportunities.[25] A study of community schools in Baltimore indicated that schools that had been implementing community school practices for five or more years had statistically significant higher rates of attendance and lower rates of chronic absence when compared with non-community schools.[26]

Some research has looked at factors influencing the implementation of the community school model. In early work on community schools, for instance, Lawson and Briar-Lawson found that services often were add-ons to school sites without intentional efforts to integrate them within the school, and that co-locating service providers did not necessarily lead to better quality of services.[27] In a 2013 study of community schools in New York City, Rao finds evidence of "organizational hybridity" by which schools and partner CBOs shift from an approach where responsibilities are divided as each organization works toward its own goals, to one in which each knows its role as all work collectively toward a shared goal.[28]

Other evaluations examine the operation of community school components. Richardson outlines a model of highly effective community schools that focuses on principal leadership, community

partnerships, and organizational development (consisting of resources and staff available for programming as well as capacity for
managing resources related to community school implementation).[29]
Based on research that applies Richardson's framework in exploring
components of effectiveness in three full-service community schools
in an urban school district, Sanders highlights several necessary
conditions if FSCSs are to be transformative learning environments
for socially and economically disadvantaged children and youth.[30]
Sanders notes that principals must possess a comprehensive understanding of leadership in order to administer community schools effectively, that community partnerships are at the core of FSCSs, and
that community school coordinators are critical for the development
of these partnerships. Anna Maier, Julia Daniel, Jeannie Oakes, and
Livia Lam developed four "pillars" common to effective community
schools: (1) integrated student supports; (2) expanded learning time
and opportunities; (3) family and community engagement; and (4)
collaborative leadership and practice. Their review examines evidence
to support the effectiveness of each pillar and contribution to community school goals.[31] However, they do not consider how these pillars operate together in a FSCS, noting the general lack of research on
comprehensive community school implementation and outcomes.

While research suggests that *elements* of community schools can
play a role in supporting improved student outcomes, evaluations of
community schools' outcomes and research considering their implementation and effectiveness remain limited.[32] In addition, even less
research exists that examines the district role in supporting community schools practically, institutionally, or politically as a systemic
(rather than one-off) school reform strategy. For instance, none of
the seven community schools initiatives featured by the Coalition of
Community schools as national models is district-led.[33]

PURPOSE AND ORGANIZATION OF THIS BOOK

Oakland's more than nine years of experience as a full-service community school district provides a valuable opportunity to address

these gaps in knowledge about community schools. Taking OUSD's 2011 strategic initiative, *Community Schools, Thriving Students*, as a case of system change, this book examines community schools' functioning and consequences for students, families, and educators and considers how their institutional and social contexts influence their operations and outcomes. In addition to illuminating community school efforts in Oakland, the book contributes to discussions in the broader field about the organizational capacities that a district and a community school must develop in order to facilitate the successful execution of its new role and responsibilities.

Part 1 takes up the initiative's social, economic, and political context and the challenges faced by Tony Smith, a new superintendent determined to bring about whole-child-focused system change and a new way of "doing school" in Oakland. It describes the comprehensive planning process that created the 2011 strategic plan, the backbone of the effort.

Part 2 focuses on central office implementation and the diverse tools employed to bring about district system change, and presents examples of the system changes associated with them. It examines sources of the strategic plan's remarkable stability over the course of significant leadership transitions, fiscal crises, and staff turnover.

Part 3 considers site-level implementation and outcomes of implementing the plan. These chapters describe school-level responses to the strategic plan, and the elements most critical to positive implementation.

Part 4 recaps Oakland's almost ten years' implementation of the FSCS initiative and outcomes associated with it. The final chapter summarizes Oakland's lessons for the field. It is followed by a short afterword in which Tony Smith shares his reflections on Oakland's FSCS initiative.

PART I

BEGINNINGS

CHAPTER 1

The Oakland Context

Oakland, the county seat of Alameda County, California, is the largest city in the East Bay region of the San Francisco Bay Area, and the eighth-most populated city in California. It is home to one of the most demographically diverse populations in the United States, with residents of different racial, ethnic, national, linguistic, and other cultural groups. White, black, and Latinx residents each represent about one-quarter of the population, and Asian residents make up 16 percent. About four in ten residents speak a language other than English at home and more than one-quarter of the city's residents were born outside the United States.

Inequities run deep in Oakland and profoundly impact its schools. Within Oakland, considerable disparities in opportunity and outcomes exist, largely along racial and geographic lines, with severe concentrated poverty in places, especially for Oakland's children. Among Oakland families with children, 12 percent live below the federal poverty rate ($24,300 for a family of four). However, given the high cost of living in the Bay Area, estimates of the income a family of four needs for self-sufficiency are much higher than the federal poverty threshold, and 38.1 percent of Oakland households fall below this self-sufficiency index.[1]

Children born in some Oakland neighborhoods are much more likely to suffer from poor nutrition, be subject to violence, and lack adequate health care. For example, according to an often-cited 2008 report from the Alameda County Public Health Department, a black child born in West Oakland is seven times more likely to be born into poverty, four times less likely to read at grade level by grade four, and 5.6 times more likely to drop out of school than a white child born in the affluent Oakland Hills neighborhood. Additionally, as an adult, that same black child will be at least twice as likely to die of heart disease, stroke, or cancer.[2]

During the 1970s, Oakland began to face serious problems with gang-controlled drug dealing; violence and property crime increased at the same time and Oakland's murder rate rose. Drugs and violence continued, earning Oakland a regular spot on lists of America's most crime-ridden cities. David Kakishiba, East Bay Asian Youth Center (EBAYC) founder and longtime school board member and former chair, recalls the culture of drugs, guns, and gangs that characterized Oakland in throughout the 1980s and 1990s: "It was all-pervasive back then."

Oakland also is home to tremendous civic engagement. Birthplace of the Black Panther Party, a longtime stronghold of organized labor (for example, Oakland port workers' International Longshore and Warehouse Union), and a creative center of multiracial and multi-issue organizing, Oakland has a long history of community activism. Beginning as early as the Black Panther Party's free school hot breakfast program in 1969, civic organizations have played a critical role in the struggle for more just and equitable access to high-quality education for the city's poorest residents. Not surprisingly, many of the organizations that serve and advocate for Oakland's children and their families today have played a critical role in the community schools initiative.

Despite Oakland's long history of civic activism and social justice advocacy, significant inequities exist along racial lines. The 2018 *Oakland Equity Indicators* reports that almost every indicator of well-being shows troubling disparities by race. Black residents consistently receive the lowest scores on measures of welfare reported within six themes: economy, education, public health, housing, public safety, and neighborhood and civic life.[3] According to the *Indicators*, "Oakland's

2018 Citywide Equity score, which encompasses all Indicators in the framework, is 33.5 (out of 100), demonstrating substantial room for improvement."[4]

OAKLAND UNIFIED SCHOOL DISTRICT

In 2017–2018, the district enrolled around 53,000 students in 87 district-run schools and 34 district-authorized charter schools, making it the eleventh-largest California school district. Although OUSD's student numbers have dropped slightly from around 55,000 two decades ago, student moves to charter schools account for current declines. Charters have pulled about 13,700 students from the district-run schools, contributing to costly under enrollment in many schools.[5]

District-run schools serve an increasingly diverse student population.[6] In the 2017–2018 school year, Latinx (46 percent) and black (24 percent) students made up the majority of the population, followed by Asian/Pacific Islander (12 percent) and white (10 percent) students. Nearly three-quarters (72 percent) of the student population qualify for free or reduced-price meals, and three in ten are English language learners. More than 90 percent of OUSD schools receive ESSA Title I funding.[7] These demographics have changed considerably over time, mirroring the changes in the larger community. For example, over the last decade, the number of African American students decreased by 34 percent, while the Latinx student population experienced a 30 percent increase (see figure 1.1).[8] OUSD welcomed twenty-five hundred Newcomer students in 2017–2018. Around 50 percent of OUSD students speak a language other than English at home; 33 percent are English language learners.

OUSD teachers do not reflect students' ethnicity: 47 percent are white; 21 percent are black; 15 percent Latinx; 12 percent Asian. Teacher expertise is distributed unevenly across district-run schools. Students of color are most likely to find new teachers in their classrooms and experience high levels of teacher turnover. OUSD schools with a predominately black or Latinx student body have the highest

Figure 1.1 *Enrollment over time*

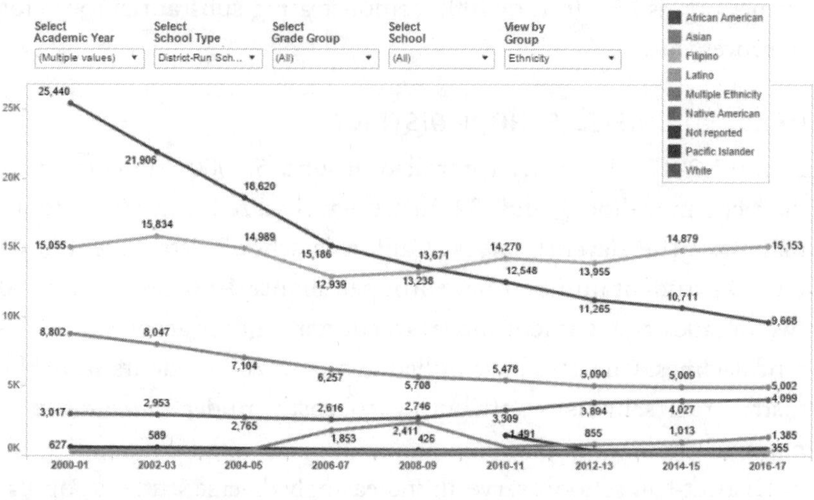

Select Academic Year: (Multiple values) ▾ | Select School Type: District-Run Sch... ▾ | Select Grade Group: (All) ▾ | Select School: (All) ▾ | View by Group: Ethnicity ▾

Legend: African American, Asian, Filipino, Latino, Multiple Ethnicity, Native American, Not reported, Pacific Islander, White

Data points (approximate):

- 25,440; 21,906; 18,620; 15,834; 14,989; 15,186; 13,671; 14,270; 14,879; 15,153
- 15,055; 14,989; 13,238; 12,939; 13,238; 12,548; 13,955; 10,711; 9,668
- 8,802; 8,047; 7,104; 6,257; 5,708; 5,478; 5,090; 5,009; 5,002
- 11,265; 4,099
- 3,017; 2,953; 2,765; 2,616; 2,746; 3,309; 3,894; 4,027; 1,385
- 627; 589; 1,853; 2,411; 426; 1,491; 855; 1,013; 355

Years: 2000-01, 2002-03, 2004-05, 2006-07, 2008-09, 2010-11, 2012-13, 2014-15, 2016-17

Source: Oakland Unified School District, http://www.ousddata.org/announcements/category/enrollment

percent of teachers in their first five years of teaching; they had 1.64 times as many new teachers as students in majority white schools. OUSD schools enrolling a majority black student body had the highest teacher turnover, averaging 38 percent of teachers leaving between the 2016–2017 and 2017–2018 school years. Majority Latinx schools were second highest at 34 percent of teachers turning over. Schools with a majority white student body had the lowest teacher turnover at 10 percent. OUSD's scores on California's State Smarter Balanced Assessment Consortium (SBAC) evaluation are significantly lower than statewide averages and lower than scores of other large urban school districts.

Overall, in 2018, 35 percent of OUSD eleventh-graders met English language arts (ELA) proficiency standards on California's Smarter Balanced Assessment Consortium (SBAC) evaluations, and 18 percent scored proficient in math. Moreover, achievement differences exist between students with different socioeconomic status. For socioeconomically disadvantaged students, 30 percent met proficiency standards on ELA and 13 percent on math. For OUSD eighth-graders, 31 percent rated proficient for ELA and 23 percent for math overall. For economically disadvantaged students, 24 percent met proficiency standards on ELA and 27 percent on math.

ENTER TONY SMITH AND A NEW VISION

In 2003, after declaring bankruptcy, Oakland Unified School District moved into state receivership and received a $100 million bailout loan from the state.[9] When Anthony (Tony) Smith arrived as superintendent in 2009, OUSD had just come out of state receivership, regained decision-making autonomy, and was in significant debt and internal disarray. An administrator commented on the chaotic district context the new superintendent encountered, especially the obligations associated with the $100 million state loan: "Out of more than a thousand school districts in California, only five or six have ever had a state loan. It's not like OUSD is part of a big club!"

Tony Smith brought a vision for making OUSD a full-service school district and strategy for achieving it that reflected both his professional and personal history. As superintendent in Emeryville, California, from 2004 to 2007, he resurrected the tiny Bay Area school district, which also had gone through state receivership. In Emeryville, Smith had developed a program to identify at-risk kids and place them with in-house social service and student-nurse volunteers from local universities; he also established the Center for Community Life to bring families and the community together around the needs of the community's youth. From 2007 to 2009, Smith served as San Francisco Unified School District's Deputy Superintendent for Instruction, Innovation, and Social Justice. He worked to focus SFUSD on the equity of academic resources and opportunities available to the district's economically and ethnically diverse student body.

OUSD board members and community leaders saw Smith as a good fit for Oakland. "By selecting me, the board is saying they want to do things differently and put kids and families at the center and design education systems that serve them best," Smith said. "We need to get really clear about what we want all of our kids to be able to do. There have been system and structural improvements, but it's time to connect with the communities and families and engage all of Oakland in this conversation."

Smith says his passion to support struggling children and offer support they need to succeed derives from his own childhood in California's Central Valley, one that included poverty and moving from home to home and school to school. Born to unwed teen parents in Stockton, he bounced from relative to relative until his high school years in Placerville. Smith credits an uncle for pulling him off a path that in sixth grade led to juvenile hall and negative relationships. "Turn it around," his uncle told him, "or you'll be dead or in prison by the time you're twenty-one." Smith turned it around: "By the time I was in middle school, I knew I had to get a scholarship to play sports or join the military. I was playing for a purpose."

The 6-foot-3, 285-pound white offensive lineman learned about race from his high school teammates of color and subsequently from his surroundings on the University of California Berkeley campus. Smith served as UCB team captain and played from 1986 to 1989. In the early 1990s, he went pro with the Green Bay Packers and San Francisco 49ers. Injuries forced his release before he could play any regular season games. He returned to UCB for his bachelor's degree in English in 1992, MA degree in education in 1993, and his PhD in the school of education in 2002.[10]

Tony Smith brought an untraditional background to a district leadership role. He had never been a classroom teacher and never obtained any kind of credential to teach or serve as an administrator. Because his vision for Oakland's students extended well beyond the classroom or school, OUSD's board waived the administrative credential California required for district superintendents. Board members and teacher leaders considered his commitment to equity, passion for uplifting kids like those struggling in Oakland schools, and vision of how to move forward to be more important than usual educational credentials. "I think he's an incredible evangelist," said Oakland school board member David Kakishiba in 2009. "He's brought [equity] to the forefront in a way that I have not seen in my lifetime—that, as a district, we're going to be very focused, diligent, and relentless on eliminating these disparities for children with less means and the legacy of racism."

Smith's lack of teaching or administrative credentials sparked pushback from some OUSD teachers and administrators. Nonetheless, he also had influential support for his nomination from the Oakland education community. Trish Gorham, president of the Oakland Education Association (OEA) agreed with the board that Smith was a good fit for the district, especially because of his advocacy for social emotional learning: "One thing I have always credited him with was his advocacy of social and emotional learning and how that is a huge part of what any urban district has to deal with—the trauma the kids come in with. He recognized that."

Smith's experience growing up taught him that the gaps in academic achievement between Oakland's poor and more advantaged students were broader and deeper than any shortcomings of the schools:

> It is intellectually complex, but also just spiritually and emotionally heartbreaking when you talk about how deep the inequity is . . . part of what I'm able to do because I know from my own history, my own experience what has to be . . . I have been there—embarrassed, not enough to eat—so I have my own fury about that . . . My sense of social responsibility is the only reason I am in this position—to do something about it.

Smith's vision of disrupting "historical predictability" resonated across Oakland as refreshingly different from the often-heard "close the achievement gap" rhetoric. Further, Oakland leaders viewed Tony Smith as authentic in his passion for educational equity and his ability to talk credibly about white privilege.

PREPARED GROUND: BUILDING BLOCKS FOR FULL-SERVICE COMMUNITY SCHOOLS

When Smith became superintendent in 2009, OUSD was a low-capacity district by any measure. Its salaries were among the lowest in Bay Area, its institutional infrastructure was in disrepair, and teacher and administrator turnover eroded school stability and morale throughout the district. The city of Oakland itself wrestled with budget shortfalls, racial divides, and civic discontent. OUSD did not appear by any account to be a ripe candidate for significant school reform.

However, despite these negatives, local history, perspectives, and experience all informed and reinforced a reform approach aiming to change radically the opportunities and resources available to all Oakland's youth and the way the district did business. Tony Smith entered a "prepared ground" compatible with his vision. Three aspects stand out as especially important to a positive local reception to his vision, equity goals, and reform ideas: Oakland's historically activist support for its schools; traditions of cross-sector collaborations around youth; and positive experience with community school–like practices.

Community Activism

Political activist Angela Glover Blackwell considered Oakland unusual in its high level of community activism. "Oakland is a town in which the non-profit community sector can make things happen."[11] Oakland has a long history of empowering families and community, as well as public and private agencies, to show up and demand things from the schools, even in the context of state receivership. For instance, Nicole Taylor, the former executive director of the East Bay Community Foundation, remarked, "Activism is in Oakland's DNA. It goes back to the Black Panthers." Oakland was home to the Black Panthers, founded in 1966 by Huey Newton and Bobby Seale to challenge police brutality against the African American community. The Panthers also involved themselves in social policies affecting black youth and founded what Lisa Villarreal, former ED of Youth Ventures JPA, termed the "first modern community school in California—The Black Panther Community School—as a vehicle for enhancing power." According to Villarreal, "Those values and the roots of that never really died in Oakland. They're here today. The equity notion also goes back to Marcus Foster. The idea that Oakland needed to be a Full Service Community School wasn't a big stretch." (Marcus Foster, a nationally known educator, became OUSD's first African-American superintendent in 1970 and was an effective advocate for improved and equitable resources for Oakland's black students. Members of the Symbionese Liberation Army assassinated Superintendent Foster in 1973.)

Oakland youth were involved as powerful actors in school transformation long before the district made its commitment to embrace community schools. Youth organizers formed a new coalition when Proposition 21, introduced in 2000, proposed changes to the juvenile criminal code that would result in significantly harsher sentences for youth, and disproportionately affect youth of color. "Schools Not Jails" became a central refrain of the movement, as youth called on lawmakers to repeal punitive criminal justice measures and invest in under-resourced public schools. Oakland's students of color were highly mobilized, organizing demonstrations in the state capital with thousands of their peers, shutting down schools and freeways across the state.

Youth activism and leadership work in schools continued to play an important role in calling attention to OUSD's shortfalls, especially disparities between hill and flatland schools. At the time of these mobilizations, Oakland's flatlands public schools had notoriously poor conditions—overcrowding, lack of adequate classroom supplies, crumbling infrastructure, and high teacher turnover, to name a few. These toxic educational experiences affected students largely along racial and economic lines and shaped students' educational and life outcomes, including high student dropout rates, poor attendance, and disengagement.

With the support of then-superintendent George Musgrove, student activists established a district "youth steering committee" charged with interrogating the high levels of dropout and disengagement and developing recommendations for district policy to redress these issues. They called their proposal the Student Power Resolution.

Oakland parents also mobilized to push for change. The Parent Leadership Action Network (PLAN), founded in 2004 to develop parent leadership and build the power of parents to transform schools, has long been a force in Oakland. Oakland Community Organizations (OCO) lent a powerful voice to community concerns. OCO emerged during state receivership with political strength in central Oakland flatlands' faith and Latinx immigrant communities and played a significant role in pushing for small schools and charters.

Oakland educators, parents, and community activists focused on questions of student engagement and leadership even as the district operated under state receivership. Meaningful student engagement (MSE) standards, adopted in 2007, emerged from the Meaningful Student Engagement Collaborative.[12] MSE standards in both intent and content set precedent for consequential youth engagement and voice and served as antecedent to the student engagement standards subsequently adopted by the FSCS strategic plan.

Some community activism took a more conventional structure and tone. In particular, the Urban Strategies Council (USC), under the leadership of Angela Glover Blackwell and then Junious Williams, provided powerful and respected support for social justice initiatives and racial equity. The USC reinforced the community's backing for equity-focused undertakings with compelling research and policy analysis.

Despite the economic challenges faced by many Oakland residents, Oakland voters have combined youth activism with a willingness to fund youth-focused measures. Voters established the Oakland Fund for Children and Youth (OFCY) in 1996 when Oakland passed the

Kids First! Initiative (Measure K), an amendment to the city charter, to support direct services to youth under twenty-one years of age.[13]

Collaboration and Partnerships

Cross-sector collaboration has a long history in Oakland. Nonprofits, local foundations, and public and private agencies have rallied to support youth even in difficult financial times, especially in response to growing violence in the flatland neighborhoods. Youth ALIVE! has worked since 1991 to respond to violence in Oakland's most dangerous neighborhoods. "[We] have worked to help violently wounded people heal themselves and their community. Our mission is to prevent violence and create young leaders."[14] Its mentors, counselors, youth leaders, case managers, and intervention specialists operate with the broad support of foundations, government grants, and corporate and individual donors, including family foundations.

As racial tensions fueled violence in East Oakland 1997, the County of Alameda and the City of Oakland made an investment in East Oakland youth by supporting a "one-stop health and human services center designed for and by youth."[15] This investment created the foundation for Youth UpRising [YU]. YU launched in 2003–2005 with a 25,000-square-foot state-of-the-art facility dedicated to direct service to East Oakland youth and families. At its inception, YU represented a public/private partnership with OUSD, local government, foundations, and local youth service agencies. These partnerships have expanded significantly to represent broad community commitment to the well-being of East Oakland youth.[16]

Oakland's Youth Ventures Joint Powers Authority (JPA), established in 2007, remains one of only around a dozen JPAs around the country. Oakland's Youth Ventures JPA operates as a partnership of political leaders and administrators from the City of Oakland, OUSD, and Alameda County and takes a collective impact approach to support improved outcomes for Oakland's children and families.[17]

The Healthy Start program, established in 1991 by the US Department of Health and Human Services, Maternal and Child Health, funded an Oakland initiative to lower infant mortality that provided prenatal care and parent education. Oakland's extremely high rates of infant mortality led to its selection to take part in this initial round of the program. The city's Healthy Start program achieved many positive outcomes for infants and their families, and demonstrated the importance of community involvement.[18] The city's successful Healthy Start program served as "prepared ground" for a FSCS initiative in two important ways: (1) it prompted the Alameda County Health Care Services Agency to apply the Healthy Start principles and practices of community involvement and integrated services to their entire county system of public health-care delivery, and (2), it led Alameda County to fund health centers in eight OUSD high schools, an investment that subsequently would become foundational to the district's full-service community schools strategic plan.

Oakland had long maintained a positive collaboration with Alameda County. A Master Agreement between Alameda County and OUSD, in place since 2004, established partnerships with several county agencies. These arrangements provided important county-funded school-based supports for students' physical and behavioral health, and general wellness and a foundation for subsequent cross-sector partnerships. Similarly, OUSD collaborated with the Oakland Housing Authority around strategies to boost students' attendance.

STATE POLICY: CALIFORNIA PROPOSITION 49 AND UNIVERSAL AFTERSCHOOL

In November 2002, California voters passed Proposition 49 (After School Education and Safety or ASES), which mandated that $550 million dollars each year be made available for K–9 after-school programs. As a push toward "universal after school in California," Prop 49 had several important characteristics that would benefit Tony Smith's full-service community school initiative. As a constitutional amendment, it was durable; it targeted low-income students; every elementary and middle school could apply. The initiative provides, in perpetuity, an annual amount of over $1 billion in cash and matching resources for California's after school programs. (Prop 49 is the largest after school investment in national history. To date, it continues to total more each year than the other forty-nine states' afterschool funding combined.) Several CBOs from Oakland and the Bay Area agreed to experiment with being "lead agencies" in partnership with the school and principal—large backbone organizations that could handle the finances, logistics, operations, and management of running multiple school site programs. Prop 49 brought a sea change to Oakland's afterschool offerings. It represented the biggest expansion and rollout of afterschool youth programs and services in Oakland's history. The model was a stepping-stone to the community school model's integration of academic, social, emotional, youth development, and community into a comprehensive approach.

Positive Experience with Community School Elements and Approaches

Many examples of an FSCS vision and likeminded practices existed in Oakland prior to Tony Smith's 2009 arrival. For instance, Sankofa, a North Oakland preK–8 school that opened during the 2004–2005 school year, offered an array of social and health services on its own, with positive academic results. However, OUSD's most significant experience with a full-service community school approach came in 2008 with the Atlantic Philanthropies' Elev8 Oakland grant to Safe Passages, a community-based organization that works with disadvantaged communities in Alameda County, to serve as lead agency for Elev8.

Elev8 presumed that young people's access to social and health services should not be limited by race or socioeconomic status and that well-supported, healthy youth are better able to learn and succeed. The Elev8 grant provided extended day academic support and mentoring, health services, and family support through a dedicated family advocate at five school campuses during the four-year implementation phase (2008–2012). Atlantic Philanthropies awarded a total of $15 million; contributions from local partners, Alameda County, the City of Oakland, and OUSD added an additional $25.7 million, bringing the project total to $40.7 million. In 2012. Atlantic awarded $3.5 million to Safe Passages for Elev8 Oakland Phase II. The goal of the thirty-six-month grant was to support sustainability and fortify the initiative's infrastructure. Among other results, Elev8 jump-started FSCS at Roosevelt Middle School and Coliseum College Prep Academy.

In 2000, OUSD signed on to the Gates Foundation's Small Schools initiative to close large elementary, middle, and high schools and reopen the campuses as smaller, themed schools. Oakland Community Organizations (OCO) effectively pushed OUSD for smaller, more intimate schools as mothers from the flatlands saw their youth languishing in crowded, chaotic schools while youngsters living in the hills received a very different education.

Oakland's prepared ground meant that Tony Smith had much to build on in attracting support for his ideas and developing his strategic plan. More than one observer of the district post-receivership scene has speculated that without this existing environment, Smith might not have come to OUSD, or could not have been successful in developing and passing a FSCS strategic plan so soon after his arrival. As one community leader said, "There was a huge mess; donors and funders did a lot of cleanup. Without that, Tony wouldn't have been able to put a plan in place [when he did], because he would have still been cleaning up. He probably would not have come to Oakland. A bureaucrat, more of a typical bureaucratic leader, might have taken the job, but not a vision-driven leader like Tony."

However, while the Oakland context Tony Smith entered contained significant building blocks and support for his FSCS plan, it also contained what one observer dubbed "ankle weights" for him to carry. State receivership legacies figured prominently among them—low staff morale, distrust of "Central," and of course the

$100 million state loan. But OUSD's pervasive leadership culture presented even more difficult challenges for Smith to navigate. The Gates-funded small schools movement created a competitive school leadership ethos in which principals looked out for their own piece of the pie. It also exacerbated the have/have not school cultures of the hill and flatland schools, but also among flatland schools when some received grant funds from Atlantic, Gates, or other funders to develop new practices and schools that did not receive grants fell relatively further behind. One district leader reflected, "The small schools movement taught us a lot about the tools and practices we wanted for FSCS, but did so in an environment and culture of market competition and charters. They were the right tools, right practices, for the right students—but [rooted in] the wrong perspective." As a consequence, while Tony Smith urged Oakland's educators to move from a stance of "me to we," and imagine a *unified* school district culture, the district's existing leadership culture pushed hard against this vision.

The next step toward implementing Tony Smith's vision, he and his advisers believed, lay in undertaking a comprehensive, authentically collaborative planning process to develop the FSCS plan and rally wide-ranging support for it. As we will see, this planning approach turned out to be key not only to the plan's implementation in the short term, but also to its stability in the long term.

CHAPTER 2

Developing a Full-Service Community Schools Strategic Plan

New OUSD Superintendent Tony Smith spent 2009–2010 walking around Oakland, meeting with residents in the city's diverse neighborhoods, visiting schools, drafting ideas, and asking: "Coming out of seven years of receivership, what is it this district needs at this moment?" Smith's analysis also drew on Alameda County's 2008 report *Life and Death by Unnatural Causes*, which detailed how regions, neighborhoods, and zip codes determine life expectancy for children and students who are furthest from opportunities.[1] Smith often said, "the district is necessary, but not sufficient"—and this perspective permeates all of the *Community Schools, Thriving Students* work.

Smith's year of observation, thinking, and writing resulted in a concept paper that formed the heart of the subsequent strategic plan. It laid out his vision for comprehensive, whole-child reform in Oakland and strategies for achieving it over time. Smith's reform ideas centered on organizing and marshaling *all* community resources to work in concert with the district to prepare and support Oakland's children, youth, and families. Talking about how FSCSs could address the inequities evident in the resources and supports available to Oakland's students, Smith focused on system change at school, district, and community levels. He held that "The common good requires uncommonly good public systems."

During this time, Smith began bringing on senior-level staff to support the reform plan. His first hire was New York City curriculum and instruction expert Maria Santos. Next, to help with planning, was Perry Chen, a longtime Oakland nonprofit leader, community activist and well-known consultant. In 2010, Nicole Taylor (East Bay Community Foundation), Lisa Villarreal (San Francisco Foundation), and other local funders provided resources to bring on a partner to help Smith with the strategic plan's thinking, writing, and logistics. They believed that Chen was the best person to help do that thinking.[2] Chen remembered, "Nicole and Lisa and a select set of funders wanted to show their support, trust, and faith in Oakland and in Tony as the new superintendent. They designed a creative and flexible fund of pooled monies for Tony to use for strategy and community engagement, and asked me to meet with him to see what could be possible."[3] Although Chen knew of Smith, he had never met him. The two men clicked immediately, energized by their shared vision and values around Oakland's schools and youth and pragmatic "grab time when you can" working style. Chen came on board as a part-time consultant to Smith in spring 2010 and then full-time as chief of staff to the superintendent in 2011.

In the spring of 2010, Chen and Maria Santos worked on elaborating Smith's concept paper. Santos added instructional muscle from New York City, Chen massaged it into more of a strategic plan format. They put the plan up to the board for review in June 2010, at the end of Smith's first year. Chen recalls,

> The board gave the concept paper their preliminary stamp, saying, "Okay, let's move forward with this exploration." This was an important step—to go slow and stay transparent. We didn't want to draft it all in a closed room, run forward, and say "This is the strategic plan, and everyone needs to follow it." Rather, after a half-year incubation and research of early ideas and observations, Tony wanted the

full strategic planning process for a community schools district to be open and community-driven. Therefore, we created an engagement structure around a set of task forces because the concept paper was organized that way—around ten initiatives that ranged from effective teaching and expanded learning to facilities and assets management.

With the board's approval in June 2010, Smith and Chen then turned to the process of a full year of community engagement and direct stakeholder involvement in plan development.

FULL-SERVICE COMMUNITY SCHOOLS REQUIRE SYSTEM CHANGE

In Smith's view, a full service community school (FSCS) serves the whole child; it functions as a core that includes the community and collaborates with the community to provide comprehensive supports for students' development; it shares responsibility for student, family, and community success. A FSCS offers a coordinated and integrated system of academic and support services, provides a safe and healthy place for students and their families before, after and during school, it personalizes its supports and resources according to community needs and assets.

These ideas about the form and function of FSCSs depart fundamentally from traditional ways of "doing school" and typical school, family, and community relationships. Smith believed passionately that implementation of a FSCS model required district system change. He considered the inequities in resources and opportunities available to Oakland's schools, students, and families at root a *system* problem, not one amenable to programmatic approaches such as those many funders pursued or other more school-focused reforms. Organizational dysfunction, unequal practices between flatlands and hills schools—and even among flatland schools—significantly and consistently disadvantaged Oakland's students of color. Further, only a systemic approach, Smith argued, could lead to a "district effect" on student achievement and address the achievement gap common in urban settings. In his view, Oakland needed to move from a reform approach targeted on narrowly defined problems or a group of schools to reforming the district itself. He and others involved in planning the initiative frequently referenced "transformation" or "sea change."

An assumption central to Smith's thinking about system change held that the relevant "system" involved more than schools; it implicated a community's youth-serving sector—health and social service providers, housing and employment services, parent and family liaisons, and city parks and recreational facilities. In his view, the "system" that shortchanges poor kids goes well beyond the school, but the schools occupy the center of this system of developmental resources. As he put it, "The strategy is not to gradually improve the schools but to transform them into a system of FSCSs, a system that brings all sectors of the community into the school environment so all children can thrive."

Oakland Expresses a Different Problem Statement

Smith's system approach to tackling the achievement gaps between Oakland's poor students (generally students of color) and their advantaged peers (typically white) stands apart from the "problem statements" found elsewhere in urban districts struggling with similar class- and race-based achievement disparities. Ideas about how to address the poor academic performance of students of color living in poverty typically centered at that time on "fixing" the schools and instructional quality, but did not consider non-academic factors that might affect school performance. For instance, a clarifying assumption guiding Montgomery County, Maryland's, public schools' 1999 *Call to Action* focused on teachers " . . . because the quality of teaching makes *all* [emphasis in the original] the difference in the children's experience, resources should support teaching and learning."[4] Oakland's approach acknowledged teachers' importance, but assumed that teachers were only part of what mattered to students' school success.

Oakland's FSCS model also differed from usual school or project-based urban education reform efforts in its "neighborhood zone approach" that moved beyond school walls to its close-by community. Smith outlined a place-based perspective attentive to each neighborhood's particular needs, opportunities and assets. This approach drew on Smith's own troubled childhood and personal experience with how neighborhood poverty and violence can shape life pathways. The character of families and neighborhoods, Smith knew, could and often did derail efforts to improve academics if left out of a reform initiative.

BUILDING TOGETHER, ENGAGING THE COMMUNITY: PLANNING 2010–2011

"There was an intentionality from the beginning. Tony knew where he wanted to go," said Perry Chen. Smith launched the FSCS planning process *Building Together, Engaging Community* with a compelling "why" and clear strategy of how to proceed.[5] "You need to start with the North Star, with the vision, not with the structure," he said. Smith understood a major goal of the planning process in terms of mobilizing broad community support for his plan and creating "positive contagion" for it.[6] Strategic planning in Oakland was not the top-down, consultant-driven, behind-closed-doors process found in many urban districts. From the outset, Smith insisted that FSCS planning be transparent and accessible to all. He firmly believed that "it takes a city" to meet the needs of all of Oakland's children and that a FSCS approach required adults to buy into a "systems approach."[7] A district leader recalled, "Tony always talked about 'Purpose, Policy, Practice.' Your plan has to be purpose-driven, but you still have to have the policy and then the practice. A policy is not just what the board decides to do, it must be strategic." Smith's approach to planning also represented his conviction that significant system change could not be mandated from the top. As he explained: "Everyone in the organization needs to subscribe to the whole child mission, everyone. Not just teachers, administrators and partners, but also facilities, nutrition, legal services and so on."

Smith also subscribed to the view that "Change is likely to be systemic only if it comes about through the mobilization of a broad set of players in a concerted effort to alter what has been labeled 'a culture of failure.'"[8] A system perceived to be running well, or at least one wrestling with only a few minor problems, seldom inspires system change. A culture of failure certainly pervaded Oakland post-receivership as educators, parents, and community members reflected on the district's inability to retain control of its schools' and students' academic shortfalls. However, most importantly, Tony Smith was able to leverage the generally negative feelings about OUSD expressed across Oakland and residents' frustrations with the schools to generate broad community buy-in for the planning process. Perry Chen put it this way: "The district and community felt that we're in a context, just coming out of receivership, where they had little voice. Tony knew that for us to have a very successful strategic planning process, it must feel different. It must come from a place where the community is at the table as early and as often as possible." Both Smith and Chen worked to create that inclusive planning process.

Longtime observer of urban education reform efforts Clarence Stone advises that significant change "requires a master politician who knows how to draw together disparate groups, provide clear and direct benefits to cooperation, define an inclusive vision, and pragmatically zero in on doable goals and tasks."[9] The East Bay Community Foundation's Nicole Taylor, like many Oaklanders, saw Smith as that master politician: "Tony has galvanized cross-sections of the Oakland community—not just folks within the school district but business leaders, nonprofits and community leaders, parents and families." Researchers Michael Fullan and Joanne Quinn identify seven leadership competencies they find essential for successful whole school improvement: that a successful educational change leader: "Challenges the status quo; builds trust through clear communications and expectations; creates a community owned plan for success; focuses on team over self; has a high sense of urgency for change and sustainable results; builds external networks/partnerships."[10] Tony Smith embodied each these competencies from the outset.

Oakland Community Organizations (OCO) and other community organizing groups were, as Perry Chen put it, "important critical friends. They helped us understand what parents and families were experiencing and saying." Developing a FSCS strategic plan made intense demands on all involved. Smith put Chen in charge of the Friday three-hour district cabinet and community leadership sessions. Here, individuals weekly shared their ideas about a FSCS initiative and told their personal leadership stories. Chen recalled:

> Early on, various central leaders would evoke the adage that "culture eats strategy for breakfast." These Fridays very expensive and different meetings [in terms of people's time] and they did lead to a culture change. It was a way for people to get to know each other, to work better together. Sharing their personal leadership stories was often very emotional. Tony focused on building trust because that was broken amongst a lot of people in the system [coming out of state receivership]. In that sense, these Friday meetings were also very healing.

Smith, Chen, and others engaged in supporting the planning process knew that while a compelling vision for system change was essential, alone it was insufficient to bring about change. As Johnson, Uline, and Perez write, "Leaders must also help everyone who plays a role in accomplishing the vision to see the vision as appealing and worth the requisite effort."[11] To achieve commitment to the FSCS vision and concrete engagement in plan development, the yearlong planning process involved ten strategic initiatives addressed, supported, and informed by fourteen task forces. Strategic initiatives fell into two general categories: high-quality effective instruction; and readying the organization for FSCS structure and systems. The task forces took up issues key to building systemwide change. They held responsibility for such topics as school site governance; quality community schools standards; social-emotional learning (SEL) standards;

student and family engagement standards; and a first read on equity policy. Smith and Chen stressed that these policies sat at the core of system change and affected every district school, whether or not it had a community school manager, as did the first cohort of eight FSCS, "early adopter" schools (these schools were selected because they were among the district's neediest). The fourteen task forces focused on developing goals and strategies associated with the ten initiatives central to the 2010–2011 strategic plan, shown in figure 2.1.[12]

Figure 2.1 *Strategic plan initiatives*

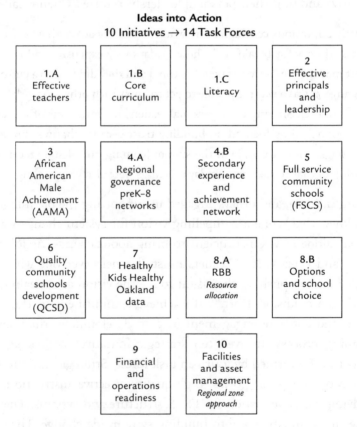

Ideas into Action
10 Initiatives → 14 Task Forces

1.A Effective teachers	1.B Core curriculum	1.C Literacy	2 Effective principals and leadership
3 African American Male Achievement (AAMA)	4.A Regional governance preK–8 networks	4.B Secondary experience and achievement network	5 Full service community schools (FSCS)
6 Quality community schools development (QCSD)	7 Healthy Kids Healthy Oakland data	8.A RBB *Resource allocation*	8.B Options and school choice
	9 Financial and operations readiness	10 Facilities and asset management *Regional zone approach*	

Source: Perry Chen, "Community Schools Thriving Students: Strategic Work Update," PowerPoint presentation, OUSD Board of Education, December 11, 2011

Chen and Junious Williams, then executive director of Urban Strategies Council, designed the task forces to represent multiple stakeholders and perspectives—"tree-tops" and grassroots, nonprofit leaders, public agencies such as social services and the mayor's office, advocacy organizations such as Oakland Community Organizations and the Urban Strategies Council, educators and community residents, and youth and families.[13] Task force leadership was intentionally designed to have at least one leader from the central leadership team and one community-based leader. Each of the task force leads had a mandate to create a group that was reasonably representative of Oakland in terms of demographics and perspectives and to ensure the groups most impacted by the subject had a presence at the table. Each task force's composition reflected the specific demands of their task; there was no universal task force member selection or uniform task force size.[14] Task force leaders issued an open call to either general or selected populations to get involved and start developing a chapter for the strategic plan.

By spring 2011, with the upcoming board meetings to review and vote on the plan, Chen recalls his worries as numerous task force reports and notes from the many community engagement sessions accumulated and he was unable to find any extended sit-down time with the superintendent. Smith's calendar was packed—meetings with funders, community leaders, and state and federal policy makers: "I was anxious because there was just reams and reams of input and ideas. Tony had no bandwidth in his calendar to sit down and think about how all of this works. So I looked at his calendar and saw that he was flying to DC. I told him that I was going to book myself to sit next to him and we were going to use all that plane time—just to think for six hours each way."

The resulting FSCS plan was not without critics. Some administrators and teacher leaders worried that the proposed system approach and comprehensive whole-child focus would distract teachers from classroom work, or prompt some to excuse academic shortfalls in terms of non-school factors. Other critics expressed concerns about central office capacity. "There were those," said Smith, "who believed that the central office was the problem . . . that what we needed was enough smart, good people to have their own schools. However, I honestly believe that the role of the central organization is to hold a vision of equity and to take responsibility for targeting resources where they are most needed. Equity can never be achieved on a school-by-school basis . . . we're going to make a public system to interrupt that." The three-hour Friday sessions and other community engagement opportunities provided critical opportunity for taking up these issues and for Smith, Chen, Williams, and others to respond to them concretely. As one observer said at the time, "Tony is helping them to heal and believe again [in their work], by virtue of what he is and genuinely cares about."

Smith from the beginning underscored the "unified" part of OUSD and urged educators to "move from *me* to *we*." But "we" was challenged. Individuals who took part in these discussions recall that a "secret" group of around fifteen principals met to consider "seceding" from the district and becoming charters. Many worried that "unified" would compromise the successes they had achieved as part of the small schools initiative and that their schools would lose out in terms of resources. Most of these principals decided to stay with OUSD, but two left to head up new charter schools.

In short, Oakland's planning process differed in both conception and scope from most urban education reform planning processes. Commentators on urban school reform efforts highlight their typical "project focus" and incremental change goals.[15] Rather than the system perspective Smith advocated, urban education reform proposals typically feature the addition (or elimination) of various initiatives, such as professional development, an updated curriculum, or new accountability structures. These reform efforts take a tactical rather than the broad strategic approach to education change seen in Oakland. For instance, typical among many accounts of urban education reform approaches is a step-based, problem-solving approach to design and implementation. Former Boston superintendent Tom Payzant called out eight such tasks: identify the problem; analyze the problem and diagnose its causes; develop a theory of action; design the strategy; plan for implementation; implement the strategy; access progress; adapt and modify for continuous improvement.[16] A tactical approach may bring innovative and productive practices, but it comprises incremental, not radical, change and typically serves to sustain or merely tweak status quo arrangements. Education historians David Tyack and Larry Cuban long ago dubbed this approach "tinkering toward Utopia."[17]

Tony Smith and, Perry Chen intended to nurture change in culture and operations at all levels of the system by posing questions that could nudge participants out of their institutional boxes to focus on broad goals. They guided each task force to ask, "What do we want for students? What must change? What do we need to build?" An aim of broad stakeholder participation had to do with culture, relationships, and creating understanding that the FSCS concept was not business as usual, but went beyond individual organizational agenda and perspectives. Looking across the failure of urban education reform efforts undertaken in Atlanta, Baltimore, Detroit, and Washington, DC, Jeffrey Henig and colleagues conclude that it fundamentally reflects insufficient civic capacity, or "the ability to assemble a broad-based set of community actors who might have collective capacity to design and implement educational reform."[18] For Smith and Chen, broad, concrete stakeholder involvement in the planning process represented the most promising strategy for building and extending wide-ranging civic capacity essential to support FSCS.

Intensive stakeholder engagement in the FSCS planning process and responsibility for drafting the strategic plan achieved that goal. As one community leader put it, "Community partners saw the relationships established as part of planning and the FSCS vision as a sea change . . . the district coming out of state receivership, to taking care of the whole community." Several principals commented on the value to them of participating in plan development after the negative context of state takeover. In addition to enabling mobilization of support for FSCS, Tony Smith and colleagues explicitly designed the planning process to provide opportunities for capacity building and problem solving that would benefit the initiative as sites and the central office moved to implementation because participants had been required to think through implications for action.

FSCS Planning Differs from Typical Community Schools Planning

The planning process underlying the FSCS initiative also differed significantly from typical community schools' planning efforts. Community schools advocates such as Joy Dryfoos and Sue Maguire underscore the critical role the planning process plays in the effective community school implementation, and the importance of inclusiveness: "The more people and groups involved at the outset, the firmer the foundation for a comprehensive program."[19] However, these planning recommendations focus the development of *individual* community schools and generally are silent on implications for host districts. *Building Together, Engaging the Community*, in contrast, addressed FSCS implementation at the district and system levels as well as at school levels. "It's not just the school that disadvantages poor kids," said Smith. "It's the whole network of services, resources, and opportunities needed to support their health development. The school is the hub, but the change needed goes way beyond the individual school. It's not about a new program here or there, but about a coherent system of supports for kids." Smith's approach assumed that significant and sustained change required understanding of the underlying design principles needed to guide practices adopted at individual schools and agencies. In his view, significant system change needed individual implementers to work out their own meaning; each school's implementation would and should look somewhat different. Tony Smith refers to this purpose-driven but adaptive approach to planning and subsequently to implementation as "targeted universalism," referencing the work of UCB professor john powell.[20]

District and community advocates closely managed the planning process and task forces to foster buy-in and broad support for FSCS across the community. Junious Williams (then head of the Urban Strategies Council), the initiative's designated community intermediary, recalled this role as very hands-on and attentive to "who might go off the wall and wreck the whole thing. The whole process was carefully orchestrated."

"It was important to have an African American elder [Junious Williams] centrally involved with the process," said Perry Chen. Reflecting on the planning year, he points out that "a number of things lined up in 2010–2011 for Tony, Maria, and me. We incubated ideas for the first half of the year; we got the go-ahead from the board to continue; then we designed a comprehensive community engagement process. We didn't know it was going to grow into something like five hundred people over the whole period, but it gave us the plan—some real authentic grounding and political protection."

Focus on Coherence

Their ability to shepherd the district's new strategic plan through a broad, positive community engagement process enabled Chen, Smith, and others to move from fostering support for the plan to concentrating on the plan's coherence. They promised task force participants that their voice and vision would be prominent in the resulting strategic plan. OUSD's strategic plan would not be the result of closed-door central office sessions or consultant's proposals, but represent the community's priorities, concerns, and perspective. Perry Chen faced the challenge of keeping that promise to the fourteen different task force leads who had responsibility for drafting chapters of the strategic plan while also creating an internally coherent strategic plan to guide the vision of system change underlying the FSCS initiative. For a plan to have coherence, it must not merely represent a collection of perspectives and priorities but recognize that all policies within a system are interrelated and affect each other. A coherent plan sets out shared goals, frameworks for action, and support structures. As education researchers Smith and O'Day explain, a coherent system requires "mutually reinforcing policies designed to build capacity and focus to ensure . . . [that] top-down direction was combined with bottom-up discretion, knowledge, and professional energy of school people and their communities."[21]

OUSD's fourteen-task-force approach to planning and commitment to broad community engagement created a management tension. How to achieve coherence while also showing the "voice" and the contribution of multiple stakeholders? Chen addressed that challenge in two ways. First, he focused task force conversations on what mattered to the kids and the conditions that connected stakeholders about purpose, rather than on particular program elements or tactics. Keeping the focus on goals for kids, Chen believed, promoted collaboration across agencies and departments and brought attention to policy coherence across and within domains. Chen and others called this approach "a push against adhocracy; everything had to align with core goals; coherence had to be achieved at the receiving end [schools and kids], not at the delivery end [district programs and policies]."

Second, Chen managed the spring 2011 writing of the strategic plan with an eye to the shared language, goals, and perspectives essential to a coherent plan. Each task force lead held responsibility for writing a chapter of the plan—Tony Smith insisted that participants, not just district staff, take part as authors. Chen remembers,

> It was like incredibly stressful and time-consuming. I knew everyone [task force leads] was stressed out and working so hard. My role didn't have departments to run or schools to oversee, so I tried to think creatively and pragmatically, to make it as easy and focused as possible for them. I engaged a friend of mine who is a great writer and educator; we interviewed [all of the task force leads], recorded and transcribed those conversations. I sent everyone both the audio file and the transcription so they could have drafts of their own words and write their chapters faster.

Looking back at his role, Chen stresses the importance of his ability to concentrate on plan development, coordinate disparate elements and interests, and be available to meet with Smith when and wherever possible: "I know of few if any other [district] chief of staff positions that don't also include running programs, overseeing projects or a bunch of other daily responsibilities that make it impossible to focus on developing a strategic plan." This capacity was part of the original design—the philanthropic funders who underwrote a chief of staff position wanted a dedicated strategist and community engager for Smith.

When the chapters came in over the spring, Chen and colleagues "raked through them and connected everything . . . so that the writing was coherent and flowed, more like a novel and not like a short story collection . . . finance can't be saying something totally opposite from what early childhood wants to be done financially. We created massive spread sheets where things were visible and locked together." Chen underscored the importance of retaining participants' voice and resolving missed connections among chapters so that the plan would be both coherent as a guide and authentic as representative of the participants' positions: "I didn't want to write the whole thing! The process is as important as the substance, right? How you do it matters as much as what you did." By June 2011, when the strategic plan went to the board, *Community Schools, Thriving Students* was internally consistent and enjoyed broad community buy-in as well as unanimous board support. Chen reflected, "Admittedly, it was a big, thick plan with a community-built framework to hang everything on. Other strategic plans I have seen are more like pamphlets. Those documents are easier to manage because everyone can just hew back to the district's three principles or whatever, sometimes without really considering purpose, policy or practice."

The process of developing OUSD's new strategic plan took care to connect stakeholders' perspectives to each other and to the initiative's broad goals. *Community Schools, Thriving Students* differed consequentially from "typical" district strategic plans in its authentic and broad engagement of stakeholders, in the implementation definitions developed for various goals, and in the deep, informed support constructed for it. As we will see, this investment of time and resources in creating this admittedly hefty strategic plan paid off importantly in both short and long terms.

PART II

IMPLEMENTATION:
SYSTEM LEVEL

CHAPTER 3

A New Strategic Plan

Creating System Change

In June 2011, Oakland's school board unanimously adopted a new five-year strategic plan: *Community Schools, Thriving Students*.

Introducing the new strategic plan, Superintendent Tony Smith wrote in his letter to the Oakland community:

> Our efforts in the Oakland Unified School District (OUSD) are now clearly focused on serving all of our children in every neighborhood by providing high quality community schools where children, adults, and community thrive. We are committed to creating, and sustaining, a district of community schools capable of supporting the unique needs of each child while creating caring school communities that link every Oakland neighborhood. We believe that each child in Oakland must be ready to succeed in college and careers that lead them to healthy and happy lives. The OUSD school board believes that Oakland must become a city known for how well our children are cared for and how well they are educated. We have a great legacy and we acknowledge and honor past efforts to serve children. We also know we have a long way to go to become the public school district and city all our children need today for a secure and healthy future tomorrow.
>
> It's with these beliefs that we engage in creating a Full Service Community District filled with Full Service Community Schools, in which schools act as resource and service hubs that connect with local partners to help build healthy and vibrant schools and communities.[1]

Oakland's Five-year Strategic Plan:
Community Schools, Thriving Students

VISION

All students will graduate from high school. As a result, they are caring, competent, and critical thinkers, fully-informed, engaged and contributing citizens, and prepared to succeed in college and career.

MISSION

Oakland Unified School District is becoming a Full Service Community District that serves the whole child, eliminates inequity, and provides each child with excellent teachers for every day.

GOAL AREAS

Every student in the Oakland Unified School District will:

· Attend a SAFE, HEALTHY, and SUPPORTIVE SCHOOL, that collaborates with civic and community partners to reduce violence in the community and schools, thereby creating secure campuses where a culture of calm prevails.
· Learn the knowledge, skills, and abilities to be PREPARED for SUCCESS in COLLEGE and CAREERS when they graduate from high school, to ensure that they can read, write, speak, think critically, and reason mathematically for post-secondary success.
· Have HIGH QUALITY and EFFECTIVE INSTRUCTION with excellent teachers for every day of the school year.

The Oakland Unified School District will:

· Become a FULL SERVICE COMMUNITY DISTRICT that is in service of and fully supporting the success of community schools and thriving students.
· Be ACCOUNTABLE for HIGH QUALITY for its schools and in its work across the organization.

Source: Oakland Unified School District, *Community Schools, Thriving Students: A Five-Year Strategic Plan,* Summary Report, Version 2.0, June 2011, www.thrivingstudnts.org.

A triangle—adapted from that used by the Children's Aid Society and the National Center for Community Schools—symbolized the plan's mission and goals (see figure 3.1). Thriving students are at the center as the focus and goal of the plan. The sides of the triangle emerged from task force discussions and community ideas about key themes and core principles. The plan explained: "With these 'sides' in place, we developed and mapped our major goal areas along these themes—emphasizing our Board's priorities for children and youth."[2]

IMPLEMENTATION TIME LINE

The strategic plan outlined a five-year rollout (2011–2016) based on task force design work (see figure 3.2).

Whereas many districts' strategic plans stick to bulleted points and brief text, Oakland's is a hefty document. True to Smith's intent that the plan be community-generated, its sixty-one tightly packed

Figure 3.1 *Oakland's community school model*

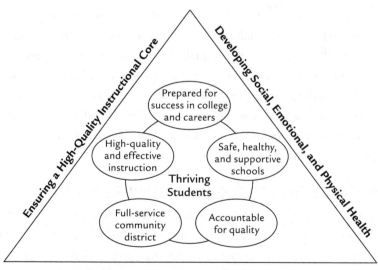

Creating Equitable Opportunities for Learning

Source: Oakland Unified School District.

Figure 3.2 *OUSD strategy timeline for 2009–2016*

Seven Years, Four Phases, Five-Year Strategic Plan (2009–2016)

Source: Oakland Unified School District

pages pull together task force recommendations based on the "chapters" task force leads produced. According to Smith,

> This strategic plan basically sits on top of all of the task force work and weaves it all together. *Community Schools, Thriving Students* elaborates a set of school quality standards. This is the first time the district has ever adopted a set of quality standards. It was a product of the task forces. This organization has said "This is what good looks like." Even though it's going to take different types of work and supports to have a quality school in every neighborhood, that needs to be the main mission of the central organization. We need a coherent, protected pathway for our kids.[3]

FUNDING COMMUNITY SCHOOLS, THRIVING STUDENTS

How does a high-poverty district pay for these expanded FSCS activities and responsibilities? The biggest source of funds that support Oakland's array of FSCS system services is public dollars, including federal, state and local. From 2011 to 2018, OUSD leveraged more than $450 million in public funds primarily to support health centers/mental health/nutrition (about $300 million) and afterschool programs (about $140 million).

Although Oakland has deep poverty, the Bay Area is resource-rich. In its robust nonprofit sector, many CBOs write their own grants and provide staffing and other resources to FSCSs. Private funds from individuals, local institutions and foundations provide important and flexible support. The FSCS initiative received about $65 million in private funds from 2011 to 2018. Finally, many school leaders chose to spend some of their budgets on community schools managers (CSMs) and restorative justice staffing. From 2016–2018, these decisions generated nearly $10 million in FSCS support. Further, these school-based allocations were tied to the Local Control and Accountability Plan (LCAP). (The LCAP is a state school finance tool that enables local educational agencies to set goals and leverage federal, state and local resources to meet those goals.)[4] Because they are allocated at the school level, LCAP funds are protected and cannot be included in general district budget cuts.

The FSCS funding story is largely one of expanding the pie to include public and private dollars outside of traditional school budgets, especially for health/mental health, as well as philanthropic dollars. Since 2011, OUSD has leveraged significant resources to support community schools: ~$66.7 million in private funds (including foundations and individual donors); ~$461 million in public funds including federal, state and local programs; ~$9M in school-site contributions toward CSM and restorative justice facilitators (beginning in 2016).

THE SHIFT: FROM A COMMUNITY SCHOOL TO "A DISTRICT OF COMMUNITY SCHOOLS"

For Smith and FSCS advocates, taking a school-centered model such as community schools and evolving it into a strategy for a unified school district entailed adapting the body of community school theory and thought to the "district system." The community schools

movement typically focused on change at the school level but provided much less guidance on implications for schools' broader context—districts or cities. For Smith, the plan and its visual model
embedded this shift with one side of the triangle—creating equitable opportunities—representing his vision for the FSCS district that
would change to support all schools to become community schools:
"New work requires new tools."

Smith knew that changing whole systems as the strategic plan detailed required "all of us to work in right relationships and in new
ways to reach our vision." Reform initiatives that include the whole
system as Oakland's did aim to bring about change not merely by
adopting a promising new program or eliminating an unsuccessful one. System change requires thinking about where changes in
structures can lead to significant, enduring changes in the underlying, reinforcing arrangements associated with the problem. Peter
Senge advises that system change means "learning to see underlying
'structures' rather than 'events' . . . thinking in terms of processes of
change rather than 'snapshots.'"[5] System change calls for diagnoses
in cause-and-effect terms, rather than just looking at the symptom
as "the problem to fix." Senge counsels that "the essence of systems
thinking lies in seeing patterns where others see only events and
forces to react to . . . see the forest not only the trees."[6] In other words,
get the right "drivers" and see the causal loops.

Smith also recognized that the superintendent has the most influence and authority at the district level. For a wall-to-wall, full-scale
plan like that outlined in *Community Schools, Thriving Students*, the locus most amenable to change is the district and central offices. Thus,
during his tenure, the central office and the larger district organization were the two areas where Smith concentrated his efforts regarding
what he called "systems change and doing different." He considered all
departments—from instruction, complementary student services, and
school oversight to finance, operations, human resources, and facilities—as implicated in the new strategic plan. To become a FSCS district
that supports all schools to be FSCSs signaled a major transformation

for the district system—asking all central office departments to work together, to challenge and change their way of working.

A Shifting Paradigm for the Central Office

The strategic plan called for different approaches, perspectives and relationships in OUSD's central office. It highlighted the need for the central office departments to "learn the community school model for the central district . . . Both the community and schools have often seen the central office as a drain on the resources and an obstacle to education . . . dealing with 'the district' is often challenging . . . the Central office must re-invent itself in order for the district to achieve its vision of *Community Schools, Thriving Students*.[7]

Throughout its discussion of the central office role, the strategic plan features the district "in service of" FSCS practices and resources.[8] The model, designed in partnership with the OUSD Board of Education, lays out the "Planning Paradigm Shift" required to convert the district's support systems and services into not just a service organization but "an organization in service of . . . " (see table 3.1).

Table 3.1 *Changing the role of central office in a community school model*

THEN	NOW
School closure a single solution to academic/fiscal challenges	Multipronged approach to create equitable opportunities
No clarity regarding "To what end?"	FSCS goal: Community health and well-being
Looking at individual schools	Looking at entire regions
No consideration of assets	Maximizing assets informs decision making
Tactical	Strategic
Short-term	Long-haul
Equity-neutral	Equity-centered
As a system of schools	Becoming a school system

Source: Oakland Unified School District, *Community Schools, Thriving Students: A Five Year Strategic Plan.* Summary Report. Version 2.0, June 2011, p.38.

SYSTEM CHANGE TOOLS

Following the June 2011 board approval of *Community Schools, Thriving Students*, implementation proceeded simultaneously at both district and site levels. To advance and reinforce that implementation, Superintendent Smith and Perry Chen set about considering policy levers and organizational changes needed to support the system change foundational to the new initiative. "Imagine a system that puts the whole child at the center," said Smith. In contrast to the "adopt a model, pick a site" approach seen in many community school initiatives, Oakland leaders systematically considered aspects integral to a FSCS districtwide implementation. They knew it was not possible to approach the question of system change in a piecemeal fashion, but rather that "all means all." FSCS was not an "opt in or opt out" proposition; all OUSD schools would be community schools. Even though they could not do everything at once, the district, not individual schools, comprised the unit of change as they thought about moving forward. As Chen put it, "Everything had to align with the plan's core goals. We addressed problems as interrelated and symptomatic of deeper issues. They had to fit together like puzzle pieces. How to translate FSCSs into whole-district change? We knew we had to think at scale, confront all of the issues, from the outset."

Across the strategic plan and over the past nine years, district leaders used a variety of "system change tools" in combination and across topic areas to make things happen. To begin the journey with "system change" explicitly meant deploying a mix of these tools from the start. Three figured prominently in Community Schools Thriving Students planning and implementation from the beginning:

- *Use process to change culture:* Involve stakeholders to build the climate, culture and spirit: charge and inspire with responsibility and urgency
- *Use levers:* A range of hard/soft and internal/external tools that pragmatically blend "opt in" and compliance

- *Change structure:* Reimagine typical departments and divisions, to break down old silos and foster cross-work

The remainder of this chapter considers the first of these tools—how district and community leaders used process to change minds and culture about education and relationships in Oakland, and shift ideas about strategies for making it more equitable, more effective and more inclusive. Chapter 4 takes up the subject of the levers used to bring about system change, and chapter 5 details a critical structural change—a new department dedicated to supporting *Community Schools, Thriving Students'* districtwide school-level implementation.

USING PROCESS TO CHANGE SYSTEM CULTURE

Chapter 2 detailed the 2010–2011 years and the eighteen-month planning process with fourteen task forces, more than thirty-five hundred participants, and ongoing communication with stakeholders. This scale of planning had not been done before in Oakland and has not occurred since. It featured the meta-consistency of a large-scale community process (listening, input, collaborating) to create a wide-scale community school plan. The process created a powerful culture of inclusion and buy-in to the resulting strategic plan, commitment that contains clues about why the plan has endured through so much churn over the years.

Another important inclusionary tactic involved naming all OUSD schools as community schools along a spectrum of supports—even the most distressed schools were lifted up for some positive community school practices and benefits. The power of including everybody proved significant. FSCS was not a typical education reform approach that would build slowly and ask schools to wait five to ten years before they were included. Perry Chen recalls going to "forgotten schools" to talk with principals, teachers, and parents about the plan, and seeing their eyes light up when somebody said, "You are a full-service community school already. You do some extraordinary things here." This inclusion and recognition, Chen says, made them felt seen and turned many into advocates for this new plan.

Superintendent Smith acted quickly to put the processes and structure in place that could change central office communication, planning, and culture. When Smith arrived, OUSD, like most urban districts, functioned in departmental silos that communicated poorly, if at all, and operated with departmental goals, not district goals, as their primary reference. Typically, a district's central office operates as two sides of the house—schools/instruction and finance/operations. Smith reimagined many parts of the central office and, in order to create a FSCS district, required all leaders to be responsible and accountable to, and designers of, the strategic plan. He believed the writing of chapters and reconciling differences that emerged from task forces would create accountability across the system.

Smith instituted new internal procedures—obligatory Friday meetings—to promote communication across departments and central office "houses." These meetings of the OUSD cabinet (twenty individuals) and senior leadership across all departments (forty individuals) focused on collaboration and meaning-making supportive of the new planning process and strategic plan. This new central office process was not without pushback, resistance, or conflict. Moreover, it was not without varying levels of buy-in and accountability over the years. But it did represent a different and changed central office culture and meant that departments and their leaders were "doing different" from the start.

The superintendent also moved to alter existing and often negative district and community conceptions of the central office. State receivership had left OUSD educators resentful of top-down mandates and apparent inattention to their school contexts, issues, and needs. Smith heard soon after his arrival that many educators and community members saw the central office as a significant source of OUSD's problems because of poor spending decisions, isolation from schools and families, and generally low capacity. To change those conceptions, he and others instituted a number of advisories and committees to move decision making and oversight into the community and "re-culture" relationships between schools, community, and district to be collaborative and respectful.

CHANGED EXPECTATIONS AND ACCOUNTABILITY FOR LEADERS

Community Schools, Thriving Students highlighted the importance of principals' roles in transitioning to full service community schools. Initiative 3B of the strategic plan states that some elements of the principal's role would change and that "we must have a common definition of what a Full Service Community School Leader embodies."[9] Prior to 2011, OUSD had no systematic process for supporting school leaders or a clear definition of school leadership. A 2009 review of OUSD's No Child Left Behind (NCLB) practices instructed OUSD to develop a principal evaluation procedure. Smith and others recognized the need to focus on leadership development and expectations in establishing the Effective Principal and Leadership task force. Based on focus groups, the task force concluded: "Not unlike many districts, we have multiple interpretations of 'effective leadership.' The expectations, foci, and goals for leaders change frequently and vary across the district. Leaders experienced these inconsistencies as barriers to their learning."[10]

The development and implementation of the Principal Leadership Framework resulting from taskforce work involved significant changes in how school leaders understood their responsibilities and assessed their effectiveness.[11] A Leadership Task Force (LTF) begun in 2011 convened to develop a "homegrown" framework for effective leadership consistent with the district's vision of what a FSCS leader represents. The LTF included principals, assistant principals, teachers, district leaders, and community partners; participants defined six leadership dimensions of practice central to OUSD leaders' effective support of the district's FSCS vision. (The LTF included more than fifty OUSD administrators over the years.)

The resulting Principal Leadership Framework embodies another instance of process changing culture to create system change (see figure 3.3). Though the leadership framework has roots in NCLB's evaluation requirements, its broad acceptance by OUSD leaders reflects the process of development, not the more typical pro forma compliance responses. "This document has been designed using a democratic engagement process that includes the persons who use and will be most affected by the development of the professional learning tool and evaluation instrument." Launched in 2011 as an outgrowth of the Full Service Community Schools Strategic Plan, the OUSD Leadership Task Force (LTF) developed a homegrown framework for effective site leadership, the Leadership Growth and Development System (LGDS), supported by district and national research. The district explains: "The overarching purpose of the LGDS is to

Figure 3.3 *OUSD Leadership Growth and Development System*

Source: Oakland Unified School District, https://www.ousd.org/domain/3423.

ensure all schools are equipped with highly qualified and effective leaders. This practitioner-created evaluation system facilitates this goal by: (1) supporting leaders' growth and development through the annual goal-setting process and cycle of inquiry, and (2) producing valid and reliable data using transparent measures of assessment."[12]

Lynda Tredway, founding coordinator of UC Berkeley's Principal Leadership Institute, was a founding member of the LTF and served as a co-facilitator for three years.[13] District staff acknowledge, "Her vision, expertise, knowledge, ability to both listen and push, and forward thinking propelled the members to think deeply and critically about their practice and how to support our district and peers in systematizing leadership development following an asset-based cycle of inquiry practice."[14]

The framework development process Tredway led proved critical to participants' commitment to and comfort with the new LGDS, which sought no small shift in mindset and culture following the punitive climate of state receivership and a "climate of fear." Commenting on the development process and OUSD administrators' buy-in to the framework, Tredway noted that the peer-based process of meeting, discussing, developing, piloting, and evaluating proved essential: "The new framework was not something done to them, or handed down from central. It was theirs and they owned it." The "secret sauce," Tredway continued, "was their deep, deep to the core commitment to being bigger than your school. They were charged with the spiritual dimension of the [FSCS] initiative."

In 2014–2015, the district and the union, the United Administrators of Oakland Schools (UAOS), launched a districtwide pilot to learn how to revise protocol and tools to better support principals' growth and development. (The district extended the pilot for the 2015–2016 and 2016–2017 academic years to continue revisions and fine-tuning.) In 2016–2017, the district piloted the LGDS with assistant principals and modified it for central office leaders. In June 2017, the union formally adopted the LGDS process for all certificated UAOS members.

Ultimately, the process launched by the 2011 LTF resulted in a new districtwide leadership growth and development system that includes all OUSD leaders, not just principals. Current Chief of Staff Curtiss Sarikey observed: "We have said we are a full-service community district. This is the operating frame for all principals to lead by. It doesn't matter if you have the support to be a full service community school, you've got to be working on these elements." The same leadership framework now applies to central office leaders as well.

Oakland's experience planning for and rolling out the new strategic plan shows how respectful, authentic, and broadly inclusionary processes can change culture and mindsets. The extensive planning process created broad, enthusiastic buy-in for the goals and system changes the plan represented, despite the cynicism and low morale shared by many OUSD stakeholders at the outset. Likewise, the "democratic" processes of the LTF moved OUSD school leaders from their generally anomic positions and individualistic leadership culture to broad support for a common definition of an effective leader and measures of leadership quality.

However, Tony Smith and his colleagues understood that process could not move some Oaklanders' attitudes and perspectives, especially about relationships between district procedures and structures and his foundational goal, equity. Change in thinking about equity would require stronger levers for system change.

CHAPTER 4

Levers for System Change

What do we want for students?
What must change?
What do we need to build?

The district leadership and task force participants explored these three central questions in the planning process as they developed recommendations for their particular topic area. These questions directed them to consider the system changes and levers capable of bringing about needed change in their associated underlying structures, policies, and practices. Task force participants considered which needed modification to work better or differently, and which needed to be created in order for the strategic plan to achieve its goals. To carry out the plan outlined in *Community Schools, Thriving Students*, the leadership team also sought levers that affected the district's relationships with students and families, teachers, and school leaders; altered the negative, unsafe school context many students encountered; and forged stronger, more consistent relationships with community partners. These goals required both new ways of doing the district's business, but also new mindsets about "doing school" in Oakland for the central office, schools, and community partners.

Levers for system change involve actions or changes that might lead to significant and enduring changes in system structures or conditions of concern. They range from simple to complex; they exist inside and outside the district. Some levers internal to the district might involve setting up a model of practice and having schools opt in; others might involve mandates issued from the superintendent or school board. External levers—state and federal policies and philanthropic grant requirements—typically feature compliance and aim to "make us do what we need to do" to increase equity and capacity across the system. They may, over time, influence the thinking that produced the problem in the first place as compliance brings system change.

LEVERS FOR SYSTEM CHANGE: A MATRIX

Even before the strategic plan's June 2011 authorization, Tony Smith, Perry Chen, Junious Williams, and others involved in constructing Oakland's Full Service Community School District initiative wrestled with questions of how to move OUSD toward its vision. These deliberations centered on the tools, or levers, that could bring about the system changes underlying task force participants' responses about goals for students, needed changes, and new practices.

A variety of levers existed for OUSD district leaders and school board to consider—from the "hard" accountability stance of mandates and requirements, to the "soft" accountability of capacity-building measures and new frameworks (see figure 4.1). OUSD's 2009 complex fiscal and system conditions and culture—right out of state receivership—highlighted the need for different types of levers to spur system change. Some focused on institutional culture; some featured collaboration; some encouraged educators and community leaders to opt in; others pushed down, requiring compliance with mandates. Smith knew that potentially effective system change levers existed at different levels—federal, state, and local—and that choices needed to be made with careful consideration of policy across levels of government, as well as Oakland's local political, social, and economic context.

State and federal policies generally turned on external compliance and set out actions OUSD had to take—fiscal and programmatic

Figure 4.1 *Levers for change*

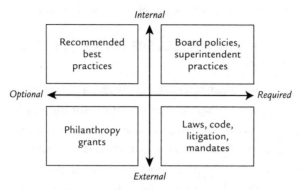

Internal

| Recommended best practices | Board policies, superintendent practices |

Optional ← → Required

| Philanthropy grants | Laws, code, litigation, mandates |

External

accountability, governance, services provision, for instance. Some philanthropic and government system-building investments turned on built-in accountability measures and time lines, others offered funds and supports to educators who bought in. These levers pushed on inertia in a most gentle and positive way: "You don't get a piece of the pie if you don't accept this grant." Practitioners and OUSD leaders did not want to leave money on the table and so usually went along with grant goals and requirements. Board policies also set out "have to do" changes but relied on internal accountability and administrative oversight for teeth make changes happen.

Targeted Universalism

In addition to evaluating various levers in terms of the local Oakland context, thinking about levers also reflected the superintendent's subscription to john powell's theory of "targeted universalism" as a guide to advancing equity (versus equality). According to powell,

> This is an approach that supports the needs of the particular while reminding us that we are all part of the same social fabric. Targeted universalism rejects a blanket universal, which is likely to be indifferent to the reality that different groups are situated differently relative to the institutions and resources of society. It also rejects the claim of formal equality that would treat all people the same as a way of denying

difference . . . It is important that we focus on changing the structure that people are within, not the people within the structures.[1]

EXTERNAL AND REQUIRED LEVERS (LAWS, CODES, LITIGATION, AND MANDATES)

Federal, state, and legal systems can make a district "do the right thing" through codes, laws, litigation, and funding guidelines. They provide a regulatory push. A passionate mission to promote equitable allocation of the resources and opportunities available to Oakland's poorest students drove Superintendent Smith to pursue external system change levers and take an active role in shaping them. In particular, Smith provided substantive leadership in framing major state policy issues that subsequently served as key external levers for the strategic plan in 2012 and beyond: new state requirements for local fund allocation and new school climate and equity indicators.

Local Control Funding Formula

California's 2014 school finance reform, the Local Control and Accountability Plan (LCAP), changed the way districts allocated their funds. As described in chapter 3, LCAP enabled districts to construct budgets in ways that reflect *local* needs, priorities, and concerns. Superintendent Smith participated actively in state-level discussions about funding categories and indicators and made central FSCS elements (such as basing school funding allocations on students' needs—ELL, homeless youth, special education students, academic proficiency) part of the district's mandated funding and accountability requirements.[2] Smith played a major role in constructing the LCAP template to reflect and protect major elements of OUSD's strategic plan.

CORE and State/Federal Systems

Perry Chen commented that being a CORE district comprised perhaps the "biggest lever of all because it encompasses other key pieces—accelerates things in the strategic plan because district has to do them, there's no choice." CORE (California Office to Reform Education) involved a collective of eight California districts and represented a moment when those district leaders could influence the governor, state superintendent, and California Department of Education as well as the US Secretary of Education.[3] Piloting practices across CORE districts led to the development of expanded indicators for school and district assessment such as social-emotional learning, school climate, and school site plans for equity and budgeting. These external and required indicators, consistent with Smith's strategic plan for the district, are now embodied in the California School Dashboard, the LCAP, and the Local Control Funding Formula (LCFF; this policy was enacted in 2013–2014 and replaced the previous K–12 finance system that had been in place for more than forty years[4]).

Federal Office of Civil Rights and the Voluntary Resolution Plan

Tony Smith and USC's Junious Williams turned to federal civil rights legislation as a tool to force attention to the equity issues that had long plagued OUSD. Reference to urgency and moral purpose alone, Smith knew, would not and could not lead to the deep policy changes required to address substantive equity goals in Oakland. Rhetoric about the inequitable resources and opportunities provided OUSD's poorest flatland students had persisted for years, yet the status quo prevailed in the district's fiscal and human resource policies and in school practices. Efforts to change them consistently fell short for political reasons, as well as for lack of institutional will and capacity. Despite his firm commitment to "top-down support for bottom-up change" and principled objection to issuing central office directives to schools, Smith understood that equity-based policy changes would require a hard accountability approach—one that carried meaningful monitoring and significant consequences. Chen offers a market explanation of principals' resistance to policies that might negatively affect their resources: "They think 'I've got to do what's best for my school' in contrast to a unified approach. That's why a compliance approach is needed. The education leadership culture is 'take care of your school and do what you can to promote it.'"

Advancing the strategic plan's equity vision entailed calculated consideration of the relatively non-negotiable levers that could drive the necessary changes in OUSD. In choosing a tactic to further OUSD's strategic plan, Superintendent Smith and supporters turned to federal muscle and the US Department of Education's Office of Civil Rights (OCR). With Smith's urging, the UCS sent the data they had gathered on the disproportionate disciplinary actions and school suspension imposed on black students to OCR as evidence of OUSD's violation of Title VI of the 1964 Civil Rights Act (protecting students from discrimination in public schools and colleges). Smith, Chen, and others felt that only federal action and associated compliance requirements could compel attention to the district student group most disadvantaged by OUSD's disciplinary approaches and fiscal and human resource policies. OCR decisions carry significant and consequential weight. They are immune to local institutional or political disputes such as those that derailed past Oakland efforts to address systemic inequities. Were OUSD to be found out of compliance with Title VI, OCR could withhold substantial federal dollars—most importantly, ESSA Title I.

Upon review of the USC report, the US Department of Civil Rights instituted compliance investigation of OUSD under Title VI. OCR examined district data from 1998 to 2011, interviewed district staff, visited schools and classrooms. OCR found evidence of

exclusionary discipline practices in the recent past . . . In 2011–2012 [district data], African American students composed 31.8% of the total student enrollment and 63% of all students who received OSS (out-of-school suspension) . . . and 61% of the students who were expelled, more than double the percentage of their enrollment in the District. White students composed 10.4% of the total student enrollment and 2% of the students who received OSS; no White students were expelled.[5]

OCR also found OUSD out of compliance with Title VI:

> When similarly situated students of different races are disciplined differently for the same offence, discrimination can be the only reasonable explanation for the different treatment."[6]

The district disciplinary policies that created disproportionate suspension and harsh discipline for students of color had multiple system roots. Concerns for students' safety, violence, and disruption led to zero tolerance disciplinary policies aimed at controlling students in school. Yet in many instances, extreme discipline policies do not address root issues that foster problematic student behavior—emotional upset, trauma, feelings of insecurity and hopelessness, and safety concerns. Several observers felt that teachers lacked cultural understanding of black students.

OUSD requested a voluntary rather than mandated resolution of the OCR findings. Discussions and negotiations with OCR dominated the fall of 2012 and resulted in a Voluntary Resolution Plan (VRP) accepted by OCR. The VRP not coincidentally represented strategic, specific, and authoritative support for *Community Schools, Thriving Students'* equity goals and implementation framework. OCR staff had spent substantial time in Oakland discussing the district's strategic plan, reviewing OUSD's "innovative discipline practices," interviewing district and school administrators "involved in the creation of positive school environments," and providing "technical assistance on behavior interventions and alternatives to punitive discipline."[7] The VRP essentially required key elements of *Community Schools, Thriving Student* and core student service programs such as restorative justice, positive behavioral interventions and supports (PBIS), youth leadership, and the Manhood Development Program.

The VRP called for revision of the district's disciplinary policies, the provision of a framework for schools to review their discipline data and identify student and teacher needs for supports, and to provide specialized professional development for administrators, teachers, and staff responsible for implementing the new practices. OCR required that OUSD "immediately expand the number of elementary, middle and high schools that will implement programs to address disproportionality with respect to discipline."[8]

VRP language and direction channeled Smith's expressed vision of a FSCS district and the system changes needed. Federal staff involved in the compliance review complimented the district for its open-handed collaboration with OCR. For instance, in the US Department of Education's September 28, 2012, announcement of the agreement, Secretary of Education Arne Duncan and Assistant Secretary for Civil Rights Russlyn Ali praised Tony Smith's leadership and the cooperation of OUSD staff, calling the district's commitments "in this unprecedented and far-reaching agreement" unparalleled.[9] Smith, district colleagues, and community supporters such as the USC enthusiastically endorsed the VRP because OCR's compliance investigation forced implementation of key elements of its FSCSs and foundational system change in the district's schools.

EXTERNAL AND OPTIONAL LEVERS (PHILANTHROPY, GRANTS)

Major funders provided another implementation push; they invested considerable funds into the development of the strategic plan, so the district had to follow through with commitments or else lose funders' support.

African American Male Achievement: Grants for a New Department and Program

A particularly important example of an external and optional lever is Office of African American Male Achievement (AAMA). In 2010, a group consisting of the superintendent, the board, the Urban Strategies Council, and the East Bay Community Foundation together examined longitudinal district student data. They found compelling evidence that African American males consistently fell furthest from other student subgroups in terms of educational opportunity and had the lowest indicators in terms academic progress and attendance but highest reports of disciplinary action and out-of-school suspension. The group concluded, "Past initiatives had done little to transform the experiences, access or educational attainment of African American male students."[10]

Based on these data and the patterns of disparate student outcomes and inequitable access they revealed, Smith asked Perry Chen to write a grant to establish an Office of African American Male Achievement (AAMA) tasked to create the systems, structures, and spaces that promote success for all OUSD African American male students. john powell's theory of targeted universalism motivated this first major program initiative. The targeted universalism approach underlying AAMA started with goals for all students (having everything they need to learn and thrive) rather than for one group in comparison to another, then targeting efforts to ensure that all students met them (as opposed to starting with African American males, which is targeted but not universal). As OUSD's website describes it, "OUSD's theory of action . . . asserts that by transforming the system to support successful outcomes for OUSD's lowest performing subgroup, OUSD will create a district that improves academic and social-emotional outcomes for all of its students."[11]

AAMA was the nation's first district-level department created specifically to address the interests and needs of African American males. In 2010, it launched its signature Manhood Development Program (MDP), an academic mentoring model designed and carried out by African American males for African American males in selected schools. The MDP proved so effective during its first year that it grew from three to six sites in its second year, and now operates in fourteen schools throughout the district. The program posts impressive positive outcomes. Since 2012–2013, participants' grade point averages are 25 percent higher than for African American male students who did not take the course; the number of African American male seniors who qualify for admission to the University of California or California State University is 6 percent higher for MDP participants than for non-participants.[12]

INTERNAL AND REQUIRED LEVERS

Board Policies: School Governance

Changes in parents' role in site governance comprised the first system change following passage of the strategic plan. The major board-led policy shift on school governance referenced *Community Schools, Thriving Students'* stance on what made a community school the community's school—parent involvement in decision making and setting priorities. Parents had long complained about their lack of voice in or access to school decision making. Change in this domain involved a new board policy regarding the nature and operation of school site governance. Adopted in the spring of 2012 to further the strategic plan's goal of substantial and meaningful family involvement in school decision making, the board's School Governance Policy (AR 3625) established school site councils (SSCs) at every OUSD school. Each SSC comprised a group of teachers, parents, administrators, and interested community members who would work together to develop and monitor a school's improvement plans (also legally required for schools receiving federal Title I funds). (See "School Site Council Responsibilities.")

The new SSCs were, in the words of one observer, "not your mother's PTA." This new policy represented a major shift in OUSD's governing practices. It took the SSCs out of state and federal programs (and a checklist compliance mode) and connected them to *Community Schools, Thriving Students'* goals for family and youth engagement. The SSCs' responsibilities and authority placed them squarely in role of making decisions about school budgets, program and partner choices, and student policies. AR 3625 stated, "The central purpose of school governance is to provide leadership and decision making to support student achievement, with the ultimate goal of students successfully engaging in college, career and community. The SSC's goal is continuous improvement that will close achievement gaps and accelerate student achievement at the school site."[13]

Furthermore, the policy required principals to provide the SSCs with the information needed to carry out its role; the school network

---

School Site Council Responsibilities

The School Site Council is responsible for working with the school principal to inform and engage the school's stakeholders—employees, parents, students, and community members—to:

1. Review and analyze student outcome data;
2. Identify critical questions related to the efficacy of the school's program strategies;
3. Research effective-practices;
4. Establish student outcome goals and benchmarks;
5. Establish a data-informed theory-of-action that leads to the achievement of goals; and
6. Establish a resource allocation plan that is aligned with the theory-of-action.

Source: Oakland Unified School District, Administrative Regulations Business and Noninstructional Operations, AR 3625, School Governance, https://boepublic.ousd.org/Policies .aspx.

---

superintendents, an intermediary group that sits between the central office and the schools, hold responsibility for overall SSC implementation.[14] In the process of developing the Principal Leadership Framework, the district rebuilt principals' leadership tools to support increased family and student engagement in governance. The board policy assigned the superintendent and central office responsibility for providing the necessary resources, staffing, tools and supports to principals and SSCs.

This move to establish and support site-based governance brought change consistent with Tony Smith's vision of schools as place-based and his belief that schools should have the authority and responsibility to develop practices and policies that reflected their community's needs, assets, and priorities. The district's responsibility was to support that autonomy, a position that departed significantly from past policies and the schools' experience under state receivership.

Accountability and Quality Standards

When Tony Smith became superintendent in 2009, the district had limited capacity to produce data about school functioning beyond student indicators, and no standards with which to assess school quality. One middle school principal remarked that prior to Smith's tenure, quality standards existed in few domains. "Everybody knows that," he said, "It's no secret." Smith and the board saw new performance standards as "soft" internal levers that could undergird efforts to improve district practices.

In 2011–2012, the district piloted a School Quality Review (SQR) process in fifteen schools. SQR spelled out districtwide school quality standards and functioned as the main systems-level driver for continuous improvement. In 2013, the board passed the BP 6005 Quality School Development Policy. BP 6005 directed OUSD to:

> Establish a school quality review process in which all schools, through their school governance team and in collaboration with District leaders, are accountable for:
>
> a. Assessing the state of their school in relation to established performance quality standards and student outcome goals.
> b. Identifying key priorities for school improvement.
> c. Establishing a school improvement plan.[15]

The board quality review policy also incorporated the district's Balanced Score Card (developed in 2011–2012 based on the strategic plan) for district (board level), central offices, school sites, and a strategic management system that translates vision into specific metrics and actions to guide system-level quality review and standard-based change, consistent with the strategic plan. Clear internal standards and accountability, district leaders believed, precede and establish a school's response to external accountability. Several new sets of quality standards emerged. As part of this shift in accountability measures, the district has developed Student and Family Engagement Standards that set out clear goals and standards systemwide. With these standards in place, quality engagement represents a system goal, not merely an activity that varies by schools and leaders' preferences.

INTERNAL AND OPTIONAL LEVERS: PROFESSIONAL DEVELOPMENT AND LEARNING COMMUNITIES, COACHING, LEADERSHIP DEVELOPMENT STANDARDS

Community Schools, Thriving Students described a new way of "doing school" in OUSD. In the early years, not everyone was on board with its whole-child centered vision, and many preferred "traditional" practices both inside and outside the classroom. Many of the district activities undertaken to promote and expand practices consistent with the FSCS initiative feature "soft" levers focused on learning, professional development, and culture change. For instance, network superintendents and district staff worked with site administrators to create strong SSCs and encourage significant family engagement. District staff provided extensive, ongoing professional development opportunities as well as mentoring to introduce teachers and site administrators to the FSCS model and implications for their professional roles. Chapter 3 describes the considerable contribution of the peer-based Leadership Growth and Development System (LGDS) to shifting the mindsets about effective leadership and standards of practice in OUSD. Over time, OUSD's investments in "soft" internal levers such as these have paid off significantly. Oakland educators, families and community leaders widely subscribe to shared ideas about how to "do school," and express deep support for FSCS's goals and strategies. Arguably, these levers played an essential role in changing the prevailing OUSD culture about the role and responsibilities of district schools.

MULTIPLE LEVERS FOR AN AREA: SOCIAL-EMOTIONAL LEARNING

OUSD remains the only community school initiative in the nation to explicitly include social-emotional learning (SEL) in its formal goals and prioritized activities. Multiple levers make SEL a district priority and featured districtwide practice. SEL is embedded in two strategic plans—*Community Schools, Thriving Students* and its updated successor, *Pathways to Excellence*—and in board policy.

SEL's prominence in *Community Schools, Thriving Students* signaled fundamental system change in establishing district priorities about what needs to be learned beyond academic instruction and commitment to integrating it into all aspects of the district—from the classroom to the boardroom.[16] The Bechtel Foundation supported this work for several years, and OUSD's partnership with the Collaborative for Academic, Social, and Emotional Learning (CASEL) signaled its SEL leadership nationally. OUSD has adopted three signature SEL practices districtwide—community building, check-in, and optimistic closure—and has incorporated SEL indicators into district benchmarks.[17] Ultimately, OUSD's SEL programs and standards have informed California School Dashboard measurements and climate indicators.

Significant progress on *Community Schools, Thriving Students'* big-picture goals assumed significant system change, changes made difficult by Oakland's political and social context, the fiscal shortfalls, assumptions both inside and outside the district about "doing school," and traditional roles and relationships between central office and schools, within schools and with partners. Smith and colleagues knew that implementing the strategic plan was not a simple question of adopting a new program or designating some schools as community schools. The system change sought required strategic thinking about levers of different sorts—external, internal, mandated, and optional—and the choices made generally have proven effective. These different levers have resulted in meaningful system changes; among them, new school governance policy that gives voice and authority to parents, discipline reform, new quality and accountability standards, SEL, and equity-focused school finance strategies.

"Unwinding" these system changes, embedded as they are in local, state, and federal polices, would be extraordinarily difficult.

Superintendent Smith and his advisers knew, moreover, that compliance alone, or buy-in alone, could not promote productive implementation of the strategic plan absent necessary human knowledge and expertise as well as organizational capacity. The strategic plan states: "A Full Service Community School District in Oakland provides and implements the infrastructure and systems to support full service community schools including policies, practices and funding."[18] Meeting that district responsibility, Smith believed, required structural change in the central office—the creation of a new department. Chapter 5 takes up the development and operation of this new OUSD department.

CHAPTER 5

Structural Change

A New Department

From the beginning, Tony Smith's system-level change vision involved creating new infrastructure to provide aligned supports for *Community Schools, Thriving Students*—structural system change tools. The superintendent called for consolidation of the many FSCS-relevant services and supports then scattered across the central office under a new Family, Schools, and Community Partnerships department. The strategic plan outlines the new department's role in the FSCS implementation process:

> The Family, Schools, and Community Partnerships Department coordinates with all Central Office departments and units to provide seamless systems of services and supports to school sites and community partners engaged in FSCS development. It facilitates cross-boundary relationships between sites, regions, and school district departments to support integration, effectiveness and efficiency of academic and learning support services . . . it works with the leadership of public systems, major institutions, community-based organizations, the business sector, philanthropy and other stakeholders to align everyone around a common set of outcomes for youth in the city.[1]

To carry out that charge, Smith brought Curtiss Sarikey from San Francisco Unified School District (SFUSD) to OUSD in November 2011 to build the new department. Sarikey's professional experience and personal values fit well with Smith's: a social worker by training, he had spent ten years as a supervisor for SFUSD's Student and Family Services Department and served as the executive director of Big Brothers Big Sisters of the East Bay. Sarikey held deep commitment to Smith's view that productive educational contexts for youth must address the needs of the whole child, that students' school success required family engagement, and that youths' positive academic and social development depended on collaboration with diverse community partners. Sarikey and Smith were of the same mind: being a full-service community school district is not just about program elements, it is a philosophy, a way of doing business.

Sarikey's colleagues characterize him as an especially skilled community builder, and successful community building lay at the center of his implementation challenges in creating new department. Once in Oakland, he merged two departments, Complementary Learning and Family and Community, into the Family, School and Community Partnerships, which was renamed Community Schools and Student Services (CSSS) in 2014. Sarikey intended that this new structure would bring coherence to central office FSCS programs and services.

CSSS's reconfiguration and re-culturing of fundamental FSCS services and programs into one central office department distinguishes Oakland's approach from other district-led community school initiatives. Most community school programs operate as sub-units within other district departments—curriculum and instruction, for instance—and elements of community school programming—for example, health and extended learning—are dispersed across the central office as they were in Oakland prior to CSSS. CSSS created the infrastructure, collaboration, and leadership needed to bring alignment across FSCS components at both district and school levels. A community school manager (CSM) remarked on the importance of this coordinated support: "The foundation for FSCS is strong; the building blocks are there. The fact that there is an entire district department with a true idea of how they're going to support and build this work . . . amazing. They've got it together."

The CSSS brought together in one place the programs and services fundamental to FSCS site-level implementation; key among them, afterschool programs, attendance and discipline support, behavioral health initiatives, community schools, youth and family engagement, school-based health centers, social-emotional learning, summer learning programs, positive behavioral intervention, restorative justice, and wellness. In community-building mode, Sarikey furthered programmatic coherence with internal cross-program connections and communication, where previously little had existed in the central office. He made what he called "cross-boundary" conversations a priority:

> Whole-team meetings focused on staff getting educated about different units and looking across those units. What does Health and Wellness have to do with After School? How are nurses involved with Family Engagement? I told staff that I wanted everybody in CSSS to be an ambassador for the whole [FSCS] vision, not just the work of their own unit. Make cross-boundary connections.

Sarikey believed that featuring connections across units not only brought coherence to the department's work, but also "built opportunities for people to be creative" with their own work because they had more and different resources available to them.

Ali Metzler, who supports the Community Schools program within CSSS, sees the functioning of the CSSS department as essential to the programs' providing effective support to OUSD schools:

> In our department, we have staff working regionally who oversee multiple schools, so there's a lot of touch points of people at the district level who know the intricate needs of the school; they have really trusting relationships with principals, with RJ [restorative justice] coordinators and parent liaison, the community school manager . . . and can communicate the different needs that schools have. We can blend

understanding the district goals and with supporting the individual school goals.

Several school leaders stressed the need for this supportive central office infrastructure in order for teachers and principals to engage the mindset shifts and practice changes advanced by the FSCS initiative. As the strategic plan rolled out, one principal reflected, "Before, nobody paid attention to infrastructure. There was this focus on 'Go in the classroom and make the teachers do this, make the teachers do that.' Okay, but what about all the other things that create the conditions so that instruction goes well, so that kids come to school ready to learn? What about all this other stuff that supports the paper to pencil?" Now, he says, central CSSS supports exist for these extra-classroom needs.

Additionally, many school principals saw this focus on communication and coordination between the central office departments and schools as a much-needed change from previous practices. For example, one said: "There should have been better communication between the people who are delivering the service and those who are creating the policies for it. It is important for people in the central office to always be connected with teachers first and foremost and [with] school principals, those who are on the ground." In his view, central office staff now have better connections with and knowledge of school needs, and how best to respond. CSSS staff play a key role in that communication at both district and school levels.

FROM TRIANGLE TO TREE

The Children's Aid Society-informed triangle featured in the 2011 strategic plan (figure 3.1) represented the FSCS initiative's goals, but did not depict an approach to implementing and supporting FSCS. Its three "arms" represented objectives for district action but did not communicate anything about how to achieve them. The triangle also was context-free. Berkeley philosopher john powell might have asked: "What about the soil underneath and the air all around?"[2]

In 2014, Curtiss Sarikey and colleagues created a tree to represent OUSD's mission and programmatic interrelationships (see figure 5.1). The tree image symbolized the district's approach to community schools, and how OUSD could serve and support FSCS at scale.[3]

Figure 5.1 *The Oakland Community Schools Tree*

Source: Oakland Unified School District

The *roots* signify the district's interconnected, collective work. They provide foundational support and focus for targeted FSCS work across OUSD: Health and Wellness; Academics; School Culture and Climate; Youth Leadership; Social and Emotional Learning; School Readiness and Transitions; and Family Engagement.[4] Sarikey emphasizes the importance of Academics as a root: "We wanted to be sure that "academics" was part of our model. The tree is about creating not only wraparound elements, but well-supported educational environments and opportunities."

The *soil* contains the "nutrients" needed for the roots to strengthen and grow—Evaluation and Learning; Collaboration; Relationships; Equity; Coordination; Leadership; Partnership; and Diversity. Sarikey says the soil is his favorite part of the tree: "That's the hard stuff. Without the elements contained in the soil, the roots could just become wraparounds."

The *limbs* depict the outcomes a healthy, thriving tree would produce. Consistent with the strategic plan's primary goals, Oakland's students and families would be Healthy, College and Career Ready, Successful in School and Life, Part of a Thriving and Safe Community, and Civically Engaged. The tree metaphor also especially resonates in "Oak-land."

The seventeen programs and services operating within the CSSS department address the three broad FSCS goals: Learning, Thriving, and Together.[5]

- Programs focused on *Learning* include SEL, Restorative Justice, School wellness, nutritional education, garden education (with a garden at each school), drug and alcohol education.
- Programs and services centered on *Thriving* include health and wellness, behavioral health, school-based health centers, school nurses, attendance and discipline, transitional students/families, and physical education.
- Programs and services targeting *Together* include family engagement, the Family Resource Center, community school

managers, afterschool programs, summer learning, and community partnerships.

While the work of specific CSSS programs or services targets a particular FSCS domain (or root), in practice they interconnect with most all of CSSS work. Three examples:

- *Expanded Learning* shows up in programs and services associated with all three goal areas. It contributes to family engagement and youth leadership through afterschool programs; Health and Wellness staff lead trainings for afterschool staff and connect students with expanded earnings opportunities; Transitional Students and Families refers students to afterschool and summer programming.
- *Youth Leadership* plays a role across the CSSS department's work. Youth leaders bring voice and input to the Behavioral Health's anti-bullying work; afterschool programs offer youth leadership programs for elementary, middle, and high schools; students help decide which linked learning courses they would like to see at their schools; the LCAP student advisory enables students to interact directly with the school board.
- The *Family Engagement* "root" appears in almost all CSSS work. The SEL group provides professional development and training opportunities for parents; CSSS offers adolescent development curricula for families; family engagement specialists collaborate with CSMs to learn about the needs of families and communities; Parent Wellness Champions engage schools and communities around wellness; the Central Family Resource Center has family health advocates; and family liaisons collaborate with afterschool programs to engage families.

NEW FSCS ROLES AND SUPPORTS
Community School Managers
The community school manager's position brings a high-leverage and high-traction resource for community school implementation.

CSMs coordinate programs and services for youth, their families and the school community. The CSM job description lists twenty-three "essential functions" and highlights seventeen needed "abilities" (chapter 11 discusses CSMs' school-site work). CSMs work closely with their principal to identify needs and opportunities, cultivate new partnerships and manage existing ones, coordinate existing resources to ensure maximum impact and effectiveness, and "track" and assess the multitude of strands of community school work. While all OUSD schools have community school elements—the tree's "roots"—forty-two schools have the support of a CSM in the 2019–2020 school year, significantly up from the eight CSMs staffing the 2012 FSCS cohort. OUSD places CSMs at the highest-need schools—as determined by a complex district rubric and influenced by a site-level application process.

While CSMs' day-to-day work varies by school site, over the last several years, their role has focused on a set of five goals: (1) increasing school attendance; (2) strengthening the Coordination of Services Team (see below) and multi-tiered systems of supports (MTSS) to support students, families, and teachers; (3) increasing student access to health services; (4) increasing and strengthening partnerships; and (5) creating innovative systems and strategies to address individual school's goals, as specified in their School Plan for Student Achievement (SPSA; described in chapter 9). These common goals foster a sense of coherence in CSM work across FSCS, and enable OUSD to demonstrate broader community school impact aligned with district priorities. As CSSS's Ali Metzler explained, "Of course, we want [CSMs] to be innovative and organic at each school, but to show impact, you have to have some common threads. So two school years ago, we established the community school priorities."

The CSSS program supports CSMs in multiple ways—through learning opportunities such as professional development, coaching, and professional learning communities, but also by working on-site with principals around opportunities and expectations associated with the CSM role, reaching out to other central office departments for resources and connections, and screening CSM candidates before arranging interviews with principals.

Coordination of Services Team

Curtiss Sarikey featured the Coordination of Services Team (COST) role in full-service community schools. COST school-based teams typically involve social and health clinicians, school psychologists, school representatives, and resource specialists (although teams vary in composition from school to school). CSMs coordinate the COST at each school. The team comes together on a weekly basis to discuss how the school is providing additional services to at risk students. The team aims to coordinate schoolwide efforts focused on student attendance, health, academic experiences, and social emotional development. Teachers, staff, and families make referrals to COST to discuss and identify additional supports for struggling students. All OUSD schools now have COST support. Sarikey notes that "the implementation of COST teams at all schools was foundational to scaling community schools across the system, it's the key structure ensuring that no kid falls through the cracks—that no kid is overlooked that may need support and resource."

Services and Supports for All Schools.

CSSS staff provide professional development opportunities for *all* OUSD teachers and administrators, arrange coaching for CSMs and COST teams, work with practitioners to develop protocol, and provide frameworks and other implementation tools. CSSS staff involved in health and wellness services connect schools lacking school-based health clinics with nearby clinic services, so all OUSD schools have access to health resources. CSSS program leader Ali Metzler underscored the focus on districtwide work within CSSS:

> We're really committed to making sure that all schools have those tools [whether or not they have CSMs]. Just trying to increase access to services, increase communication . . . sharing medical records and

knowing who needs to be vaccinated, and bringing sexuality training into elementary schools. I feel like we're making some big strides through all of the [FSCS] elements, whether it's social-emotional learning or family engagement or health and after school.

NEW CENTRAL OFFICE SUPPORTS AND OVERSIGHT

The new CSSS department also brought first-hand central office support and oversight for fundamental components of the strategic plan's vision—health and wellness and community partners. While both elements had played an important role in Oakland schools for many years, neither had a significant central office presence prior to the new strategic plan. CSSS changed that by locating these key functions within the new departmental structure.

Health and Wellness

OUSD had school-based health clinics prior to Tony Smith's arrival. In 2008, the number of school-based health clinics expanded from seven to fifteen, but they received little central office support or supervision. *Community Schools, Thriving Students* pledged that *all* schools would be healthy environments, and the new CSSS featured a Health and Wellness department. Mara Larsen-Fleming, who has been at OUSD since 2009 and heads up CSSS's health and wellness efforts, said, "Becoming a full-service community school district really did help us build internal capacity to support and integrate all of those programs into the district. And it shifted our work with the partners. Before [the FSCS strategic plan] we never had (health and wellness) point people at the district level, so we never had anyone responsible for coordinating and integrating the school clinics." (In 2014, the addition of one school-based health clinic brought the total to sixteen.)

Health and Wellness organizes its work into three areas:

- *Health Access* includes the Central Family Resource Center, school-based health centers, and school nurses.

- *Healthy Environment* includes school wellness, the Behavioral Health Unit, restorative justice, LGBQ programs, and nutrition services.
- *Health Education* addresses nutrition and garden education, drug and alcohol education, and physical education.

The Health Access program has worked to connect each OUSD school with health resources. Mara Larsen-Fleming explains:

> We have sixteen school-based clinics, but they're expensive and we're not likely to grow the number. We're embedding referral coordinators in the schools who are able to refer students out to community-based services. So, while every school may not have a clinic, every school should be able to say that they know how to connect their students to health services and they have the systems to do that.

The Health and Wellness program undertook several initiatives with that goal in mind. It launched the Central Family Resource Center (CFRC) in 2013, in partnership with Alameda County Health Care Services and the East Bay Agency for Children. In its first five years, the CFRC enrolled 3,349 children and 3,496 adults in health coverage, and enrolled 1,436 children and 1,059 adults in CalFRESH (food stamp program). The CFRC has also provided a range of other services to ensure that the basic needs of OUSD families were met (case management, emergency food, early childhood playgroups, ESL classes, etc.). Health education staff implemented sexual health education districtwide in grades 6, 7, and 9, with statistically significant increases in knowledge, attitudes, and skills observed across all grade levels.

Larsen-Fleming described how OUSD has grown teacher leadership around implementation of the District Wellness policy. "In 2008, teachers at eight schools were funded to serve as 'Wellness Champions.' In 2018–2019, fifty-two schools had Wellness Champions. In 2019–2020, we will expand the initiative to have a Wellness Champion at every school."

Partnerships

CSSS holds responsibility for supporting and overseeing OUSD's many partnerships that provide vital supports to FSCS. Partners draw on the assets, expertise, and capacity of local public and private agencies to provide students and their families with the services and resources they need to thrive. (Chapter 9 discusses site-level partnership work.) Responding to a visitor's characterization of community partners as the "heart" of community schools, a middle school principal said, "I don't know if they're the heart so much as the legs. They need to be in place for us as a school system to accomplish this mission of preparing students for a college career, citizenship. Without the legs we're just not able to stand. We're not able to move." Yet productive partnerships are not easy to develop, manage, or sustain. Joy Dryfoos and Sue Maguire judge developing partnerships and creating governance arrangements "the most challenging aspect of creating a community school."[6]

Partnerships are not new in Oakland. The district has long benefited from supportive community partners, but typically, partners initiated their own arrangements with individual schools or responded to direct school requests.[7] Yet while significant CBO attention to partnerships existed before Superintendent Smith joined OUSD, prior to the 2011 passage of the district's strategic plan, little central office partnership responsibility existed and the district had limited knowledge of or contact with community partners. Andrea Bustamante, who now heads CSSS, recalls a 2010 conversation with Superintendent Smith as early FSCS planning was moving forward. Smith asked her, "Who are our partners? Can you tell me who they are? Can you give me a list?" She could not. The CSSS partnership role evolved from that conversation and Smith's belief that "OUSD was necessary but insufficient" to changing Oakland students' life outcomes. "We had to galvanize all of the community's assets around students."

Partnerships became a featured element of Oakland's new strategic plan: "A Full Service Community School connects the school, family, and community to support student success at the school site and through its partnerships."[8] As one CSSS administrator put it, "We realized that if we are going to be a FSCS district, we need to support that at the district level, we need to be involved in the [partnership] process—organize the process."[9] Curtiss Sarikey characterized the district partnership work as a "move from the 'wild, wild, west' to a more coherent way of understanding partnerships within the district."

With the strategic plan's focus on policy coherence within and across the district, the board requested formalization of partnership arrangements. While background clearances should have been standard, without a centralized system to manage partners, many went directly to school sites without basic requirements and accountability agreements in place. The district intended to move beyond the ad hoc partnership arrangements of the past to formalize school/partner relationships; CSSS's Partnership staff worked to align partnership arrangements across the district and clearly focused on quality and results. Andrea Bustamante worked with partners for over a year on how to manage partnerships within the FSCS framework and establish a partnership system built on quality, accountability, and results. In the partnership arrangement, interested agencies, businesses, or CBOs must complete a centralized partnership process managed and supported by the CSSS with the "hope to increase communication and alignment, uplift community school outcomes, and adhere to California Education Code."[10] Once a school or the central office has selected a partner, the partner must submit a certificate of insurance, insurance policy endorsement, and clearance letter that includes tuberculosis clearance, a criminal background check, and fingerprinting. Potential partners must complete a memorandum of understanding (MOU), which requires board approval. (MOUs existed before 2011, but were not always completed or followed.)

Partnerships vary in focus and scope. While some partners provide single services such as tutoring or recreation, many offer an array of services at community schools. For example, Safe Passages serves as lead afterschool agency at four OUSD schools and provides academic enrichment and out-of-school-time programs as well as family and community support services. The East Bay Asian Youth Center (EBAYC) partners with more than fifteen OUSD schools to provide expanded learning programming and foster community engagement; its staff work with schools to strengthen school climate and attendance. La Clínica operates six school-based health clinics in OUSD elementary, middle, and high schools, with a focus on culturally and linguistically responsive community health.

Partner arrangements have evolved over time through ongoing communication between district staff, site-level educators, partners, and CSMs. Many partners and their schools now complete a letter of agreement (LOA) that describes the logistics and expectations for the partnership. An Annual Community Partnership Evaluation encourages schools and community partners to reflect on their shared goals, strategies, and efforts.[11] The LOA and annual evaluation aim to promote mutual accountability and deepen school/partner relationships. CSSS's partnership office provides a range of tools and supports for both partners and CSMs on each of these practices, including "Partner Check-in" guides and rubrics for issues like communication, integration, alignment, and logistics (see the appendixes at the end of chapter 9).[12] These systems and tools formalize key elements of school-partner relationships. However, OUSD partnership work has always been less about compliance with new procedures and protocol and more about shifting culture and expectations around partnerships.

Martin Young joined the CSSS team in 2015 to provide support for the partnership processes and CSMs' work with partners, and to develop a partner database that could facilitate the approval process, provide an up-to-date partner registry, and inform quality control. The Community Partner Platform enables parents, teachers, students, or community members to learn more about partner organizations and the programs they provide, and see the number and focus of partnerships for any OUSD school.[13] Young finds that schools without CSMs are less likely to communicate about partnerships, participate in an annual evaluation, or to sign off on an MOU: "Principals don't have time to focus on community partnerships and enrichment programs."

CSSS community schools staff, especially CSMs, have forged productive relationships with partners and partnerships with OUSD schools that continue to grow. In school year 2018–2019, more than 225 partners engaged with OUSD schools; 150 "approved" community partners participated in community schools; and another 75 are "pending approval" (awaiting bureaucratic review) but active in schools. Several of these partnerships represent collaborations of many years. These long-term relationships not only allow partners and their schools to deepen their collaboration, but they also enable partners to develop significant connections with the students and families they serve. For instance, the EBAYC has collaborated with Oakland schools to provide afterschool programming for more than thirty years.

OUSD's partnerships extend beyond CBOs to public-sector partners, which have played a significant role in the collective work of community schools, integrating and aligning resources. The five-year agreement with the Alameda County Health Care Services Agency covers everything from behavioral health and health clinics to juvenile justice detention centers and community schools. An agreement with the Oakland Housing Authority focuses on reducing chronic absenteeism, engaging families, and building parent leadership. The Oakland Fund for Children and Youth works to align its investments in OUSD with the FSCS model.[14]

Partners bring assets to the FSCS initiative in part by leveraging resources and funding streams not usually accessed by educational institutions. Their long-term relationships with families provide an important resource of another kind for schools. David Kakishiba, EBAYC founder, school board member, and former board chair, sees these long-term partnerships and associated family relationships as critical sources of school stability, especially in the face of significant teacher and administrator churn. "We've known many of these families for a long time and they trust us. Our parent contact is high; we can get families engaged in school, paying attention to attendance." Because of EBAYC's involvement in afterschool learning and mentoring, he said, staff learn about students' home situations: "The father just died in prison, and mother is whacked out with a crazy boyfriend who's just going in and out, and the kid is just angry." EBAYC staffers can let teachers know about home issues, and they work directly with youth after school about issues they face. Kakishiba said, "I think our biggest contribution has always been around the tamping down the worst parts of the school climate issues . . . " That contribution requires significant relational trust.

ESTABLISHING PRIORITIES FOR ACTION: ROLLING OUT THE STRATEGIC PLAN

Implementing OUSD's new strategic plan required choices about action to take within its broad vision. Curtiss Sarikey's CSSS department provided coordinated assistance and oversight to FSCSs and worked with *all* OUSD schools to adopt elements of the FSCS model. Sarikey describes how he managed the districtwide stance that "all means all" in a context of tight OUSD resources:

> Every year, we said, "All schools are going to focus on these things, community school manager or not." But people can't do everything all at once, and we certainly couldn't with our capacity constraints. One year, for instance, we had family engagement and alignment of school-day/afterschool as the priority. Every year, we'd take two or three other elements and say, "We can support all schools . . . no matter what you're doing, you can be better at putting these pieces together and starting to think about whole child systems . . . Here's the support, let's zero in."

Given the district's practical and fiscal limitations, Sarikey underlined the importance of being intentional and strategic in building out program elements year by year, always keeping *Community Schools, Thriving Students'* broad, long-term system change goal in view: "Our plan was to get fifty schools with a full-service community school core [especially a CSM] by 2020. So, we said [to the CSSS team], 'What do we really want to do? What are some of the big things we can move that would be systemwide?'"

OUSD's CSSS department provides essential support and oversight for core aspects of the FSCS functioning at the school level. For instance, the long-term partnerships seen in OUSD community schools and the growing list of community partners reflect the effective work of CSSS's partnership and community school programs. Likewise, the focused attention given health and wellness resources in *all* OUSD schools, whether or not a school-based clinic operates on site, results from CSSS Health and Wellness staff's ongoing engagement with schools, students, families, and service providers. This active central office backing for foundational FSCS elements sets OUSD apart from other district-led community school efforts, most of which lack this coordinated, district-level oversight and sponsorship.

Also notable in the urban school district universe is the sustained development and institutional persistence of CSSS. Created by Tony Smith and Curtiss Sarikey almost ten years and four superintendents ago, the CSSS department brought structural change to advance Tony Smith's strategic plan; Curtiss Sarikey collected, coordinated, and aligned initiatives core to *Community Schools, Thriving Students.* In many (if not most) urban districts, significant redefinition of the CSSS departmental mission (if not its existence) likely would have accompanied revolving-door superintendents as new leaders brought new agenda. Yet CSSS has persisted in the face of superintendent turnover and budget crises that brought deep cuts in central office programs and staff. That departmental perseverance has paid off. CSSS's continued operation since 2011 has allowed staff and sites to learn from experience, scale core elements of the FSCS model—for example, COST, SEL, Extended Learning, Wellness Champions—and place CSMs at more than forty schools as demand for their services grew. That departmental continuity and growth aimed at system change also sets Oakland apart from other urban districts. Chapter 6 takes up the question of stability in the face of leadership change.

CHAPTER 6

Transitions, Change, and Stability

OUSD has had five superintendents in the ten years from 2009 to 2019. Urban superintendents' typically short tenure—on average, 2.5 years—stands as a consistent refrain in accounts of urban education leadership. Moreover, experience teaches that with the arrival of each new superintendent usually comes a new agenda. A consequence of this leadership turnover is a continual revolution in district priorities, goals, and approaches. Moreover, district staff often feel "This, too, shall pass" and resist investing deeply in the latest agenda. Oakland's experience prior to Smith's arrival was no different. Discussing the agenda of OUSD's seven superintendents between 1962 and 1990, former OUSD superintendent, board member, and education historian Gary Yee writes that as superintendents came and went, "attention shifted again and again . . . few [programs] lasted beyond the superintendent who initiated them."[1]

However, while OUSD has experienced greater than usual leadership turnover in the past decade, in contrast to the agenda change associated with superintendent change in most urban districts, Oakland's commitment to the FSCS mission has remained relatively stable. This chapter takes up the sources of this exceptional stability of a system-change agenda, and considers the how and why the original vision has persisted.

SUPERINTENDENT TONY SMITH RESIGNS

"It was like a balloon popped," said Curtiss Sarikey of Superintendent Tony Smith's unexpected April 2013 resignation. Smith's announcement surprised the board and his central office staff. His resignation was prompted by his father-in-law's illness and plans to move to Chicago in June so his wife could support her parents. *San Francisco Chronicle* reporter Chip Johnson wrote on April 8, 2013, that Tony Smith had his "priorities straight" and would be hard to replace: "One thing's for sure: When he leaves in June, the school district will be in better shape than it's been in nearly 20 years. Under Smith's watch, test scores have risen, graduation rates have improved and finances have stabilized . . . Smith has set forth a reform plan that the school board supports. The challenge to replace him will be finding someone who can place their own ego aside and continue the work that Smith has begun."[2]

In addition to these family considerations, 2012–2013 had proved a difficult year for Superintendent Smith professionally. In an effort to begin to "right-size" OUSD in the face of declining enrollments, Smith closed seventeen schools and programs.[3] Many were small, alternative programs located on existing school campuses and launched during the small schools movement initiated with Gates Foundation funding. In each of these programs or schools, low student enrollment no longer justified their operating costs.

Smith argued forcefully that the money saved at these sites would be better spent at schools serving more students, and that affected students would have stronger instructional programs at the larger schools. Even though nearly everyone acknowledged that OUSD had too many schools, board sessions to discuss closures became shouting matches, and parents pled passionately to save their neighborhood schools. Tony Smith became the object of verbal abuse, was called a racist, and received death threats. Occupy Oakland, a protest group that had staged a series of protest demonstrations and occupations starting in October 2011, weighed in on the charges that Smith's school closures intentionally targeted black students.[4] To protest Smith's decisions, Occupy Oakland members carried out drive-by visits to Smith's home and gathered on his porch, frightening his young daughters.

OUSD educators generally concurred that while Tony Smith's 2013 resignation was unexpected and upsetting, the FSCS mission would continue. One community school manager summed up her reaction and that of her colleagues:

> Tony announced his leaving and it did not stall the work. It was like, "Okay, he's leaving. That is terrible!" We were blindsided, but we said, "Okay. Moving on. Let's keep this going." The dialogue after that first district meeting was, "We hate to lose him. We understand the reasons given. We wish him the best. But we are in this knee-deep and we're not turning back."

A longtime OUSD administrator and FSCS supporter shared similar feelings about culture change in the district and commitment to *Community Schools, Thriving Students*:

> I have been in this district for a very long time. I never thought I would see this day. I was there for the principals' meeting where Tony told everybody that he was leaving. I never really thought that there was going to be a moment where I saw everybody was like a collective . . . everybody was physically facing towards him, everybody was emotionally and mentally connected with him. And I never thought I'd see that in Oakland. I never thought in a district that's so divided and so chaotic in so many different ways . . . I never thought I'd see a group of administrators have this collective intake of breath at Tony's announcement, like, "Oh, my God!" And you could tell in that moment that we were all on the same page [about keeping on with FSCS].

AN INTERIM SUPERINTENDENT CONTINUES THE WORK: GARY YEE (2013–2014)

Gary Yee, a longtime Oakland resident and educator, agreed to serve as interim superintendent for one year. Yee had served more than ten years as an elected school board member; he was president of the board that passed *Community Schools, Thriving Student* and was serving a second term as president when Smith resigned. Yee's family counts over one hundred years of OUSD service—his mother was a food-service worker, he and his late wife Caroline had been teachers, principals, and district leaders; his children and grandchildren all had attended or were attending Oakland schools; and his daughter led a school-based health center. As one observer put it, "Gary's *bona fides* were untouchable, and his roots in the diverse Oakland community, especially across black, Latinx, and Asian lines, were incredible. He had unanimous board support, love, and unique capital to make things happen."

The board chose Yee as interim superintendent for many reasons, and one was his expressed commitment to *Community Schools, Thriving Students*. Yee characterized his tenure as "finishing off Tony's five years. I wanted to be as faithful to the strategic plan as possible, so he would get a full five-year run on it. I wanted to do something purposeful and meaningful without undermining Tony." One OUSD high school principal talked about the shock everyone felt at Smith's announcement, their worries about someone coming in with a new agenda, and relief at Gary Yee's appointment: "The board's ability to move on having Gary Yee come in as the interim I think is actually a pretty powerful statement. And to me what that said was: 'Hey, we like the trajectory we're going. We want to continue to move in that direction and we're not in a hurry to go out there and get somebody new. Let's keep staying to our plan.'"

As interim superintendent, Yee focused on the policy questions important to him and compatible with Tony Smith's vision. Like Smith, equity issues figured prominently—equal opportunities, equal resources, equal access. Moreover, like Smith, Yee knew these would be difficult to address absent policy levers to reinforce them. Referencing the strategic plan's underscoring the need to "modernize" the district's results-based budgeting (RBB) system (put in place by Randy Ward, the state-appointed administrator responsible for running

OUSD during state-receivership) to include such criteria as funding an adequate core program, differentiating funding for different student needs, transparent implementation to eliminate bureaucratic frustration, Gary Yee developed a new budget allocation strategy.[5] He wanted "radical change" from existing RBB policies, in which the dollars follow the student, to one more consistent with LCAP that would guarantee schools support for basic core services, even if their enrollment declined. He said, "It is like the reform of the past [RBB] becomes the problem of the future." He knew a budget proposal's new allocation procedures would encounter fierce opposition from some schools and would be politically problematic to pull off; he turned to broad engagement and open communication as a way to win support. A Principal's Advisory established as part of a district budget advisory committee played a central role.

Yee told the board, "I am only here till June. If you support this budgeting change, we have to get it done now." He believes that, in the end, he was successful largely because of his relationships with board and community. "People would assume a positive intent— nobody would ever question whether I was doing this for myself . . . they might disagree with the kind of construct, but not with the intent." He also credits the state LCAP deadline—an external, required lever—for accelerating the need to pass a new proposal before June if a new budget allocation strategy was to inform budgeting for the next school year.

Thinking about "major accomplishments" in his tenure as interim superintendent, Yee pointed quickly to the major midyear budget reform he pushed through, and then to the CORE waiver and LCAP. He also counts as a major accomplishment the balanced budget he achieved "even at the end of a recession" and passed on to the next superintendent.

Looking to the end of his year as interim superintendent and the arrival of a new superintendent, Yee reflected on the question of a new leader linking past practice and aspirations to the present and implications for *Community Schools Thriving Students*. When he took on OUSD leadership, Yee said, the strategic plan was in place, he was committed to it, and keeping with it was "easy enough for me to do. The question is, can the next superintendent put aside his own designs, professional pathway and embrace the strategic plan developed over the last few years . . . adopt a position of being an implementer of what's happened in the past?" Although former board colleagues and others urged him to sign on as superintendent, Yee remained firm about his "interim" status, and the search for a new superintendent got under way early in 2014.

UPDATING THE STRATEGIC PLAN:
ANTWAN WILSON, 2014–2017

Denver's Antwan Wilson became that next superintendent. The OUSD school board sought an implementer: " . . . a strong, dynamic superintendent who will lead the District forward in helping to achieve the vision, mission, and goals in its strategic plan."[6] In the spring of 2014, Wilson emerged from a pool of twenty candidates as the board's choice to lead Oakland's schools. His successful work with struggling schools as an assistant superintendent in Denver attracted the OUSD board, and he appealed to Oaklanders as a "take action" educator who would focus attention on the district's lowest-performing schools. A black man raised by a single mother in poverty and neighborhood violence, Wilson expressed a deep personal commitment to social justice and educational equity, values foundational to OUSD's FSCS initiative. He said he saw himself in many of Oakland's students. He received a four-year contract with a July 1, 2014, start date.

Wilson's entry plan explicitly incorporated the OUSD language and mission of the strategic plan: "Every Student Thrives! . . . all students graduate from high school as caring, competent, critical thinkers and fully informed, engaged, and contributing citizens prepared to succeed in college and career. I embrace this vision for the OUSD!"[7] Accepting the existing vision, Wilson framed his responsibilities in terms of action: "My role is to assess the obstacles that stand between OUSD and its vision, identify and prioritize the resources that will help us overcome them, and oversee their successful implementation in the service of schools and students."[8]

On November 19, 2014, a little more than four months after arriving in Oakland, Superintendent Wilson released a new strategic plan for the district: *Pathway to Excellence—2015–2020.*[9] Wilson wrote that his new plan provides a "roadmap for the next five years as we uphold our moral obligation to the students and residents of Oakland." *Pathway to Excellence* outlined three district goals: effective talent programs, an accountable school district, and quality community schools. Perry Chen, who held responsibility for drafting the plan, recalls, "Antwan really wanted brevity and conciseness because his whole orientation coming in was 'We're not writing a new strategic plan, we're just getting focused.' The *Pathway to Excellence* was really just an update [of *Community Schools, Thriving Students*]."

Wilson's personal style contrasted with Tony Smith's "go slow to go fast" approach. "Go fast to go fast," he believed—a stance he saw as compatible with his board-prescribed "implementer" role. Curtiss Sarikey worked with Wilson on FSCS language and mission, and his coaching paid off. In his greeting to Oakland educators at the start of his second year as superintendent, Wilson framed the district mission and vision in terms of working " to expand and accelerate the work of transforming OUSD into a Full Service Community School District focused on high academic achievement, eliminating inequity, and providing each child with excellent teachers, every day."[10]

Wilson's Unexpected Resignation

Wilson described his first year's work in Oakland as highly successful: "Overall, and in collaboration with the OUSD team, we have met the goals outlined in my Work Plan:

- We are two years into the implementation of our strategic plan, *Pathway to Excellence.*

- We gained national recognition for our collaborative work on the Oakland Promise, an initiative that aims to triple the number of college graduates from Oakland.
- We are receiving national attention for launching the Equity Pledge, a partnership between District and charter leaders to create a more equitable school experience for all Oakland children.[11]

Wilson's May 2015 work plan featured similar "shared accomplishments" and assured the board of his commitment to OUSD. He wrote, "I look forward to continuing my service, building on the collective successes we have achieved in just 11 months working together, and continuing our steady progress toward becoming a district that prepares *every* student for college, career, and community success."[12]

Nonetheless, despite these assurances to the board, Wilson was to have short tenure in Oakland. On November 22, 2016, OUSD school board president James Harris announced that Superintendent Antwan Wilson would leave Oakland in the spring to become chancellor of the District of Columbia Public Schools in Washington, DC. Wilson would not be leaving Oakland with a record of "shared accomplishments" but instead with a legacy of serious budgetary and administrative challenges. Just a month before his February departure, it became clear that the district was suffering a severe fiscal crisis and disarray. After a two-and-a-half- year tenure, Wilson left OUSD with a $30 million deficit, the result of rapid program and staff expansion and overspending in both central office and school-based initiatives, and a $10 million loss in expected state funds due to student enrollment declines. As the district wrestled with challenges of preserving fiscal solvency after Wilson's departure, reports appeared that showed he had overspent budget on administrators and consultants by as much as 100 percent.[13]

However, OUSD's fiscal mess was years in the making, and the deficit was ultimately the board's responsibility. The dysfunction of the district's fiscal management enabled Wilson's overspending and produced the deficit through poor accounting practices, inadequate data, and technical incapacities. To keep out of the budget red in 2017, district administrators cut $46.7 million from its 2017–2018 budget.

There was another, more positive, consequence of Antwan Wilson's tenure: stability of the district's vision. Wilson came to Oakland as an implementer, not with an articulated agenda of his own. His strategic plan, *Pathway to Excellence*, did not challenge *Community Schools, Thriving Students'* comprehensive whole-child vision or goals for the district. The spirit of FSCS and buy-in to its vision remained intact. On Wilson's departure, Devin Dillon, who had worked with Wilson in Denver and came to Oakland via Los Angeles to take the post of Chief Academic Officer, assumed responsibility for leading OUSD as interim superintendent, and the search for a new superintendent began.

AN INTERNAL CANDIDATE TAKES THE REINS:
KYLA JOHNSON-TRAMMELL (2017–)

The board named Oakland native Kyla Johnson-Trammell superintendent in May 2017. She had been the district's interim Deputy Superintendent of Academic and Social Emotional Learning, as well as the district's lead network superintendent of elementary schools. Johnson-Trammell had also served the district as an elementary school teacher and principal, director of talent development, and Associate Superintendent for Leadership, Curriculum, and Instruction. As one OUSD staffer put it, "She's got perfect Oakland cred."

By replacing Antwan Wilson with Kyla Johnson-Trammell, the board ensured that OUSD would retain *Community Schools, Thriving Students* vision. As a first-time superintendent, Johnson-Trammell was very much in what she called "learning mode." She had been part of the original *Community Schools, Thriving Students* planning team and was deeply familiar with the thinking and aspirations that created it. She saw FSCS as the "Oakland brand." One central office leader said, "She's worked in Oakland for so long and has deep understanding of the district and the community. She's very much behind the mission to create a full-service community school district, but not completely recreating the mission and the strategic plan, but building on it."

Superintendent Johnson-Trammell says that her "true passion has always been working with young people"; she is a strong instructional leader at core. Following college, she returned to Oakland to teach in an elementary school a block from her childhood home. "It was there that I fell in love with teaching," she said. With Smith and Yee, she expresses a deep commitment to equity and the quality of all Oakland schools, most especially the under-resourced flatlands schools. Tony Smith comments: "We were—and Kyla is—committed to healing historic inequities by nurturing the development of whole healthy children in schools that are inclusive and caring. She is really, really thoughtful. She is well prepared as a leader. Her training and preparation is not just *in situ*; she's got a broad perspective."

As a black woman who grew up and taught in Oakland, Johnson-Trammell had firsthand experience with the trauma, safety concerns, and uneven school resources and opportunities that Oakland's students of color often encounter in their neighborhoods and schools. Her priorities for OUSD schools reflected these concerns about equity, school quality, and the district's fiscal capacity to address these issues. Johnson-Trammell took on OUSD leadership well aware of the district's fiscal crises and labor unrest. As Perry Chen reflected, "The fiscal problems Kyla faces right now have been thirty years in the making. I think Kyla is great for this position now and so suited to understanding and knowing what the right things are to do."

Superintendent Johnson-Trammell walked into a district in crisis when she took office in 2017. Budget shortfalls required deep cuts in programs at both central office and site levels, and laid bare serious problems in the district's finance and business operations. She made several personnel changes in the operations side of the house. She brought Curtiss Sarikey (who had left OUSD in 2015 during Antwan

Wilson's tenure) back to OUSD as her chief of staff to assist with those management challenges but also to work on the Blueprint for Quality Schools and the Community of Schools Citywide Plan that would inform implementation. As a key implementer of the system changes assumed by Tony Smith's strategic plan, Sarikey served as a vision-keeper for *Community Schools, Thriving Students*. Johnson-Trammel's mission statement mirrored that expressed in the 2011 strategic plan: "To become a Full Service Community School District focused on high academic achievement while serving the whole child, eliminating inequity, and providing each child with excellent teachers, every day."[14] Her Oakland roots and experience, she said, called for a FSCS model: "Because I was here, I deeply believe in the role of public schools is to serve the whole child. We have to have a full-service community model where we are working with the cities, business, philanthropy, health care, and the county to support students' quality of life."

The June 2018 Board Policy 6006 directed the superintendent to develop a citywide plan that promoted the sustainability of Oakland's public schools that "represent quality and equitable educational options."[15] BP 6006 called for a plan to reduce the number of OUSD-funded programs. As Johnson-Trammel laid out the issue in her letter introducing the June 2018 Citywide Plan, "The bottom line is that OUSD has too many schools for the number of students we serve . . . students will not be served by a quality school in their neighborhood unless we correct . . . currently 11,000 seats are empty across our District-run schools."[16]

These corrections would affect more than twenty programs—some would be merged, some would be expanded, some would be closed in what the superintendent termed a "redesign." The district Research, Assessment, and Data (RAD) office developed a citywide map that considered assets management, feeder patters, and quality school standards and laid out a timeline for the board.[17] To make program closure decisions, the district convened an ad hoc Blueprint Engagement Committee that brought the community into the process, Oakland-style. The board made decisions about the first cohort of schools to be closed in the fall of 2018. In February 2019, an extended teachers' strike disrupted the board timeline; the board made decisions about the second cohort in fall of 2019. Throughout, OUSD's guiding mission—"To become a Full Service Community School district"— remained constant.

Heading into the 2019–2020 school year, Kyla Johnson-Trammel expresses two major priorities. One is to address finance issues of revenue enhancement, cost efficiencies associated with "rightsizing" the district, and improved budget development practices. The other is a focus on instruction: "Our #1 Job: Effective Instruction . . . the transformation of teaching practices, leadership practices, and organizational practices is the precondition for continuous improvement of the student learner . . . While we have made some progress, our work is far from done."[18] OUSD educators across the district acknowledge that students' academic performance falls short, but also believe that strategies to improve instruction must reflect the Oakland way. "We are not going back to the traditional 3 Rs," said Johnson-Trammell. The vision, mission, and core values of a FSCS district continue to guide that work.

STABILITY IN THE FACE OF LEADERSHIP CHANGE

Many of the key elements of *Community Schools, Thriving Students* endured over five superintendents and more than nine years. Conventional wisdom and experience hold that leadership change derails districts' strategic plans and the goals they represent. A long-time OUSD administrator recalls how "folks on the ground" experienced the district's substantial leadership turnover in the district—twenty-two permanent, interim, or state-appointed district leaders since 1970: "It was like, 'Well, whatever, next' . . . with each new person there was a huge shift and something new." So how did this strategic plan manage to survive? The answer to this question about the extraordinary persistence of FSCS vision, goals, and strategies in Oakland evokes a complex mix of decisions and events.

Planning for a System Change Effort

Arguably, an overarching explanation for the vision's persistence lies in the power of approaching the FSCS initiative as a system change effort, rather than a one-off or silver bullet solution of program adoption, new models, or tactics. "You start with philosophy; you don't just start having schools," said Sarikey. "Your whole system has to change." The initiative's comprehensive, inclusive planning process built a strong base of support for *Community Schools, Thriving Students*. This support has deepened and expanded as promising FSCS building blocks emerge—from eight to forty-two community school managers, for instance—and critical elements of the Voluntary Resolution Plan, such as restorative justice, show success. Continued commitment to the strategic plan's vision enabled fundamental FSCS elements to take root throughout the district. One central office administrator said, "Every time you go into the community to ask, 'What do you want, what do you need?' the FSCS model comes up immediately. People understand that we need a whole-child approach." Sarikey reflects on the significance of this buy-in: "A plan means nothing if the people in the district don't care about it . . . and a plan means nothing absent policies to back it up." In Oakland, the external and internal, mandatory and optional levers used to advance system change are now embedded in district policies and practices in ways that would be difficult if not impossible to "unwind."

Middle Management on Board

The continuity of Smith's FSCS initiative in the years after his departure also reflects stability of OUSD's middle management. The network superintendents, a group that sits between the central office and the schools, organized by district region/school level, include individuals with extensive OUSD experience and acknowledged success at Oakland elementary, middle, and high schools. "They grew up with FSCS," said Sarikey. "They were born into it. It's how they think about school."

Several OUSD central office leaders have been with the district for many years, participated in the FSCS planning process, and remain fully on board with the vision. Andrea Bustamante, now executive director of CSSS, has been in the district since 2009, took part in planning efforts and collaborated with Sarikey to build the district's partnership model. Mara Larson-Fleming, who also has been in OUSD since 2009 and now heads up the CSSS Health and Wellness area, said, "We are still using *Community Schools, Thriving Students*. It provides a coherent model that lets you look at the big picture, weave everything together, and integrate it into the educational setting. We haven't shifted our strategic plan, and that enables us as staff to really continue to build instead of shifting around." Curtiss Sarikey's 2017 return as chief of staff provided critical reinforcement for Superintendent Johnson-Trammell's intent that OUSD continue as a FSCS district.

Major Funders' Ongoing Support

The continued backing of major funders contributed fundamentally to the FSCS's persistence. Kaiser Permanente Health Care's consistent backing has been especially important. Kaiser sees its support for various OUSD health-related services as part of its "corporate partnership" with Oakland. As one Kaiser official put it, "Contribution to the health of the community is in our DNA—it is a shared mission, it starts at the top." The long-term investments of philanthropic partners such as Kaiser provided especially critical backing to OUSD as the ending of other grants threaten the continuation of practices that rely on "soft" money, especially as budget crises force cuts in personnel and service.

THE COSTS OF LEADERSHIP SHIFTS

Despite the stability of core the FSCS mission, central office leadership churn imposed costs. Although site-level leaders generally see FSCS as "the way we do schools in Oakland," central office departments remain unevenly engaged with *Community Schools, Thriving*

Students and its whole-child model. Departments on the instructional side of the house mostly carry the FSCS torch, but departments on the operational side lag in implementing practices and policies consistent with the FSCS district vision and have little engagement with it.

The central office department alignment outlined in the strategic plan remains largely aspirational because district leadership did not pursue it once Tony Smith left. In the turbulence following Smith's departure, central office focus on coherence eroded and the operational departments never bought in. The district leaders following Tony Smith were supportive of FSCS but paid little attention to promoting consistency across central office departments or undertaking the community-building required to achieve it. Budget crises, labor disputes, high rates of teacher turnover, and other difficulties demanding a superintendent's immediate notice unquestionably eclipsed attention to the community-building needed for the central office to function as an "in service of" FSCS district model.

To what extent has the FSCS initiative led to system change at the school level? Part 3 takes up that question.

PART III

IMPLEMENTATION: SCHOOL LEVEL

CHAPTER 7

Full-Service Community Schools in Action

Community schools represent a complex weaving of programs and practices into the fabric and structures of the school. Full-service community schools build on each school's unique set of strengths and community context. As schools begin to implement new practices and strategies, the FSCS elements work together and mutually reinforce each other. Necessarily, distinct elements of implementation are difficult to disentangle. We open part 3 of this book with three case studies from mature OUSD community schools. These examples bring to life the complex and unique adaptations of OUSD's FSCS model in three different school contexts.[1]

ROOSEVELT MIDDLE SCHOOL

Roosevelt is located in the heart of the San Antonio District, a 2.5 square mile neighborhood that is one of the most diverse areas of Oakland. It is home to nearly 36,700 residents, roughly 45 percent of whom were born outside the United States. Because of the area's large newcomer population—18 percentage points higher than the citywide average—the San Antonio District is also known as the immigrant gateway to Oakland. Roosevelt reflects the multicultural and multilingual richness of its surrounding neighborhood. Walking through classrooms or visiting the cafeteria at lunch, visitors may hear as many as a dozen different languages, as nearly one-third of its students—and even more parents and guardians—are learning to speak English. Many students are newcomers to the US, including refugees fleeing violence and poverty in their home countries of Guatemala, Nepal, and Burma.

In 2018, Roosevelt served nearly six hundred students, 97 percent of whom are socioeconomically disadvantaged and 33 percent English language learners. Seventeen percent of Roosevelt students are black, 40 percent Asian, and 33 percent Latinx. Since Roosevelt became a FSCS, chronic absence and suspensions have been declining—they currently hover at 6 percent and 4 percent, respectively. Mathematics performance has been improving; and in 2018, Roosevelt made the CORE list of "schools to learn from" (schools where students had demonstrated rapid academic gains).

Roosevelt's FSCS provides the tightly integrated services and supports that are vital to students' success. An on-site health center offers easy access to medical care. The afterschool program is a seamless extension of the school day, providing a safe and affordable place for students to receive academic support, enjoy a hot meal, and explore enrichment activities. Over the years, students and their families have received a range of services through Roosevelt's web of partnerships, including counseling, tax preparation support, and food and housing assistance. It is that tight integration of services and supports, together with its team approach to addressing challenges, that earned Roosevelt Middle School the 2014 Community School Award from OUSD. In 2018, the Coalition of Community Schools honored Roosevelt principal Cliff Hong with its Educational Leadership Award.[2] "We want our neighbors to see Roosevelt as an asset and as a center for the community," says Hong. "Roosevelt should be their school . . . a place where they are welcomed and supported."

With a history stretching back nearly fifteen years, the Roosevelt Student Health Center is one of OUSD's most well established and tightly integrated school-based clinics. The center, located in the basement of the school, is managed by La Clínica, a leader in the city and throughout the country in providing community-based health services. At Roosevelt, the health center is not simply located in the school; it is part of the school. Health center staff participate in school committees and leadership structures to facilitate communication between the clinic and the broader school community and to bring a health perspective to schoolwide concerns or challenges. Clinic staff work closely with school leadership to integrate health services into the school culture and the school day, with minimal disruption to classroom learning. For example, every morning, classroom teachers receive a list of students who have appointments in the health center. The introduction of this simple yet high-impact system enables teachers to coordinate class projects and testing, and reduces the need for disruptive phone calls to classrooms.

Roosevelt also counts on the longtime partnership of neighborhood CBO East Bay Asian Youth Center (EBAYC). It would be difficult to find a community partner more deeply connected to a school than EBAYC is to Roosevelt. Through personal relationships, strategic participation in the school leadership structure, and support for key programs and services, the EBAYC staff provide the glue that connects Roosevelt to the larger San Antonio community.

Many EBAYC leaders at Roosevelt grew up in the San Antonio neighborhood and understand both its assets and its challenges. Over the years, EBAYC has offered a range of programs and services to fit the changing needs of the community—from starting the school clinic, to launching a Saturday program to introduce students to college and career options, to providing programming and counseling supports during the school day. "Most of our staff are from the neighborhood, and we have worked hard to build relationships here at school and to build trust with parents," says the EBAYC site coordinator.

EBAYC is perhaps best known for its afterschool program. During the critical 3 p.m.–6 p.m. time slot every school day, EBAYC staff provide students with academic support, enrichment activities, and a safe place to spend time with their classmates. The program is deeply connected to classroom teaching and learning. Afterschool mentors also work in classrooms during the school day and monitor students' academic strengths and challenges. These connections add to the program's impact on both building community and extending learning time, particularly for struggling students. EBAYC staff have also played a critical role in Roosevelt's parent outreach efforts, the introduction of classroom advisories, and in providing counseling and related services to young men needing additional support. In fact, the organization is so tightly integrated with the school that it's difficult to know where Roosevelt stops and EBAYC starts. EBAYC staff say they wouldn't have it any other way. As the EBAYC site co-ordinator puts it, "If you know something needs to be done or you see a gap somewhere and you have the means to make things better, then why not step in and do it?"

COLISEUM COLLEGE PREP ACADEMY

Coliseum College Prep Academy (CCPA) sits on a shared campus that serves students and families from transitional kindergarten all the way through high school. The school is located in the Havenscourt neighborhood, a twenty-five-square-block area that is home to predominantly Spanish-speaking families, including many immigrants from Mexico and Central America.

CCPA is a 6–12 school created through a community-based design process. It opened in 2006 as one of two neighboring schools to replace Havenscourt Middle School. A team of parents, staff, students, and community members contributed to the design of the school with extensive input during a visioning, research, and planning process. The result is a community school with a deep commitment to collaborating with families and a tightly integrated web of supports and services to help students and parents be college-ready by the end of twelfth grade. In 2018, CCPA served just under five hundred students, 96 percent of whom are socioeconomically disadvantaged and 30 percent are ELLs. The student population is primarily Latinx (83 percent), with 13 percent African American students. In 2018, 97 percent of all students graduated, and 95 percent considered "college- and career-ready." Fewer than 3 percent of students were suspended.[3]

The original vision statement of the school—designed by parents and teachers—imagined a school where parents would be welcome and supported, with staff who spoke Spanish (the primary language for 83 percent of the parents), and a dedicated space for parents to meet and learn together. Years after that original vision was crafted, home-school partnerships continue to provide the foundation for CCPA's success. Not only are parents welcome at school, but the calendar is packed with opportunities for them to learn and engage with other parents and with school staff. Teachers are accustomed to parents dropping in to observe instruction. They also rely on their partnership with parents to maintain the school's rigorous schedule (students typically stay until 5 p.m.) and its family-focused discipline policies and practices. Potluck dinners for students and their families, parent gatherings with the principal, and parent and family workshops are a few of the ways in which CCPA creates space to build community. A health center on campus provides medical and dental services for students, and its staff lead parenting support groups on issues of common interest, such as maintaining a positive relationship with adolescent children.

CCPA's Family and College Resource Center (FRC) is the hub for many of these programs and activities. Four mornings a week throughout the school year, part of the space becomes a classroom for parents learning English as a second language through a partnership between CCPA and the district's adult school. Childcare is provided free of charge for the (mostly) mothers in the class. On the second Friday of every month, the classroom space hosts "Coffee with the Principal," an informal gathering for parents to ask questions or express views on any topic. In addition to the structured events, the FRC is a place for parents to seek out and receive individual support on everything from navigating the school's online student information system to communication with a teen or a teacher. It hums with activity throughout the school day as parents and students stop by to ask questions, inquire about resources, or just to say a quick hello to the FRC staff. Sometimes, all a parent needs is another parent to listen and provide support. Other times, staff connect parents to services offered by community-school partners, such as tax or legal help, counseling services, or information about food-assistance programs.

In addition to the myriad programs and services available at the school, teachers visit the homes of students once a year, a foundational practice that sends a powerful message to parents and families about the school's commitment to partnerships. Home visits provide a different context for conversations between parents and teachers and help teachers better understand how to support and motivate their students. Home visits also give parents the opportunity to meet in a space that is more comfortable to them.

Parents have played a pivotal leadership role at critical junctures in the school's history, including petitioning the district to expand CCPA from a middle school to a high school, successfully advocating to retain the adult education program on campus and monitoring district budgeting to ensure the school has sufficient resources. CCPA parents were key community leaders in the campaigns for Measure N and Proposition 30, local and state ballot measures that have substantially increased the school's budget and ability to build and provide programs for students. "Without our parent community and their direct advocacy for schools in Oakland, we would not be able to improve and grow the school for the kids the way we have been able to over the past years," says Principal Amy Carozza. CCPA has been purposeful about reaching out to all members of the school community to make them feel welcome and supported.

OAKLAND TECHNICAL HIGH SCHOOL

Oakland Technical High School (Tech), established in 1915, is nestled in a bustling neighborhood where many cafes, restaurants, and small shops line the main streets in the area. As the district's largest comprehensive high school, Tech attracts students from all over

Oakland, and its student body reflects the city's racial, cultural, economic, and language diversity. Tech serves just under two thousand students, 29 percent of whom are African American, 16 percent Latinx, 20 percent Asian, and 24 percent white. Forty-nine percent qualify as socioeconomically disadvantaged, and 6 percent are considered ELLs. In 2018, 89 percent of all students graduated, and fewer than 2 percent were suspended.[4]

Like many other OUSD high schools, Tech offers students linked learning pathways—sometimes called "career academies"—that bring together strong academics, demanding career technical education, real-world experience, and integrated student support systems. These combine to create experiences for students that are personally relevant and engaging. Academies begin in tenth grade and continue through twelfth grade (students apply in ninth grade). Tech's pathways include: Computer Academy; Engineering Academy; Fashion, Art, and Design Academy; Health Academy; and Race, Policy, and Law Academy.

For years, Oakland Tech has been working to remove systemic barriers to college and aims for career-ready graduation for all its students. In 2013–2014, through analyzing enrollment patterns, staff saw that black and low-income students were underrepresented in the school's prestigious academic programs, which also boasted the highest graduation and college acceptance rates. On average, Tech students enrolled in a pathway had higher grades (3.0 GPA compared with 2.6) and graduate at higher rates (96 versus 85 percent) than their non-pathway peers. Students in pathways were also more engaged, with better attendance and fewer disciplinary issues. The suspension rate, for example, was just 2 percent for pathway students, compared with 5.5 percent for non-pathway students in the 2013–2014 school year. Participation in career pathways varied significantly across race and ethnicity groups, with black males among the least well represented. In the 2013–2014 school year, nearly two out of three black male students were not enrolled in a pathway.

In response, the school began requiring that all freshman take California Studies, a rigorous yearlong interdisciplinary course linking history with literature—and a prerequisite for the school's prestigious pathway programs. Tech also instituted a ninth-grade "house" system to provide incoming ninth-graders with a ready-made community to ease the transition to the large comprehensive high school.[5] Making California Studies, and later biology, part of the standard freshman curriculum was an important step toward establishing a common foundation of knowledge, skills, and expectations from the outset.

The freshmen team also developed a plan for the 2014–2015 school year to talk with freshmen early and often about their pathway options, beginning with an overview at the start of the school year. Leading up to the application process in March, the team held a pathway fair and scheduled presentations by students enrolled in each pathway. School leaders developed an information packet that detailed the application and selection process for each of the options. However, equitable access to rigorous curriculum was not enough. Staff also developed companion supports and practices that would be critical to student success, particularly for students who arrived at Tech without strong reading and writing skills. Tech teachers now provide drop-in tutoring every day before and after school, and peer tutors provide additional academic support. Teachers design classroom activities and devise seating plans to foster equity and collaboration, to encourage students to both seek out and provide assistance, and create a classroom culture where questions are acceptable and encouraged. The house system loops students in the same house together for two core classes, and gives house teachers a common prep period once a week to coordinate and communicate.

Tech has engaged other targeted supports to help all its students succeed. In a unique partnership, for example, the African American Male Achievement (AAMA) program partners with Oakland Community Organizations (OCO) and the Department of Social Justice at Oakland's Holy Names University to increase college-readiness and access for black males. Through the college's early admit program and with support from OCO volunteers, young men participate in workshops, receive peer mentoring from African American male college students, and join trips to area colleges and universities. Students who participate in the program are eligible to receive early notification (in the fall of their senior year) of their admission to Holy Names and a scholarship of at least $9,000.

This partnership is one more piece of a focused and sustained effort to write a new narrative about what it means to be a black male in Oakland. The program, part of a districtwide initiative that has earned national praise and attention, begins with the Manhood Development class, primarily for freshmen, and includes additional college-prep courses and companion co-curricular activities. "The focus is on students' social and emotional development," says the administrator who heads up the AAMA program at Tech. "We create a safe space to build a new type of dialogue about what it means to be an African American man."

The AAMA program leader, besides serving as instructor and mentor for young men in the AAMA program, is part of Tech's Co-ordination of Services Team (COST), a critical community school mechanism for connecting students to the resources they need to be successful. Teachers and other school staff refer students to COST, which meets every Wednesday to review referrals and to devise an individualized plan for each student. This cross-cutting team also includes staff from partner organizations, such as Lincoln Child Center and the TechniClinic, as well as the school's nurse, the parent liaison, the community school manager, and other school administrators.

Tech's efforts to develop and reinforce a positive school culture also include students. Student leaders have developed and refined four "Pillars of Oakland Tech"—Positive Expression, Honor, Focus, and Community—an expression of the school's core values and expectations. They reinforce these values through work inside classrooms and at schoolwide events. Each month, Tech students organize First Friday events, centered around one of the four pillars: the events feature food, music, and a variety of games and activities designed to bring the whole school together and build community. The pillars are now posted prominently throughout the school.

Full-service community school implementation is complex and multifaceted. FSCSs include a range of supports and opportunities for students—the "roots" of the OUSD FSCS tree. They also include essential conditions that support schools' growth—leadership, partnership, collaboration, and equity. In chapter 8, we begin to disentangle FSCS site-level implementation, including how the initiative scaled, key site-level strategies, the district's role, and progress toward outcomes.

CHAPTER 8

Site-Level Implementation

Community Schools, Thriving Students' site-level implementation began in 2012–2013 with a cohort of nineteen full-service community schools. The first schools designated for FSCS implementation already had infrastructure and funding streams for components of the model in place. This cohort included the six existing Elev8 sites, funded by Atlantic Philanthropies, which already functioned as community schools. It also included thirteen sites with school-based health centers, funded by Kaiser Foundation in a major 2012–2013 expansion of its existing investment. These schools were primarily middle and high schools, and reflected high-need priority areas based on equity data. The idea was that the community school managers could leverage the existing investments and deeply integrate health centers, afterschool programs, and family engagement into the core work of schools. Elev8 sites already had CSMs, and Kaiser funds provided resources to hire new CSMs, or designate a CSM among existing staff. While Kaiser and Elev8 funded the majority of CSM staff salaries, OUSD funded some of the first CSM cohort as district staff and others as contracts to community-based organizations.

In early FSCS implementation, Community Schools and Student Services (CSSS) staff walked a line between respecting schools' autonomy and differences while also providing some standardization and supports. CSSS staff saw the CSM as a chief conduit to effect site-level implementation. Yet the heterogeneity of funding streams and different models for integrating school services posed a challenge. CSMs received their funding from multiple sources: many were funded by partner organizations, and therefore were not direct employees of, nor directly accountable to, the district.[1] In the spirit of top-down support for bottom-up change, CSSS staffers Andrea Bustamante and Mara Larsen-Fleming established a professional learning community (PLC) for CSMs. The PLC brought CSMs from very different school ecosystems into a shared conversation about community school implementation. The PLC also helped establish a common identity of being a FSCS and a professional identity as a CSM. It provided CSMs with training and support and created some clarity and structure around the role that was not dependent on who was signing the paychecks. This "hybrid model" set the tone for CSSS's approach to community school implementation henceforth: working "in the service of" sites, creating standards and guides to help ensure quality and alignment, seeking ongoing feedback and engagement, and allowing for variation and autonomy.

Over the subsequent years, CSSS staff expanded implementation to include additional cohorts as grant funding allowed. Consistent with the district's strategic plan, CSSS staff saw 2014–2015 and 2015–2016 as a time for tuning and refining the model (see chapter 3). The first cohort of community schools were important pioneers and laboratories to tease out promising practices that would inform subsequent scale-up. Partners, CSMs, and school leaders all provided ongoing feedback to CSSS staff to help develop quality standards for partnerships, create a clear job description for the CSM role, systematize new coordinating structures (e.g., COST), and implement flagship programs and services (e.g., restorative justice, attendance teams).

In 2014–2015, OUSD received a major grant that allowed expansion of a new cohort of schools. Funding from the US Department of Education provided resources to expand the FSCS model into elementary schools. The federal grant prioritized increasing health access, addressing student attendance and chronic absence, developing strong family engagement linked to learning, and intentionally supporting successful transitions to from elementary school to middle school. Schools were preselected based on feeder patterns that could help establish "proof of concept" for intentional elementary-middle FSCS transitions. The Department of Education proposal was also the impetus for establishing the community school priorities that now span all OUSD's FSCSs.

The following year (2016–2017), OUSD received another substantial grant to support scale-up. The funding came from San Francisco Foundation's Oakland Opportunity Grant, part of which was designated to sustain and scale community schools. Unlike in prior years, CSSS staff used an application process to select this cohort of schools. They prioritized schools with high chronic absence/suspensions and high free and reduced-price lunch rates that were willing to develop aspects of the FSCS model, such as facilitating regular Coordination of Services Team (COST; see chapter 5) teams and developing strong shared governance practices. By design, the application itself gauged the school's readiness and ability to successfully adopt the model: principal applicants were asked to read a set of case studies about current OUSD FSCSs and reflect on what aspects of the model most inspired them. The application also asked principals to identify one to three specific school goals, existing areas of strength and challenge (in relation to community school priority areas), and potential priority work areas to designate for a CSM. According to CSSS staffer Ali Metzler, who was brought on board to support FSCS expansion and scale-up, "It's been really a successful way to make sure the principals are bought into becoming a community school." Sharing leadership with someone, having another administrator on site as a partner, can be a challenge for some school leaders. "We wanted schools that were ready for that and willing to do that, schools that were willing to make sure their COST was super robust, making sure that schools were committed to having strong parent, student, and family governance structures." Based on the priority criteria, nine schools were invited to apply and six (five elementary, one middle) were chosen to receive funding.

The 2016–2017 year was also the first year that the district asked each FSCS to contribute to the funding of its CSM from the school-site budget. Both the US Department of Education and San Francisco Foundation grants asked FSCS sites to enter into a cost-sharing agreement to fund their site's CSM. In year one, the district would fund 100 percent of the CSM's role; in subsequent years, that distribution would decrease by 25 percent, so that the school would gradually take on the full cost of the CSM position. According to CSSS staff, some schools paid for the position 100 percent from the start because they prioritized the role. As of 2019–2020, all schools are paying 50–100 percent of the salary of their CSM. Beginning 2019–2020, there were forty-two schools with CSMs.

OPERATIONALIZING "THE TREE": CORE IMPLEMENTATION STRATEGIES

Shortly before launching the second cohort of FSCSs, CSSS engaged the John W. Gardner Center for Youth and Their Communities at Stanford University (Gardner Center) to inform initiative scale-up. The Gardner Center started by working with CSSS staff to create a theory of change, or a Community Schools System Strategy Map (SSM), that would operationalize the OUSD FSCS tree (see figure 5.1) into (researchable) objectives, strategies, and outcomes (see appendix 8a at the end of this chapter).

The SSM helped CSSS articulate its strategy within the broader district system. As a FSCS district, technically, the entire district was operating under the FSCS umbrella. However, in an education climate focused on academic test scores, CSSS staff sometimes struggled to define and articulate the department's contribution to student "success."[2] Academic data typically did not show immediate improvements in desired student outcomes at FSCSs. While proximal indicators like discipline and attendance sometimes showed swift and dramatic improvement, this was not always the case. In an environment of growing fiscal crisis, principals needed to make tough choices about the value to students of every dollar spent.

While most FSCS programs relied on external funding, the new FSCS cohort model required schools to assume increasing financial responsibility for their site's CSM salary. The SSM helped CSSS staff articulate their impact and focus their efforts.

Community schools in Oakland are more than a program or tactic. They require complete system change. The SSM also helped CSSS staff articulate the type of school systems they were trying to build. While each group within CSSS had their own benchmarks, indicators, and accountability mechanisms—for example, after school, behavioral health, and family engagement necessarily have different metrics and outcomes—the the SSM allowed CSSS to create a coherent set of goals that cut across groups and articulated the broader mission of "Thriving Students." As described in the SSM, the CSSS office aimed to "ensure that every OUSD community school (1) offers each student the culturally relevant and appropriate services and opportunities they need to learn and thrive; (2) provides a safe, supportive, and engaging environment for teaching and learning; and (3) is staffed by adults who are culturally competent, collaborative, and actively working towards equity . . . so that each student graduates college, career, and community-ready." All the groups in CSSS—and in fact, many stakeholders in the FSCS initiative—could see themselves and their work within these broad, shared goals.

Additionally, the SSM surfaced a set of organizational practices at the school-site level that became system change tools. Gardner Center research conducted in 2014-2015 and 2015-2016 across early implementing sites identified that strong FSCSs (schools showing positive shifts in student outcomes and identified by CSSS staff anecdotally as "positive examples" of FSCSs) shared a set of common practices:

- Developing strategic partnerships
- Coordinating and integrating student services and supports
- Including partners, families, students, and community in collaborative leadership
- Using data to inform priorities and programs

While each of these areas refers to a distinct set of practices and strategies, in reality, they are often interwoven and mutually reinforcing. For example, strategic partnerships depend on inclusive leadership approaches to make room for partners at the table in schools. Data-driven discussions can activate students and families in school planning; they can also be catalysts for critical conversations about alignment between partners and school leaders. COST can help integrate partners with school staff, as it uses data to monitor individual students and assess schoolwide wellness needs. These four elements became identifiable best practices in FSCSs that work to shift culture and change structures at the site level.[3] They are now well-recognized standards of practice at FSCSs across the district.

WIDESPREAD IMPLEMENTATION AND UPTAKE

The OUSD community schools initiative catalyzed a widespread shift in culture and practice across school sites. While each FSCS necessarily reflects the character of its own community and school context, the practices described above—strategic partnerships, co-ordinated and integrated student services, collaborative leadership, and data-driven improvement—are widely shared as common expectations of quality community schools.

The success of widespread FSCS site-level implementation reflects many of the conditions and system-level decisions discussed in part 2. The "prepared ground" of a robust civic sector provided a network of community partners that could be coordinated and that aligned within the FSCS framework. (Site leaders also reflected district staff's creativity by braiding diverse funding streams in the service of an overarching vision.). The elaborate and inclusive strategic planning process that activated school and community members around a common and increasingly focused set of goals set the tone for collaborative leadership at the site level. District leaders' early decision to leverage external accountability measures (e.g., Office of Civil Rights compliance and the Voluntary Resolution Plan) as change levers carried over into site-level strategies. CSSS staff have undertaken a similar strategy, linking community-school implementation to state-mandated accountability processes such as the School Site Councils and School Plan for Student Achievement required under LCAP and LCFF. (The following chapters go into this topic in more detail).

Widespread FSCS implementation also owes much of its success to the efforts of central office staff, who have provided "top-down support for bottom-up change." CSSS staff provide a very specific set of supports to FSCS school sites. They work with community organizations to administer and develop community school programs, and have brought millions of dollars to the schools through a wide range of grants and district-level partnerships. CSSS provides site-level staff with goal-aligned professional development and support; for example, trainings for all program staff in the dozens of afterschool providers serving schools across the district; annual partnership orientations for new partners; and ongoing professional development and support to CSMs. CSSS staff have also taken on the role of communicating districtwide standards of practice, structures, and systems. Best practices such as COST or MTSS, piloted and refined at school sites, are shared and explicitly included as expectations (and supported with training) for site-level staff.

CSSS staff have worked to demonstrate the impact of the FSCS work in relation to district goals—for example, identifying and leaning into the five priority areas that now guide all CSMs' work (increasing school attendance; strengthening COST and MTSS; increasing student access to health services; increasing and strengthening partnerships; and creating innovative systems and strategies to address individual school's goals). Lastly, CSSS has taken the "targeted universalism" approach embodied in the initial strategic planning. As grant monies make new programs available, CSSS makes decisions about resource allocations that are determined, first and foremost, on the basis of need. "All means all" equates to targeting resources and supports where they are most needed to address equity gaps.[4]

SITE-LEVEL ACHIEVEMENTS

The initial cohort of nineteen FSCS schools has more than doubled to forty-two sites. While some schools have been FSCSs for nearly eight years, others are in their first or second year with a CSM. However, in OUSD, the amount of time a school has been a FSCS does not necessarily equate "maturity." Some of the long-time FSCSs have struggled with leadership change and staff turnover, both of which can destabilize relationships and dramatically effect implementation. Additionally, as FSCS expectations and support tools have become more explicit and robust over time, newer FSCS schools may actually have an advantage, as they begin their journey as FSCSs with more guidance and resources at their disposal to help them navigate the transition.

Ultimately, OUSD FSCSs' site-level implementation has catalyzed important shifts in school culture and practice that support conditions for learning. Due to the gradual rollout of FSCS cohorts, it is difficult to assess impact at *all* FSCSs across the district. The site-level descriptions highlighted in this book primarily draw from in-depth qualitative research at nine FSCS sites. This includes five "early adopters" from the first cohort of FSCSs, as well as four schools designated in later cohorts. In total, the schools include three elementary schools, four middle schools, one high school and one "span" school serving both middle and high.[5] While implementation and outcomes vary across sites, the following four areas of schoolwide outcomes reflect trends found, to some degree across all FSCSs in the district.

Integrated and Coordinated Services and Opportunities

FSCSs facilitate greater integration of student and family support services to the school's academic goals, even in "emerging" schools. All FSCSs provide a range of services and opportunities to students, including afterschool programs, linked learning career pathways, clinic visits, dental exams, vision testing and eyeglasses provision, and behavioral health services. Many schools seamlessly integrate partners and services into the fabric of the school. FSCS teachers report widespread use of community school resources and, further, that they understand and actively engage in key community school practices, especially referring students to supports, engaging directly with families, and enacting positive discipline practices.[6] The CSM plays an instrumental and essential role in supporting teachers' use of community school resources.

Conditions Allow Teachers and Principals to Focus on Instruction

FSCS teachers report that community school resources address student barriers to learning, improve school climate, and enable teachers to focus more directly on teaching. FSCS services and supports diminish classroom disruptions and student absences. They provide culturally relevant tools for teachers (e.g., positive discipline practices), which makes for higher quality instructional time. Additionally, community partners and the CSM "take the load" of nonacademic responsibilities at the school, freeing up more teacher and principal instructional time. While teachers' knowledge and use of community school resources vary quite a bit by site and individual, we find widespread agreement in the extent to which teachers and principals perceive that community school practices support conditions for teaching and learning.

Enhanced Collaboration and Partnership Between Adults at the School and at Home

OUSD full-service community schools show high levels of collaboration and partnership between adults at school and at home. In many schools, principals and CSMs cultivate a school culture where families and partner organizations become integral to the schools' functioning and success in fostering student achievement. More than half of FSCS teachers surveyed agree that partners contribute positively to their school's goals. In high-functioning FSCSs, staff often do not distinguish partners from school staff. Adults regularly communicate about student progress, attend professional development sessions together, and engage in shared goal-setting and planning. Teachers actively communicate with families around student learning—for example, calling families at home to share positive news about their child, texting families, holding classroom parent meetings, looking at data with families, and communicating with families about their hopes and dreams for their child.[7] Some schools have changed practices to be more inclusive of families—for example, transforming standard parent-teacher conferences with Academic Parent-Teacher Teams scaffolds data-based conversations, shared goal-setting, and skill-building with families, teachers, and students. Families are active contributors to school improvement and decision making; parents play important roles in School Site Councils and setting SPSA goals.

Climate of High Expectations and High Levels of Support

FSCSs aim to create a climate of high expectations and high levels of support for students. This goal means that adults at the school show understanding of students' behavior in light of the norms of the communities in which they have grown, respect all students as learners with valuable knowledge and experience, and demonstrate the expectation of student success. At some of our focus schools (typically those who have been FSCSs for longer), school leaders are innovating with new instructional practice that hold students to high standards of success—for example, increasing the rigor of career pathways or piloting new 21st Century Science curriculum. Principals credit the strong culture/climate work with freeing up their attention to focus on instructional rigor and innovation.

FSCS teachers largely recognize and celebrate the richness of students' diverse backgrounds. In a Gardner Center survey of FSCS teachers, nearly all indicate they actively prioritize building positive relationships with their students. Most use some form of positive discipline practice to manage classroom behavior: nearly all use restorative justice circles, and the majority report using trauma-informed practices.[8] The majority indicated they actively considered their students' life experiences in class planning and instruction. (However, less than half felt they understood what their students' lives were like outside of the classroom.) Given the disparities in cultural, racial/ethnic, and linguistic background of many OUSD teachers in relation to those of their students, building teacher knowledge of and empathy for their students' lives is an important achievement of the FSCS initiative.[9]

What aspects of FSCS implementation are most important to bringing about these changed practices and mindsets at the site level? How are core community school elements—for example, partnerships, CSM role, integrated student supports, and family engagement—implemented in OUSD schools? What role does the district play in each of these arenas? In the remainder of part 3, we dive into specific aspects of FSCS implementation to elaborate what each looks like at the site level.

Appendix 8a

Oakland FSCS System Strategy Map

Problem Statement: Persistent inequalities, institutional racism, and a lack of culturally appropriate educational opportunities have contributed to inequitable academic and life outcomes for Oakland students and their families.

Goals: To ensure that every OUSD Community School: (1) offers each student the culturally relevant and appropriate services and opportunities they need to learn and thrive; (2) provides a safe, supportive, and engaging environment for teaching and learning; and (3) is staffed by adults who are culturally competent, collaborative, and actively working toward equity . . . so that each student graduates college-, career-, and community-ready.

CS Programs
· Health and wellness
· School culture and climate
· Family and youth engagement
· Expanded learning
· Social and emotional learning
· Academics
· School readiness
· Equity and responsiveness

District Strategies
· Partner with community to administer and develop community school programs.
· Provide site-level staff with goal-aligned professional development and support.
· Communicate district-wide standards of practice, structures, and systems.
· Drive equity-focused resource allocation, continuous improvement. Align CS efforts with other district initiatives.

Stakeholders
· Students
· Principals
· Teachers
· CSMs
· Partners
· Families/community
· District staff

School-Site Strategies
· Develop strategic partnerships to support school/student goals
· Coordinate and integrate student services and supports
· Include partners, families, students and community in collaborative leadership
· Use data to inform priorities and programs

Necessary Conditions
1. Teachers have resources and support to provide quality instruction
2. Ongoing resource allocation and prioritization at by district, schools, and community
3. Collaborative partnerships with Alameda County, City of Oakland, public & private funders, and community organizations.

Long-Term Outcomes
· Scaled and sustainable community schools support equitable outcomes for all OUSD students.
· Schools have the conditions to support high quality teaching and learning.
· Improved social-emotional and academic learning for students.
· Families are partners in student's success in high school, college, and beyond.

Short-Term Outcomes

District:
· District training is accessible to school-site staff
· District communication is effective and systematic
· District programs and tools are in place and responsive to school-site needs and district priorities.

Schools:
· Schools provide culturally responsive services, opportunities, and supports that meet student needs.
· Schools have high quality community school systems and practices.
· Principals and teachers access services and understand their roles in developing community schools.
· School staff have capacity to meaningfully engage families in student learning, school improvement.
· Partners provide resources aligned with student needs and school goals.

Students/families:
· Students know how to access supports, services, and opportunities to help them succeed.
· Families feel welcomed, valued, supported to participate in their student's learning.
· Students and families have the confidence and opportunity to engage in school site improvement efforts, advocacy, and decision making.

Intermediate Outcomes
· Distribution of district (and community) resources reflects school and student needs.
· District strategy, accountability, and decision making reflects cultural responsiveness and equity orientation.
· Community school workstreams are integrated into and fully funded in LCAP and district plan.

Schools:
· Seamless integration of services and opportunities to support learning.
· Conditions allow teachers and principal to focus on high-quality instruction
· Adults at the school work together to support students.
· Climate of high expectations and high support for student learning.

Students/families:
· Students feel valued, are engaged in school every day.
· Students and families consistently access supports, services, and opportunities to help them succeed.
· Students and families participate in school governance and district policy.

CHAPTER 9

Strategic Partnerships

[Our partners] are behind every single initiative that we do
that I would say falls under community schools . . . It's not that
there's a [partner organization] and [our school], it's the [part-
ner organization] at the [school]. We're just one team. So,
I never think of [so and so]—any of that team—as an outside
agency coming in. They're the core of our school.

—OUSD principal

Partnerships are fundamental to FSCSs because they allow schools to
provide more resources, supports, and opportunities to students than
schools could on their own, and create an important link with the community. OUSD community schools are supported by several hundred
community-based organizations providing a range of services and supports to students and families from pre-K through high school. These
partners include large health-care providers and public entities (e.g.,
Alameda County Public Health Department); midsized organizations
such as the YMCA; neighborhood development corporations; mental
health and social service providers; public health clinics; afterschool
program providers; youth development organizations; reading, math,
STEAM, and enrichment-focused providers; and small grassroots
groups or informal organizations such as Soccer Without Borders.
Schools with strong partner connections are staffed by adults who, regardless of the "shirt" they are wearing, are working to serve students.

While some partners provide single services, many offer an array of services on community school sites. For example, Safe Passages serves as lead afterschool agency at four OUSD schools and provides academic enrichment and out-of-school-time programs, family and community support services, family resources support, tutoring and mentorship programs, and youth urban arts and ethnic study courses across a variety of others. Safe Passages serves approximately four thousand Oakland students and families each year. The East Bay Asian Youth Consortium (EBAYC) partners with more than fifteen OUSD schools to provide expanded learning programming and community engagement; its staff strategically collaborates with school staff to strengthen school culture/climate and attendance. EBAYC serves over three thousand young people daily. La Clínica operates six school-based health clinics in OUSD elementary, middle, and high schools, with a focus on culturally and linguistically responsive community health. Services include primary medical care, family planning, immunizations, care for chronic illness, on-site dental services, individual and group behavioral health services, vision services, and clinical health education. In 2017, La Clínica provided direct services to more than sixty-six hundred students and families, and reached hundreds more with campus-wide health promotion programming.

In addition to providing direct services, many partners play a critical role in school leadership and organization. Health and behavioral health partners participate in the school's weekly COST meetings, where they triage and respond to student and school needs. Expanded learning providers may attend training with teachers, and sit in on departmental meetings. CSMs (who are in some cases funded by partners) are typically part of the school's instructional leadership team, and serve as high-level administrators working closely with the school's principal. Many partners—whether they provide afterschool programming, health clinic, or mental health services—include a family engagement component to their work, strengthening the school's capacity to support families.

Strong partners bring resources to the school and are responsive to its needs. In one school, the afterschool program coordinator also leads the school's African American Parent Advisory Council, helping to plan meetings and working alongside the principal. The principal observed, "It's not like some partnerships, where they'll say, 'Oh, we're funded to do X, Y, Z' and not take on anything outside of that." At another school slated to become a designated receiving school for district newcomers, the health partner stepped up and offered to identify and coordinate a range of resources for newcomer students and their families, including legal aid, targeted medical screenings, and mental health supports. The school's principal reported, "That's huge for us, and it makes us feel like we don't have to take the burden of that weight, which also makes us more open to serving high-needs kids." School and students needs are always changing, thus being responsive requires constant adaptation and flexibility. At many FSCSs, partners become part of the team of adults serving students, contributing well beyond the specific services they deliver.

In this chapter, we discuss some of the important practices that support FSCS strategic partnerships, as well as the critical role the district plays in fomenting these elements as widespread practice.

DEVELOPING SHARED GOALS

School-community partnerships can be complex, involving distinct organizational cultures, accountability systems, communication styles, and perspectives. For example, a school may be accountable to the state for decreasing chronic absence and improving third-grade academic assessment scores, while a partner agency may be focused on increasing the number of individual children served reported to their funders. Without meaningful communication and alignment, each entity may focus on their separate goals and contexts, missing the opportunity to leverage efforts.

In OUSD, examples of FSCSs working with partners toward shared goals abound. One elementary school had been working diligently to improve second-graders' reading levels. Its primary literacy partner, supported in part through AmeriCorps volunteers, provided tutors in the classroom to teach reading interventions throughout the day, including pulling out students needing specialized support. Although the program required the school to do additional fundraising to cover costs, the partner collaborated in raising the money. Another school leveraged its family resource center, financed by a core partner agency, to help meet its goal of reducing chronic absence by 10 percent. Through establishing an attendance team that included core partner staff and by engaging with families, the school decreased its chronic absence rate by nearly 10 percent. The attendance team diligently reviewed the district-provided data, grade by grade, week after week, and provided targeted interventions.

Shared goals and expectations start with schools' ability to identify, define, and articulate their own set of goals to share with partners. As one principal stated, "The question I ask myself is how clear were we on what we needed and how much do we follow up? [If] I can't answer those questions with fidelity, then I can't hold that partner as accountable, right?"

In OUSD community schools, the School Plan for Student Achievement (SPSA) has become a focal point for community school goal setting and plans. Goal setting is not new to FSCSs. Prior to California's Local Control Funding Formula (LCFF) and LCAP, school staff focused on identifying and aligning resources to support their school's "big rocks." With the introduction of LCFF and California Department of Education's Code 64001-65001 (and aligned with federal ESSA accountability requirements), every school receiving ESSA Title I funds must develop a SPSA.[1] The SPSA is developed by the school's site council (SSC) (see chapter 4). District guidance around strategic partnership prompts school leaders and partners to discuss the school's SPSA goals and align resources in support of those goals. Tying community schools' goals to the SPSA process has added a layer of accountability and became an important lever (external, required) for creating a culture of data-driven goal setting at school sites. It creates an explicit agenda around which partner resources can be leveraged and aligned.

SHIFTING PRACTICE

In many FSCSs, both partners and school staff adapt their practices in the service of common goals. At one elementary FSCS, the principal initially struggled to build a relationship with one of her school's core partners. She thought they were "too touchy-feely," and not adequately supporting academic goals. When the partner held community nights, the principal would ask, "What are the goals of this night? I need to know the outcome." Over time, partner staff shifted their practices to be more "outcomes driven." They continued their "feel-good" family nights, but aligned them more tightly with priority academic goals; for example, by incorporating targeted literacy training that bolstered families' ability to read with their kids at home. According to the principal, "That built trust for me. You're willing to change your practice, you're not just here to say 'the school needs to do better.'"

The shift in practice goes both ways. At a middle FSCS, the core partner dramatically modified its staffing schedule so that afterschool program mentors could "push in" to the classrooms and support teachers as co-advisors during advisory. When both the afterschool mentors and teachers indicated that they needed more common planning and prep time, the principal made shifts to the entire school's professional development calendar, holding times for mentor-teacher collaboration within the master schedule. In response, partner staff extended their daily mentor hours so that mentors could arrive on campus at 9:00 a.m. to increase the time available for daily common prep with teachers.

Principals play a significant role in shifting school culture to include partners, especially as partners participate in spaces previously exclusively for instructional staff; for example, department staff meetings, professional development days, or even classroom conversations. This shift in culture can also produce hiccups. Partner staff at FSCSs often experienced resistance, at least initially, when they began participating in traditional school spaces. One partner remembers that at one of her first staff meetings, a teacher stood up and asked, "Why is [this partner] in this meeting? We don't want them here. We're a faculty. We're professionals. And we should be able to have our own meeting and talk about things as teachers, as professionals, without having non-teachers here." The partner recalls how the tone shifted when the principal immediately responded, saying, "That's not an option . . . [this organization] is our partner, and they do belong in this meeting." For partners, this positive tone around their involvement was crucial. As one partner put it: "Partners need to feel like they're wanted, included. I think that's a team job, but because [our principal] has that attitude, it makes the team know that they're allowed to have that attitude, too. So, she's a tone-setter."

STRUCTURING COMMUNICATION

At FSCSs, partners and school staff have multiple channels for structured and ongoing communication. FSCSs hold all-partner meetings, at least once a year, often quarterly or monthly. These meetings typically include an update from the school's principal, a discussion of shared priorities for the year, and a review of data. Sometimes meetings are thematic; for example, all the health/behavioral health providers will meet together, or all the expanded learning partners will gather.

All-partner meetings also allow partner staff to build personal and professional relationships with each other and gain a better understanding of school priorities. At one school, the CSM organizes a retreat with school leadership, teachers, and all the partners prior to the start of the school year. "We look at our data, we talk about our goals. Same thing with the partners. They talk about their goals and their mission and why they're in the work. And then just follow up on how we're doing, things that need to be timed up and [the] like, so that everybody's also aware of what's coming up next." Partner meetings are a "win-win" for both schools and partners: schools get partners to more deeply align to school priorities and partners feel more engaged. Typically, partners are eager to have communication and want more alignment and understanding of the school's needs.

Often, the CSM serves as a conduit between school leadership and partner staff. The CSM will typically meet with each partner monthly to check in, trouble-shoot issues, and/or review progress towards goals. While not all FSCSs implement all communication practices to the same extent or in the same way, these practices represent a set of shared expectations that help integrate partnerships into the fabric of the school and allow for successful collaboration toward shared goals.

CONTINUOUSLY ASSESSING THE PARTNERSHIP

Leaders in FSCSs have learned to be discerning with community partnerships. Veteran principals counsel, "Not every partner is a good partner, and not every partner is a partner a school needs. It takes time to develop a partnership, so being picky and choosey is important. Don't just be desperate with your partners. Set up a relationship where as much as you need them, they need to demonstrate their value, not just be there." While many partnership relationships are dynamic and able to shift as school and student needs change, sometimes relationships with partners dissolve when there is no longer a good fit. As one seasoned middle school principal stated, "Our three big rocks are literacy, safe and secure school climate, and teacher effectiveness. If you're not partnering with us on these three, then this is not going to work."

Some FSCSs have ended partnerships that no longer are a fit. One middle school went through the difficult process of parting ways with a longtime afterschool provider that they felt was not supporting their school's culture/climate goals. For well over a year, school leadership had been hearing concerns from staff around "lax" behavior expectations in the afterschool hours. School staff felt that this undermined the site's intentional work to create consistent behavioral expectations with students during the school day. As the principal put it: "[I]f kids are just blowing out after school and doing whatever they want, it's really hard to reinforce with those same kids the next day that they can't do that in class. So that was our biggest issue . . . The behavior expectations, being consistent and just uniform." School leaders brought the concern to partner staff members multiple times over the course of a year, including in an annual evaluation. However, despite stated intentions, the partner was unable to change. Ultimately, the school's CSM worked with CSSS staff to find another afterschool provider that would align its afterschool programs more tightly with the school's behavioral and academic goals.

Partnerships take time to cultivate. To be worthwhile for both schools and the partner, the relationship must meet the needs of both. Continuously assessing the partnership ensures that partnerships are on track. While sometimes partnerships are dissolved and replaced by others, continuous assessment often prompts productive communication that leads to improved results for the partnership.

DISTRICT SUPPORTS FOR STRATEGIC PARTNERSHIPS

Chapter 5 described the formation of CSSS, which included district (system-level) supports for community school partnerships. CSSS formalized the MOU process and, under the leadership of Community Partnerships Manager Martin Young, created a central database or "registry" of Oakland partners. CSSS staff also created an array of partnership tools, guides, and rubrics to standardize partnership practice across sites.[2] We describe three of the most frequently referenced tools and practices below.

Partnership Assessment Rubric

OUSD's partnership assessment rubric provides a common framework for understanding quality partnerships. The rubric was developed by OUSD's Community Partnerships Workgroup immediately out of the strategic planning process. The workgroup included a diverse committee of CBO, health, and funder partners, as well as leadership across OUSD departments, including CSSS, College and Career Readiness, and Adult Learning. Over the following years, the rubric was adapted and refined, based on site feedback. (See appendix 9a, "Partnership Assessment Rubric," at the end of this chapter.)

There are several important features of the rubric. First, it distinguishes between different kinds of partnerships that a school may engage. *Specialized partners* are partnerships that might be engaged for a specific, targeted purpose. *Aligned partners* will be aligned to school goals, but may not play as active of a role in their co-creation. *Core partners* will be closely aligned with, and in many respects, co-creators of many school goals and priorities. Clarifying the different degrees of partnership provides a vocabulary to use in discussing expectations from the outset of a partnership. For example, school leaders may not expect the same level of involvement from a partner providing weekly reading buddies as they would for a core afterschool partner.

Secondly, the rubric articulates quality standards, including many of the expectations outlined above. These standards include: alignment of vision and goals, engagement in program planning, participation in site decision making and FSCS implementation (e.g., COST, school climate, attendance teams), using data and an equity lens to identify community needs and disparities, using communication systems and structures and employment of data-driven decision making and engagement in continuous improvement. The rubric discusses each of these criteria in relation to specialized, aligned, and core partnerships, with the expectation that partner and school staff both contribute to the partnership assessment. The assessment rubric also includes a conversation prompt for assessing current partnership strengths and challenge areas, action steps to strengthen the partnership, and a commitment to next assessment. The partnership rubric represents a set of collective expectations and priority areas for OUSD partnerships. Especially for new FSCSs, the partnership rubric can be an important tool for understanding norms and practices.

Letter of Agreement

The district's letter of agreement (LOA) template provides a companion document to the legal agreements covered in a memorandum of understanding (MOU) (see appendix 9b at the end of this chapter). Essentially, it prompts concrete discussion and agreement on specific aspects of the partnerships, such as annual targets, communication practices, space sharing, and logistics. The LOA requires the school to identify its SPSA goals and the agency to (briefly) describe its mission. Together, they identify the targeted outcomes and metrics used in the partnerships, and who will provide the specific data points used. Both parties identify frequency and modes of communication (e.g., weekly check-in, email updates). Will the partner participate in COST meetings? Will partner announcements be included in the school newsletter? The parties discuss staffing practice—for example, any shared hiring or supervision of staff, or a substitute policy for staff absences. They discuss space-sharing issues: Will the school provide custodial services to the partner space? Who is responsible for maintaining the refrigerator?

These talking points may seem hyper-specific and mundane, but in practice, they can be sources of tension if left unaddressed. One principal described frustration with not obtaining the data she felt the school needed from a partner: "You're pulling students out of class once a week, twice a week, but we're still seeing the student is having chronic absence problems, they're not doing well academically—or behaviorally, they might not be improving." The LOA anticipates this tension and prompts for agreement around student pull-outs: Will students be pulled from core classes to receive services?

CSSS staff developed the LOA based on direct input and feedback from site-level partners and staff, including the issues they felt were important to discuss up front. By addressing them directly as part of the LOA, community school staff have the opportunity to preemptively address any differences, and work toward shared understanding and agreement. The LOA as such has been in use for only a few years. While not all schools submit LOAs to the district office, the tool captures the nuances of important conversations taking place between school and partner staff across the district and is seen as a best practice to guide schools and partners as they engage in the messy work of working together.

Annual Evaluation

At the end of the year, CSSS staff send all CSMs a prompt to conduct an evaluation with their partners (see appendix 9c at the end of this chapter). Partners and school leaders (usually the CSM) complete a partnership evaluation form on the district's Google survey interface. The form prompts for reflections (with Likert-scale ratings and open-response narrative) on key areas outlined in the LOA: outcomes and achievements, logistics, partnership meetings, collaboration on COST and other teams, communication and problem solving, and impact. Partners and CSM then read each other's comments and come together to discuss. The annual review is designed to "close the loop" on the agreements outlined in the LOA, and prompt discussion for any shifts or changes for the following year. Again, this practice is relatively new and not implemented across all FSCSs. However, it reflects another example of top-down support for bottom-up change and institutionalizes the practice of continuous data-driven improvement at school sites.

Strategic partnerships are a foundational strategy in OUSD FSCSs. They represent a shift in mindset and practice regarding partners' roles in the organization and operations of the school. In chapter 10, we dive deeply into two areas of student services—Health and Wellness and Expanded Learning—that illustrate how specific structures and practices help to integrate student services and supports into the school fabric, ultimately expanding access and opportunities for students.

Appendix 9a

Partnership Assessment Rubric

OUSD FULL-SERVICE COMMUNITY SCHOOL PARTNERSHIP ASSESSMENT

Overview

This assessment tool for partnerships includes a framework for establishing ANY partnership between an OUSD school or department and a non-profit, public or private partner, as well as an action plan for continuously refining and strengthening the partnership. The assessment is designed to support and facilitate the site's annual planning cycle and is also informed by the Community School Strategic Site Plan. It can be incorporated into the existing meeting schedule, with the explicit purpose of helping define, assess, and strengthen the **partnership**. It is not an assessment of the individual organization or school, nor an evaluation of the program or services being provided. The Partnership Assessment describes three categories of partnerships, all of which are valued by OUSD:

- Specialized Partnership
- Aligned Partnership
- Core Partnership

This tool is designed to:

1. Help a school and a new partner determine the type of partnership they want to build. Use it to establish expectations around goals, target populations, communication, meetings, reporting, etc.
2. Help a school and their existing partners define the category of partnership they have, and the type they want to have moving forward.

3. Clarify expectations and regularly assess state of the partnership, identifying strengths, areas for improvement and progress towards goals.

Different Partnerships and Usage

- **New Partnerships:** Organizations that are new to the District should start by using the *Community Partnership Identification Tool (included with Letter of Agreement)* to identify the category of partnership they have the capacity and interest to build. The partner uses that tool to prepare for their first meeting with school leadership (principal, Community School Manager, or designated point person) where they are exploring establishment of a partnership. Together, the partner and school use the **Full-service Community School (FSCS) Partnership Assessment** to select the type of partnership they want, agree on the practices they will implement, and expectations of each other, and to set a follow-up meeting date to review partnership progress. *Frequency:* School and partner meet twice in the first year to use **Partnership Assessment**, once for initial identification of partnership category and practices, and again at end of year to assess the state of partnership and areas for improvement. They use the **Action Plan** to distill their discussion into a one-page plan for strengthening the partnership.

- **Specialized Partnerships:** The school and partner leadership complete the **Partnership Assessment** together in their first meeting, using the tool to guide discussion about and agree upon shared expectations. **Frequency:** Specialized partners should include the **Assessment** as part of their initial meeting about the scope of work, and at the follow-up meeting after the event, activity or program is presented, to assess how the partnership has functioned and how it can be improved upon in the following year.

- **Aligned and Core Partnerships:** It is recommended that the parties agree to work on at least 1–2 criteria from each of the three large **Partnership Assessment** goal areas (Shared Leadership; Collaborative, Responsive Implementation; and Shared Accountability for Success) to strengthen the partnership, based on a joint completion and review of the assessment. **Frequency:** Partners and schools in aligned and core partnerships should meet at least twice a year, and ideally three times for a start-of-year, mid-year, and end-of-year assessment of the partnership.

Background

This partnership tool was developed by OUSD's Community Partnerships Workgroup, a diverse committee of CBO, health and funder partners; as well as leadership across OUSD departments, including Family Schools and Community Partnerships, Health Services, College and Career Readiness, and Adult Learning. Sources the workgroup considered include: the San Francisco Unified School District Partnership Tool; the School Partnership Tool (After School Knowledge Initiative, Oakland); the OUSD School Self-Assessment Tool; and the Community Partner Self-Assessment Tool (OUSD Full-service Community Schools Task Force).

Purpose

This rubric is for assessment and continuous improvement of a **partnership**, not of an individual organization or school. It is not an assessment of the organization or school, nor an evaluation of the program or services being provided. The assessment is designed to support and facilitate the site's yearly planning cycle and is also informed by the Community School Strategic Site Plan. It lays out three categories of partnerships, all of which are valued by OUSD:

- Specialized Partnership
- Aligned Partnership
- Core Partnership

How to Use

1. School leadership (usually Community School Manager, but could be lead agency or principal) and partnership leadership (site manager or coordinator) use the **FSCS Partnership Assessment** together to rate each indicator *for your Partnership Category* with one of the following:
   - **Not Applicable (NA):** Partnership is not implementing practice at this time.
   - **Emerging (E):** Partnership is implementing this practice, though inconsistently.
   - **Developing (D):** Partnership is implementing elements of this practice consistently, with evidence of developing an effective collaboration.
   - **Sustaining (S):** Partnership implements the practice consistently; it has been an important factor in establishing strong and effective collaboration.

2. After completing the assessment, partner and school leadership use it to create an **Action Plan** (see page 6), which will help them define and target specific action items to work on to improve and strengthen their partnership. The action steps they choose can help them either strengthen the existing partnership OR transition the partnership to another category.

3. Partner and school leadership incorporate this assessment into their regular meetings—using it early in the school year to set partnership expectations and create an action plan, and later in the year to re-assess the partnership and revise the action plan for the following year.

Frequently Asked Questions

Q: How do a partner and school decide when and if a partner is ready to transition to a new partnership category?

A: Each time they use the assessment, partner and site leadership should discuss if both are satisfied with the current partnership category. When considering a change, both entities need to consider issues such as partner capacity, school leadership and management capacity, and the strength of school and partner alignment. Transition to a different category may move in the direction of more engagement or less, i.e. if both parties believe their capacity or alignment in key areas has changed, they may want to consider a *less* engaged partnership category. OUSD recognizes that Core Partnerships are less common and may not be present at every school site.

Q: Should partners maintain the same partnership category at each school site?

A: No. Partners bring specific strengths to each school, and each school also has different needs and a different array of existing and new partners. Both entities need to determine the partnership category for every partner at every school site.

Q: Can the Partnership Assessment Rubric be used to terminate the partnership?

A: No. The partnership evaluation is meant to identify the partnership category, assess partnership strengths and weaknesses, and plan for continuous improvement of the partnership. It may lead to a discussion about whether the partnership is still working to serve the needs of the school community, but it cannot be used to end a partnership. That discussion would occur when the school and partner review the Letter of Agreement.

FULL-SERVICE COMMUNITY SCHOOL PARTNERSHIP
ASSESSMENT FOR: _____ (SCHOOL AND PARTNER)

GOAL AREA: SHARED LEADERSHIP

Rate each indicator in your partnership category as Not Applicable (NA), Emerging (E), Developing (D) or Sustaining (S).

CRITERIA	SPECIALIZED PARTNERSHIP	ALIGNED PARTNERSHIP	CORE PARTNERSHIP
Alignment of vision and goals	• Partner and school can identify one or more partner goals aligned with school vision.	• Partner and site leadership discuss site vision and goals with opportunity for partner input during site planning process. • Partner and site can identify at least one partner outcome aligned with a strategic priority of the school site plan.	• Partner and site leadership co-construct shared site vision and goals and are both accountable for implementation. • Both parties are responsible for ensuring alignment of other partners to shared vision and goals.
Engagement in needs assessment	• Partner and site can identify how partner is addressing needs of community.	• Partner and site leadership identify and fine-tune strategies for meeting needs of school community	• Partner engages in school-community dialogue as part of needs assessment for site. • Partner and school advise other partners on fine-tuning strategies to meet needs of school community.
Engagement in program planning and priority setting	• Desired outcomes for program/service set by partner or principal. • Partner program/service is aligned to district and state standards.	• Partner and site discuss school priorities and program plans with opportunity for partner input during planning process. • Partner and site leadership can identify at least one partner outcome aligned with a strategic priority of the school site plan.	• Partner and site together review and set priorities and desired outcomes. • Partner and site leadership ensure that agency outcomes are aligned with all strategic priority areas of school site plan.

CRITERIA	SPECIALIZED PARTNERSHIP	ALIGNED PARTNERSHIP	CORE PARTNERSHIP
Participation in site decision-making processes	• Site and partner have discussed site decision-making process and bodies and identified opportunities for input. • Site and partner decide on appropriate level and frequency of participation in a site decision-making body.	Partner regularly provides feedback to school leadership body/committee.	Partner leads or co-leads a cross-agency school leadership body (COST, etc.).

GOAL AREA: COLLABORATIVE, RESPONSIVE IMPLEMENTATION

Rate each indicator in your partnership category as Not Applicable (NA), Emerging (E), Developing (D) or Sustaining (S).

CRITERIA	SPECIALIZED PARTNERSHIP	ALIGNED PARTNERSHIP	CORE PARTNERSHIP
Using data and an equity lens to identify community needs and disparities	• School provides basic information on participants and schoolwide trends. • Partner collects and provides general participation data.	• School provides data on participants and on schoolwide trends and disparities. • Partner collects and provides breakdown of their data to support identification of needs and disparities. • Site and partner leadership meet at least twice per year to discuss participation and assessment data.	• Partner collects, analyzes, and provides their participation and assessment data by relevant categories. • School includes partner on teams where data trends are being discussed on regular basis—e.g., school leadership team, school climate—in part to identify needs and disparities.

CRITERIA	SPECIALIZED PARTNERSHIP	ALIGNED PARTNERSHIP	CORE PARTNERSHIP
Responsiveness to school community needs and disparities	• Partner has a set program based on their expertise and school's identified needs.	• Partner and school leadership meet at least twice a year to discuss program(s). • Partner incorporates feedback on unmet needs into program planning for following year (or after each meeting if possible). • If the program is not reaching target populations—and there is still capacity—partner and school conduct targeted outreach to address disparity.	• Partner and school leadership meet at least monthly (including as part of larger group) to discuss program(s). • School and partner discuss how to make adjustments and/or create new programs to address unmet needs throughout the year.
Use of communications systems and structures	• Strong communication at the beginning of partnership to establish expectations for partner and school. • Strong communication at end of event/program/activity to evaluate impact of program and share data. • Ongoing communication, as needed.	• Partner and school leadership meet at least twice a year • School and partner share and contribute to each other's communications; e.g., newsletters, flyers, brochures, events. • School and partner have explicit agreements re: communication; e.g., respond to each other within 24 hours, preferred method and style.	• Partner and school leadership have a set monthly meeting. • School and partner share and contribute to each other's communications; e.g., newsletters, flyers, brochures. • School and partner make explicit agreements about communication; e.g., preferred method, style, frequency. • School and partner have an identified process for conflict resolution and problem-solving with each other.

CRITERIA	SPECIALIZED PARTNERSHIP	ALIGNED PARTNERSHIP	CORE PARTNERSHIP
Involvement in site planning and implementation structures (COST, school climate, attendance, etc.)	• School and partner are aware of appropriate site engagement opportunities; partner participation is optional but welcome	• School involves partner in core and program-relevant committees quarterly	• Partner is part of core school groups, incl. staff, COST, and partner meetings • Partner joins program-relevant committees at least quarterly; e.g., grade-level teams, PTA.

GOAL AREA: SHARED ACCOUNTABILITY FOR SUCCESS

Rate each indicator in your partnership category as Not Applicable (NA), Emerging (E), Developing (D) or Sustaining (S).

CRITERIA	SPECIALIZED PARTNERSHIP	ALIGNED PARTNERSHIP	CORE PARTNERSHIP
Outcomes alignment: Individual contribution to collective impact	• Site leadership and partner agree there is a need at site for partner programs/services.	• Site leadership and partner agree on role of partner in impacting identified outcomes or needs of site. • Site leadership and partner together plan strategies for impacting outcomes.	• Partner and site strategies are complementary and coordinated to impact top priorities or needs of site.
Employment of data-driven decision-making	• Partner and site collect and share relevant participation and outcomes data for services/programs provided. • Data is available on request from site or partner as it pertains to needs/outcomes and services provided.	• Site shares baseline and "target" data with partners. • Partners and site share student outcome information.	• Partner has access to all relevant data concerning student and family outcomes and can collect and analyze in real time. • Partner and site identify necessary data to track for agreed-upon site priorities.

CRITERIA	SPECIALIZED PARTNERSHIP	ALIGNED PARTNERSHIP	CORE PARTNERSHIP
Engagement in continuous improvement efforts	• Site leadership and partner meet after program/service to review and suggest changes for next visit.	• Site leadership and partner meet twice per year to review data on priority student and family outcomes and fine-tune strategies together.	• Site and partner review data on priority student and family outcomes every two months to fine tune strategies for all partners linked to the outcome(s).
Leveraging resources	• Bilateral provision of resources between site and partner • Resources are applied to general district or site need.	• Partner and site access resources together to support identified site priorities. • Partner and site agree on alignment of resources to address identified priorities.	• Site and partner plan together at least twice per year for resource development and sustainability. • Site and partner together coordinate resources upon implementation.

PARTNERSHIP ACTION PLAN FOR: _____ (SCHOOL AND PARTNER)

1. Current partnership category (circle one):
   Specialized   Aligned   Core
2. Are you currently at your desired category of partnership—agreed upon by CBO and School?   Yes   No
3. **If yes**, what steps can be taken to strengthen the partnership at the current level? (complete Action Steps below)
4. **If no**, what is your desired category of partnership (circle one):
   Specialized   Aligned   Core
5. **Identify next steps below for either strengthening the current partnership OR transitioning the partnership to the desired category.**

ACTION STEPS	WHO ELSE IS INVOLVED?	WHAT IS OUR TIMELINE?
1.		
2.		
3.		
4.		

We will review this plan at our next meeting to assess our progress. Our next meeting will be: _____

Appendix 9b

OUSD Letter of Agreement

LETTER OF AGREEMENT BETWEEN SCHOOL AND PARTNER

1. Purpose of Agreement

This agreement intends to outline and formalize the mutual goals and expectations for the site-based partnership between _____ (School) and _____ (Partner Agency), pertaining to _____ (Program Name). The term of agreement begins on _____ and ends on _____.

2. Goals and Outcomes

School Priorities (SPSA)

Agency Mission

Target Partnership Outcomes

3. Program Description

1. Short Description of Services
2. Student Eligibility Requirements
3. Target # of Students/Families Served
4. Start Date: _____
5. End Date: _____
6. Daily Schedule (days and hours):
7. Outreach and Recruitment Plan:
8. Relevant Experience of Staff: _____
9. Discuss Shared Hiring/Supervision of Staff where appropriate: _____
10. Substitute Policy for Staff Absences: _____

4. Site-Based Logistics (*Check all that apply*)

The school will provide the partner agency with the following:

- Adequate and appropriate space to provide services (list rooms and/or office space, if applicable):
- Phone and/or Internet
- Mailbox in Main Office
- Inclusion in Classroom Announcements and/or School Newsletter
- Space in Hallways, on Bulletin Boards
- Equipment (please list)
- Custodial services; notify the partner agency of any changes in provision and availability of custodial services.
- Notify provider at least __ weeks in advance of closure of school campus (e.g. over school holidays, winter break, summer vacation, professional development days
- Other:

The partner will provide the school with the following:

- Administration and fiscal oversight of the program or service.
- Sign in and out at the main office (other details): _____
- Share responsibility for hiring, and supervising when appropriate, all program team members.

- Avoid pulling students out of core classes, whenever possible, to minimize impact on class participation, unless specifically identified as an accepted intervention strategy.
- Notify school promptly if program sessions need to be cancelled.
- Other

5. **Collaboration and Communication**
   - Partner and School agree to maintain ongoing, consistent communication (indicate preferred methods): _____
     _____
   - Coordination of Services Team (COST)
     – Partner will attend COST meetings regularly (please list day and time):
     – Partner will not attend COST regularly but will utilize established COST referral protocols for students in need of support (include details): _____
     – Partner will participate in school structures that strengthen collaboration and programming. For example, partner meetings, staff meetings or school teams (please list appropriate meetings, days and times): _____
       _____
   - Partner and School agree to communicate concerns and problem solve collaboratively to resolve issues in a timely manner.
   - Other: _____
     _____

6. **Data Shared and Shared Accountability**
   - How will Partner and School evaluate the outcomes of the partnership? Please list the form and frequency of the reports provided by School using OUSD data points:
   - Please list the form and frequency of the reports provided by Partner: _____
     _____

- School will provide the following student data to Partner, in accordance with and to the extent allowed by FERPA and other federal and state law. Please list what specific data is required, when and how often it will be needed, and who is responsible for delivering it: _____
- Partner agrees to submit service/participation data as requested by site.
- Other: _____
_____

7. District Minimum Partner Requirements (*Check all that apply*)
In an effort to increase communication and alignment with our partners, and uplift the outcomes of community schools, OUSD is connecting with all partners at the district level through our Annual Partnership Process. Prior to entering schools, the OUSD Board of Education requires the following items, in accordance with the California Education Code. Once the requirements are completed, eligible partners are added to our Approved Partners List.
- Register/update in the Community Partner Platform annually (Partner Database)
- Formal agreement with OUSD submitted to OUSD Board (Professional Services Contract or MOU)
- **Included in formal agreement process:**
    - TB screening of on-site workers
    - Fingerprinting of on-site workers submitted to FBI and California DOJ
    - General Liability Insurance ($1 Million in coverage)
    - Workers' Compensation Liability Insurance (*Applies to Partner with employees only: $1 Million in coverage)
- Civic Center permit (where appropriate)

Staffing and Contact Information
The program is staffed by (Please include name, title, FTE, days/ times on site, etc.):

NAME	TITLE	FTE	DAYS/TIMES ON SITE

Contact Information for Both Parties

School Site Representative Name and Email: _____

_____

Main Phone #: _____ Mobile Phone #: _____
Partner On-Site Representative Name and Email: _____

_____

Main Phone #: _____ Mobile Phone #: _____
Partner Program Administrator Name and Email: _____

_____

Main Phone #: _____ Mobile Phone #: _____

Emergency Contacts (if applicable)

District Office Representative Name and Contact: _____
Custodial Supervisor Name and Contact #: _____
OUSD Police Services #: _____

Signatures of Both Parties

_____
Authorized School Representative   Signature   Date
(Print Name & Title)

_____
Authorized Agency Representative   Signature   Date
(Print Name & Title)

Appendix 9c

Partnership Evaluation

Name of representative *_____

Are you a school or agency representative? *

☐ School representative
☐ Agency representative

Name of community partner (agency or individual) *_____

School site of partnership _____*
Choose

School year of partnership (year–year format) *_____

Description of services provided *_____

1. Please rate achievement of shared partnership outcomes. *
(Consider goals and outcomes from Letter of Agreement, if completed at the beginning of the year.)

☐ Highly successful
☐ Successful
☐ Partially successful
☐ Unsuccessful
☐ Not applicable

Narrative (please list outcomes and short explanation) *

2. Please evaluate whether partnership logistics were implemented as agreed upon. *

Examples: Use of space, equipment, recruiting and selection of students, availability of students, on-site communication, and staff issues

☐ Highly effective
☐ Effective
☐ Partially effective
☐ Ineffective
☐ Not applicable

Narrative: Partnership logistics (please highlight successes, challenges, and suggestions) *

```



```

3. Please rate your experience with regular partnership meetings. *

☐ Highly effective
☐ Effective
☐ Partially effective
☐ Ineffective
☐ Not applicable

Narrative: Partnership meetings (please highlight successes, challenges, and suggestions) *

```



```

4. Please evaluate the collaboration between partner and site on the Coordination of Services Team (COST) and/or other site teams. *

☐ Highly effective
☐ Effective
☐ Partially effective
☐ Ineffective
☐ Not applicable

Narrative: Collaboration (please highlight successes, challenges, and suggestions) *

---

5. Please rate how partner and site are communicating concerns and solving problems collectively. *

☐ Highly effective
☐ Effective
☐ Partially effective
☐ Ineffective
☐ Not applicable

Narrative: Problem solving (please highlight successes, challenges, and suggestions) *

---

6. Please evaluate the impact of the partnership as measured by data. *

☐ Highly effective
☐ Effective
☐ Partially effective
☐ Ineffective
☐ Not applicable

Narrative: Impact (please indicate the reports, data points and source of data; include data provided by OUSD if possible) *

```



```

CHAPTER 10

Integrating Services and Expanding Opportunities

So many of our kids come from places where they just don't have [access to] the services that most upper-middle-class, white kids in the United States are used to, take for granted. So the fact that they're able to come to school and get help for the smallest things . . . [it's huge]. I just don't know how we would function without it. I think what would happen is we'd have a lot more kids that were unhealthy . . . that were unhealthy and didn't have a way to deal with it. So, what we would see in our classrooms is kids who weren't focused, kids who are off-task, kids who are angry, kids who are sick—actively sick—and we wouldn't have much recourse other than to say, "Go home."

—OUSD principal

A lot of the families depend on the afterschool program for the child to get the support they need to get their homework done, because either they're not home at night or they just don't know how to help them, because either they can't read English or they just don't understand. It takes some of the weight off of you as a teacher. So the fact that a lot of my students go to afterschool program, I know a lot of them will get help.

—OUSD teacher

Community Schools, Thriving Students outlined as central goals that every student in the district attend safe, healthy, and supportive schools and that all students learn the knowledge, skills, and abilities they need to be prepared for success in college and careers. OUSD full-service community schools offer a range of services and supports for their students that extend these commitments by integrating FSCS activities within school goals and structures. This chapter focuses on integrated services, including health and wellness, expanded learning, and linked learning, as well as mechanisms such as the coordination of services team (COST) for aligning efforts to serve individual students and accomplish school goals.

INCREASING ACCESS TO HEALTH SERVICES

Nearly all OUSD FSCS high schools host a school-based health center. Those that do not have a clinic on-site affiliate with a community or school-based clinic or health center nearby.[1] Health centers offer primary care services, including physical exams, immunizations, reproductive health services, and urgent care. Many schools also provide on-site preventive dental services and vision and hearing assessments, either through the school-based health center or via site visits from health vans. As of 2016–2017, OUSD had sixteen school-based health centers, administered by different hospitals or community clinics—for example, Kaiser Permanente, USCF Benioff Children's Hospital Oakland ("Children's Hospital"), and La Clínica all administer school-based centers. Many clinics are also involved in providing health education; for example, teaching core or elective health education classes for students, or working with nutrition services on healthy eating campaigns.

OUSD FSCSs have developed innovative practices to expand access for all students. One FSCS introduces students to the health clinic through the clinic's health educator. The health educator teaches at the school, and every student rotates through the class, receiving at least six weeks of health education. As part of the course, students receive a tour of the health clinic and meet one-on-one with clinic staff, who conduct a very basic health assessment (e.g., any concerns, reproductive health questions). Students who need medical coverage can schedule a follow-up appointment with the clinic. If there is a red flag for behavioral health, the clinic can connect those students with services. Another clinic instituted a practice of screening students one or two grades at a time to identify students in need of services (mostly focused on behavioral health). According to the school's principal, the screening process increased tenfold the amount of students who receive services through the clinic. Most FSCSs have regular screenings throughout the year, incorporated into the school calendar.

Integrating school-based health and mental health services into the fabric of the school helps regularize their use. At many FSCS sites, health and wellness services are part of school culture; students and staff see using services as normal and not something to be ashamed of. In the words of one teacher: "It's been incredibly normalizing to students that if you have something going on, that you should go and talk about it. I'll have students who in the middle of class—they've got their little confidential pass, but they'll just stand up and be like 'Oh, I gotta go to therapy.'"

Many clinics also engage with families to support health access. At one middle school, the clinic partner hired two on-site Covered California enrollment staff to assist families with Medi-Cal enrollment. Another school's health partner described organizing health fairs and campaigns, and another mentioned hosting parenting classes in collaboration with the school's family resource center on topics such as adolescent development and trauma. Some clinics also treat family members—including siblings and parents—and other members of the community. Clinic staff often use school registration as an opportunity to communicate with families about services offered.

CULTIVATING SUPPORTIVE LEARNING ENVIRONMENTS

Most schools in the US now offer some kind of mental and behavioral health support services for students.[2] CSSS's Behavioral Health unit works with community providers to offer a range of critical mental and behavioral health supports for students, including crisis intervention, family therapy, and cognitive behavioral therapy. OUSD's behavioral health work stands out for its far-reaching strategies to support students' social, emotional, and mental health. School sites focus on establishing clear behavioral expectations that are explicitly taught as part of the curriculum; for example, positive behavioral interventions and supports (PBIS), are used across nearly all OUSD elementary schools.[3] As one classroom teacher shared, "The work that's happening in the classrooms around shifting the culture and the expectations in the classrooms . . . we've had a very intentional focus around how we work: 'Let's be intentional about recognizing that positive behavior, and let's be clear about what the expectations are and holding that across the board.'"

OUSD school sites also emphasize restorative practices to handle disruptions and conflict.[4] The district's restorative justice program has gained national recognition for its powerful effects on reducing disproportionate suspensions for black students and suspensions for students overall.[5] At specific school sites—middle and high schools especially—staff are trained in leading restorative circles by a site-level restorative justice coordinator. The district's restorative work has been largely credited with reducing overall suspensions as well as disproportionality within those suspensions. One school's clinic leader recounted, "In March of 2011, there were 205 suspensions at our school; 53 percent of those were African American males. Four years later, there were 45 suspensions, and 16 percent were African American males." As of 2018, a central office director, four restorative justice coordinators based in central office and about two dozen restorative justice facilitators at various schools staffed the restorative justice program. The facilitators train teachers and students in restorative justice techniques.[6]

Lastly, schools and the district have focused on building adult staff's capacity to build meaningful relationships with youth. This includes educating adult staff around trauma-informed practice. The behavioral health unit sponsors a trauma-informed care work group that identifies best practices and offers professional development at school sites and to adults across the district.[7] For example, the unit leads trainings on trauma-informed practice for school resource officers (law enforcement officials working in the school), and instructors working with newcomer populations. At the high school level, the majority of FSCS teachers surveyed indicated that they used trauma-informed practice.

These far-reaching, broad-based supports explicitly aim to bolster equitable access to learning through reducing disproportionate suspensions and providing targeted capacity-building for adults to skillfully serve all Oakland's students. One teacher reflects, "Our kids come to school with so many stories. Maybe they're hungry. Maybe they're homeless. Maybe they saw mom get arrested. I had one student who saw his dad get shot right in front of him. They've seen domestic violence, neighborhood violence, custody battles, drugs, foster care. They've gone through so much, as seven-year-olds and eight-year-olds, that no adult should ever have to go through." Trauma-informed practice and other behavioral health supports give teachers and adults at the school tools to support and engage students skillfully, so all students have access to caring, supportive learning environments.

COORDINATING SERVICES

The Coordination of Services Team (COST) is crucial for bringing together many of the moving pieces within FSCSs, including community partners, school administrators, teachers, and CSMs. While COST teams were present prior to the implementation of the community schools initiative, their role has grown exponentially in FSCSs. Most schools in the US today have some kind of process for identifying students in need of additional supports. However, referring processes typically place a heavy burden on the teacher to identify, respond, and follow up on any concerns about a student. In schools serving communities with high degrees of poverty, trauma, violence, and health concerns, the percentage of students in need of additional supports can be staggering. It can present a heavy administrative burden for teachers, as well as make consistent identification, communication, and follow-up quite challenging. COST presents a systematic process where school staff can go with concerns about a student. By including partners, behavioral health providers, and coordinating staff (e.g., the CSM) in the COST space, students' needs are discussed, assessed, and triaged rapidly, with all relevant parties in the room. This minimizes potential delays or communication breakdowns in referral and follow-up processes. Partners can say, on the spot, whether there's room in a particular program or what other interventions are available to support the student. In essence, COST allows for a rapid, streamlined response to connect students with services before the concern escalates.

By design, FSCSs vary in the extent to which teachers participate in COST meetings. In some cases, the referring teacher participates for ten to fifteen minutes of discussion about the student up front; in others, they simply fill out a referral form. Still, most student referrals begin with the teachers, and COST provides them with a clear and consistent resource to which they can take student concerns.

When teachers have a clear channel through which to triage student needs and access resources and supports for their students, it not only helps alleviate barriers to student learning, but it also helps reduce a teacher's load. Having support from other adults at the school working to address students' needs reduces the mental burden many teachers carry; it also allows them more time to focus on instruction and curriculum. As one FSCS teacher shared, "Having support services for counseling, housing, and mental health have helped [me] tremendously. It allows me to focus more on academic interventions and classroom instruction."

While COST teams have been on campuses for many years, there have been significant improvements over the last five years in the way in which these teams function and their effectiveness altogether. The CSSS's concerted efforts to systematize and support with COST process through elevating best practices, developing a "COST toolkit" for guidance, and ongoing coaching to partners and CSMs has helped improve the functioning of COST. These measures have provided the scaffolding, structures, staffing, and accountability needed to elevate COST to a signature practice in OUSD community schools. One middle school principal recalled, "COST was just sort of a huge mess four or five years ago. Now, we've . . . really started to see a lot of accountability."

Even with district guidance, strong partnerships, and CSMs' COST efforts, teams still can struggle. Sometimes the available services still do not meet the extensive demands of student need (for example, fifteen spots for individual counseling caseload in a school with much higher need). Teachers do not always hear back about the outcome of specific referral (for instance, due to confidentiality reasons or breakdowns in communication). Even with a robust COST, teachers may not feel they have the resources needed to fully support their students.

As the FSCS site-level work has matured, schools are increasingly using COST data to look at studentwide trends to inform partnerships and planning. Rather than simply being a channel for triaging individual referrals, COST teams are looking at schoolwide data to determine areas of need and consider more preventative or broad-based interventions to address those needs. For example, one school learned through analyzing COST data that 89 percent of students referred for behavioral issues also had unidentified medical issues (e.g., vision, dental, or other health concerns). Now, as a matter of practice at that school, any student identified for behavioral issues is given an automatic referral to the school clinic. As one CSM stated, "[We're really trying to] get COST to start looking at more data and seeing . . . well, not just having anecdotal stories but actual indicators that show whether or not we've been able as a COST team to move students to better places." Still, not all FSCS sites are where they want to be yet when it comes to using data to drive action. Another CSM explained, "Right now, we're only trusting that teachers are able to identify the students most in need, but we don't know for sure if they're getting all of them or if they're even getting the right ones."

EXPANDING LEARNING TIME

OUSD's FSCS strategic plan highlights expanded learning as a key component of the OUSD community school model. Expanded learning provides a vehicle for serving the whole child, and underscores the belief that "learning takes place in all contexts and does not privilege one learning environment over another."[8] Afterschool programs and expanded learning more generally are increasingly common elements of schools nationwide, and often include partnerships with external agencies. However, in many typical schools, partner agencies operate independently, autonomously, and distinct from school personnel. It is common for afterschool programs to operate at schools, yet with little connection to the school-day staff or activities. In contrast, OUSD FSCSs build structures and norms to facilitate and incorporate partnerships as part of the school and deeply integrate expanded learning partners and activities. Furthermore, expanded learning is central to the district's equity strategy, providing students with a rich array of enrichment programs year-round and all day, including morning care, afterschool programming, and summer learning opportunities. Across the district, these opportunities vary by school and include morning art classes, academic tutoring, intensive literacy instruction, credit recovery, robotics or science clubs, youth leadership development, internship placements, core subject classes, English language development intervention, and summer camp placements, among others.

OUSD supports the school-based afterschool programs through the After School Programs Office (ASPO), housed within CSSS. Most schools have afterschool programs that run until at least 6 p.m. Many programs are free to students, while others are offered at a sliding scale. When programs have limited space, school and program staff work to prioritize enrollment by highest need. As of 2018, afterschool programs were offered at eighty-one schools throughout the district (through a combination of district- and city-funded programming) that served 8,321 students. Nearly half of afterschool program participants identify as Latinx, nearly a third black, followed by smaller proportions of Asian/Pacific Islander (12 percent) and white (6 percent).[9] Black student enrollment is disproportionally higher in afterschool programs than in the school day, which suggests that such programs may be an important strategy to addressing the racial opportunity gap in Oakland.

Many OUSD elementary and middle community schools have one core partner agency that provides primary afterschool services, though multiple partners may provide more specialized programming to smaller targeted groups of students (such as literacy classes for dual language learners or dance classes for interested students). In many OUSD high schools, expanded learning consists largely of connecting students to other opportunities within or outside the school, such as the school's linked learning pathways, external internships, or other college preparatory activities like SAT prep courses or AP classes.

In FSCSs that deeply integrate expanded learning, school staff and community partners blur the lines as they work toward the shared goal of promoting student success. As the principal at one OUSD FSCS that no longer makes a distinction between school-day and afterschool programming explained, "We don't call anything 'afterschool'; there's no such thing as 'afterschool'; everything is part of what you do." In this school, where almost all grade 6 and 7 students stay after the traditional school day for activities such as STEM, coding class, and Folklorico (i.e., dance), the afterschool program is called eighth and ninth period, and activities provided by CBOs are included on students' daily school schedules. The CMS noted, "I'm working in this system that's working together . . . I don't think the kids even know that they're in afterschool because it's so seamlessly integrated." In some OUSD FSCSs, almost all students (99 percent) participate in the school's afterschool program, and overall student participation in afterschool programs is higher in full-service community schools than in other district schools (based on analysis of OUSD administrative data on OST participation).

In some OUSD FSCSs, integration with expanded learning partners extends beyond providing students greater consistency and continuity during the afterschool hours, to include the school day as well.
For example, in one middle school, a long-term partner agency's afterschool academic mentors rearranged their working hours to allow
them to participate in students' classrooms during the day (referred
to as "push-ins"). This shift allowed the mentors to understand their
students' school-day assignments and align their afterschool supports accordingly. Additionally, the mentors provided teachers with
assistance during class time, allowing for extra academic support to
individuals or groups, as well as assistance addressing behavioral issues. Afterschool staff take part in many school activities from field
trips to cafeteria lunch duty. As one teacher noted, "So our programs
are intertwined in that they're helping me during the day, and a lot of
times I'm helping them after the kids get out of school." In addition
to providing a range of youth development activities and expanding the amount of time students spend learning, OUSD community
schools in some cases increase the *quality* of instructional time by
aligning and integrating expanded learning programming with the
school-day curriculum.

Although greater integration is a goal for most OUSD FSCSs,
creating opportunities for collaboration between expanded learning service providers and core instructional staff, with their different
hours and limited down time, is no small feat and presents a real and
ongoing challenge. These efforts are crucial for building a school
culture in which adults work together to support students' learning needs, and OUSD full-service community schools take different approaches with varying levels of success. One teacher, speaking
of the challenge and potential in collaborating with CBO partners,
said, "It's like there's no system that supports accountability because
there is no structured time for us to meet or talk. So I feel like it's
underused; it could be something pretty big, pretty amazing."

This lack of communication is by no means always the case, especially in schools where partners have developed a long-term

relationship with the school. For example, at one school, afterschool program staff have one day off per week where, as the afterschool program director explained, "they don't teach a class but it's all about going in and checking with those teachers for what the curriculum is, what they're learning, what unit is going on." Additionally, concerted effort and commitment from school leadership can shift the culture, structure, and norms to make room for partners at the table. At one school, the principal blends in-school and afterschool efforts by having a common faculty meeting time for all teaching and partner staff to meet together each month. At first, some school staff were reluctant to share space with nontraditional colleagues. However, leadership commitment to include partners and shared planning and development are key levers for collaboration and alignment. These practices represent shifting norms of communication from the traditional ways of relating between school-day teachers and afterschool staff toward more integrated opportunities and services for students.

LINKED LEARNING PATHWAYS

One of OUSD's most ambitious efforts has been the articulation of college and career linked learning pathways to expand learning opportunities at the high school level. The linked learning approach joins together rigorous college-prep academics, a challenging career- or profession-themed curriculum that meets industry standards, and an opportunity for students to apply classroom learning through work-based or other real-world experiences in their communities.[10] As of 2018–2019, OUSD offered over thirty distinct career pathways (also known as "academies") functioning at sixteen OUSD high schools, including environmental sciences, engineering, hospitality, computer science, health science, law and social justice, and education. Over sixty partners support these pathways, including major corporate entities such as Intel, Salesforce.com, Wells Fargo, and PG&E; public entities like Bay Area Rapid Transportation (BART), Oakland Fire Department, Oakland African American

Chamber of Commerce, and Alameda County Health Pipeline Partnership; major medical providers like Children's Hospital and Kaiser Permanente; and community-based organizations such as the YMCA, Youth UpRising, Hack the Hood, and the Unity Council.

An unprecedented ballot measure, Measure N, funds OUSD's linked learning pathways. It allocates an additional $12 million a year (or $1,000 per student) to reduce the dropout rate, provide students with real-world work and learning opportunities, prepare students for admission to the University of California system and other four-year colleges, and expand mentoring, tutoring, counseling, support services, and transition to job training programs. Under Measure N, 90 percent of funds go directly to school sites on a per-pupil basis. High schools use this money to create customized plans to place all students in high-performing career pathways. Since 2014, the number of OUSD high school students in linked learning pathways has increased from 49 percent to 78 percent (as of 2017–2018). The numbers for tenth-graders in linked learning pathways increased from 53 percent to 85 percent.

Experienced linked learning coordinators work with high school faculty and community partners to support pathway development. These coordinators work with instructors to develop integrated curriculum units and coach community partners to make sure internship experiences are mutually beneficial and meaningful for students. They can also work with students to support workplace knowledge; for example, how to dress for a job interview, planning out transportation, and navigating other professional expectations. Internships also expose students to people and places outside their immediate neighborhood experience. One OUSD teacher, who leads her school's social justice pathway, reflected, "It's really scary for our students when they first go out to internships. We go out to community coalition meetings, to police commission meetings, and our students are so shy in those spaces. It's kind of weird. They have this deep kind of timidness around them, and that changes . . . very much over time." Exposure to hands-on learning opportunities can not only help make academic learning more relevant, but it can also boost students' confidence and life experience.

While there has been some tension at the high school level over which is the dominant framework, linked learning pathways and community schools are mutually supportive and strengthening. Linked learning pathways engage partner organizations in students' academic, technical, and workplace learning. The community school approach provides a framework for incorporating integrated student supports and families engagement as part of the students' experience in linked learning pathway development.

Integrated student supports are a pillar of OUSD full-service community schools. Innovative health and behavioral health supports— such as restorative practices and coordination of services teams—and expanded learning opportunities—such as after school programs and linked learning pathways—offer a range of resources and supports to students that have become standard practices across Oakland's FSCSs. In chapter 11, we discuss the critical role the CSM plays in leveraging FSCS services and resources to maximize support for students and schools.

CHAPTER 11

The Community School Manager

The work of the community school manager (CSM) is at the heart of what a community school is and does, yet what this role actually entails in practice is not well understood.[1] Becoming a community school requires expanding the functions within a school—for example, providing health services to students or social supports to families—which can also necessitate new processes, structures, and work streams. The CSM is the staff person who coordinates, manages, leads, and champions the smooth and systematic integration of these additional functions into the school community. The CSM plays a host of roles related to managing and integrating community school elements, depending on school/community needs and school level. But while the CSM role can look different from school to school, there are several core features: managing and maintaining the quality of partnerships; strengthening Coordination of Services Teams (COST) and multi-tiered systems of supports (MTSS); supervising and/or supporting family engagement staff and afterschool program staff; addressing chronic absence; and advocating for resources that support student and family needs. (A description of the CMS's roles and responsibilities appears in appendix 11a at the end of this chapter.) The CSM role in OUSD is a particularly powerful lever for full-service community school implementation.

THE CSM AS HIGH-LEVEL LEADER

In OUSD, the CSM role is designed as a high-level administrative position, essentially a similar classification and salary level to an assistant principal. In fact, in some smaller schools who may not actually have an AP, a family engagement specialist, or other supplementary staff, the CSM can hold a lot of that work. As one CSSS staff member stated, "They're doing climate, they're working with the partners. I mean, it's a real high-leverage position. And so we try to sell it in that the community school manager is holding all the student support services so that the principal can focus on the teaching and learning piece. Because when we hire, we hire *really good* people."

The CSM's ability to hold key aspects of the school's work is predicated on shared leadership, trust, and understanding with the principal. At mature FSCSs, the principal and CSM work in tandem. In fact, one of the most important relationships at the schools is that of the CSM and the principal. These relationships often take time to develop, but facilitate strong alignment between the academic and community work of the school. At one middle school, where the CSM and principal had been working together for five years, the CSM described the relationship this way: "So, at this point, I feel like it's really a true partnership where both of us trust each other and it's not like I need to hide anything from him or he's hiding anything from me; it's to the point where I've heard other people tell me how principals aren't sharing budgets with them. This is the year where . . . he's sharing his school's budget with me. I know exactly how the money is being spent. And same for him, he understands how [my agency] is spending our school-site funds."

The type of transparency between school and partner staff may not be typical in most schools across the country. However, OUSD full-service community school principals and CSMs described positive relationships of deep trust and respect. Most had been working together for several years, and found ways to make their roles complementary and clear. Often the principal sets the vision, and the CSM helps make it happen. The principal holds the priority on academics, and the CSM can help align resources and practices to support those goals. Yet in strong relationships, over time, the CSM and principal both learn from and adapt to one another. For example, one middle school principal credits his CSM for helping reshape the way he thinks about families as assets and contributors to the school. The relationship between the principal and CSM, and leveraging the CSM as a school leader, are critical to integration and implementation of the community school model.

As a high-level administrator collaborating with all stakeholders at the school site, the CSM has tremendous opportunity to increase their principal's capacity to work toward school goals and specifically to focus on instruction. CSMs can reduce the number of "hats" that principals have to wear by coordinating wraparound services, leveraging resources, aligning partners, and providing support for instructional staff to utilize community school practices. CSMs can address necessary conditions for teaching and learning that principals simply would not have the bandwidth to tackle on their own; taking some of these items off the principal's plate allows the principal to focus on instruction.

Some district administrators see the creation of the CSM role as an important equity strategy to ensure that *all* schools, especially those serving high-needs populations, are able to access FSCS resources. As one administrator shared, "It's really simple stuff, but they don't have the time to be like, 'Let me find you a space. Let me answer an email. Let me look at your schedule. Let me connect with the teachers.' To have somebody hold that, just even for a couple [of] partners, is huge."

SHARED PRIORITIES LINKED TO LEARNING

While all CSMs work to address the unique priorities of their school, the district has also determined a set of common priorities for all CSMs, focusing largely on building systems and practices to support conditions for learning. For the last several years, CSSS staff have coached CSMs to organize their work around five priorities: increasing school attendance; strengthening systems to support students, families, and teachers; increasing student access to health services; increasing and strengthening partnerships; and creating innovative systems and strategies to address their school's goals. These priorities ensure that CSM efforts are tightly aligned to CSSS (and district-wide) priorities; they also provide strong examples of how CSMs and the FSCS model supports conditions for learning.

Increasing School Attendance

Attendance is one the most pressing issues in OUSD schools. While chronic absence is widespread across most of the nation's school districts, it disproportionately affects schools serving low-income and minority students. In California, where school funding is tied to pupil daily attendance, OUSD loses millions of dollars a year tied to student absences; as a consequence, there is less money available to serve students with the resources they need to be successful. The CSM brings a unique skill set to the table in tackling student attendance. While a traditional school may have an attendance clerk or registrar following up on student absences, the CSM is able to leverage community partnerships, family relationships, and systems thinking to engage the school community in collaborative efforts to shift practices and norms to support student attendance.

One OUSD FSCS elementary school has worked over the last several years to reduce chronic absence. Of the school's 652 students, 93.4 percent are considered socioeconomically disadvantaged and 60 percent qualify as English language learners.[2] Like many low-income schools in the district, it experienced high chronic absence rates. Previously, chronic absenteeism was being addressed by the school outreach coordinator, from a fairly traditional mindset. With the support of the CSM, the school was able to reduce chronic absence from 11 percent to 5 percent over the course of three years. The principal recounts, "A more traditional model of schooling says,

'You know, it's a parents' job. Get your kid to school or don't.' And in a community schools model, we say, 'No, it's the school's job to partner with the parents to get kids to school.'" Under the leadership of the CSM, attendance became a schoolwide campaign. At monthly all-staff meetings, the CSM would share the latest attendance data provided by the district's student information system. They developed systems to incentivize student attendance, aligned with the school's PBIS system and reinforced through daily announcements and periodic assemblies. Students who required more intensive supports were monitored and/or case managed by one of two family advocates from the school's CBO partner. Each family advocate managed a caseload of students and families through ongoing outreach and communication, family conferences, the Student Attendance Review Team (SART) meetings, and home visits, as needed. Under this approach, the school developed structures and systems to reinforce school attendance, as well as dedicate resources for follow-up case management for those students who continue to struggle. During the 2017–2018 academic year, thirty-four students were actively managed on a caseload. The chronic absence rate continued to hold steady at around 5 percent.

Strengthening Systems to Support Students, Families, and Teachers

While in many community school models, CSMs function as case-workers or program coordinators, in OUSD, there has been particular emphasis on the CSM as a builder of systems. Two of the clearest manifestations of that are the COST and MTSS. COST is a team of staff members who come together on a weekly basis to discuss how the school is providing additional services to its at risk students. In essence, COST bring together partners and school staff to identify student needs, triage student referrals, use data to track outcomes, follow up on individual students; and look at school population-level needs. This work includes building teacher capacity and familiarity with COST, as well as ongoing cycles of inquiry to assess gaps and bring in new supports. While CSMs may indeed end up doing a fair amount of case management, the goal is to create structures and systems to address student needs broadly. These efforts are often closely linked to academic goals and require working closely with instructional staff, who are often on the front lines of identifying students who are struggling.

Increasing Student Access to Health Services

The community schools approach posits that meeting children's physical and mental health needs enables learning. Especially in low-income communities, where access to health resources can be limited and poverty-related illness rates may be higher, increasing student access to health services becomes a core equity issue. The CSM helps with this by increasing student access to health services, including managing relationships with co-located medical clinics, ensuring that student referrals are responded to in an effective and timely manner (for example, via an effective COST), and cultivating partnerships with additional service providers. The CSM often arranges visits from vision and dental services. During the 2016–2017 academic year, one community school manager arranged for 255 dental screenings (15 of which received follow-up treatments), 215 vision screenings (17 of which resulted in glasses received), and 314 vaccinations.

Increasing and Strengthening Partnerships

The CSM plays an important role in aligning partner activities to support key conditions for learning and school, often articulated in the school's SPSA goals. Nearly all CSMs have some responsibility for recruiting, managing, and coordinating with partner agencies on campus. CSMs facilitate the letter of agreement process and hold year-end reviews/evaluations with partners. Moreover, they assess partnerships in terms of their alignment with and contribution to school goals, which sets an expectation that the partner's role is to contribute to the core teaching and learning goals of the school rather than to simply provide stand-alone services. Over time, these processes have become more formalized as district staff have developed rubrics/protocols, reflecting CSMs' shared experience and feedback at district-hosted professional learning communities.

Creating Innovative Systems and Strategies to Address Individual School's Goals

The CSM at one school was fondly referred to by the principal as a "problem-solving machine." The CSM role has been cultivated to view challenges as opportunities to build systems of support and engage in a broader range of stakeholders in supporting student success. This aspect of the CSM's shared priorities allows them the flexibility to focus on emergent priorities at the schools site, reflected in the school's SPSA. These often, but not always, tend toward academic goals; for example, to increase outreach to incoming kindergarten students or to boost second-grade boys' literacy. These goals are typically data-driven, and linked to school and district systems through the SPSA framework. For example, at one school aiming to improve reading levels, the CSM helped to organize three events targeting Latinx students, black students, and preschoolers.

These five goals help to develop coherent and widespread implementation of priority areas across the forty-two full-service community schools, while still allowing for adaptation and variability. Further, they give CSMs a language to use when talking about their work with school staff and leaders that underscores its value in relation to student learning.

BUILDING STAFF CAPACITY

Increasingly, over the last several years, CSMs have started to focus more and more on building school-site capacity with FSCS flagship practices. CSMs often hold much of the work that previously fell on teachers or administrators. As one FSCS teacher stated, "Now that we're a FSCS, you don't have to be social workers or coaches. You don't have to worry that you don't have those resources because we have partners. We have a CSM." As with principals, the FSCS model certainly can reduce the hats that teaching staff wear, and make it clear that teachers are not on their own when dealing with the challenges of serving diverse urban communities. As one principal remarked, "I would hope that our teachers feel if they run into a challenge with a student or a family or a particular situation, there is additional support here to help them."

By building systems and introducing new practices, CSMs not only remove some of the load from instructional staff, but they also increase the tools and resources available for adults at the school. Over recent years, many CSMs have been making more of a concerted effort to build staff capacity to integrate and implement FSCS practices. For example, whereas in previous years, a teacher might have expected the CSM or restorative justice coordinator to drop in and lead a circle for them, now the CSMs work to build all school staff's capacity and confidence in conducting restorative practices on their own. Especially as schools need to make difficult budgeting choices, it becomes important for practices to not just "live" with one person. As one district leader shared, "How do we build the capacity of a school site so that all teachers and staff embody FSCS practices? Restorative justice—that should be everyone's job."[3]

DISTRICT SUPPORT FOR THE CSM

Unlike many traditional school roles, the CSM role requires a wide variety of skills and experience. In many community schools throughout the country, CSMs may be left largely on their own to negotiate their role and responsibilities at their school and to figure out how to best partner with school staff, CBO partners, and families. In Oakland, the district provides critical support in both constructing and supporting the CSM role. These supports have evolved over time, largely shaped by ongoing feedback and reflection from the CSMs themselves.

Screening, Hiring, and "Matching" a CSM

An important district site-level support the district provides is in the hiring and "matching" of CSMs. CSMs reflect a broad diversity of background experiences and skills. This is an intentional part of the design of the role. A CSSS administrator sees the variety of CSM backgrounds as a "brilliant part of our model" because they bring different lenses to their FSCS work. CSMs include professionals with backgrounds in social work, family engagement, afterschool programming, youth development, and even teaching and school administration.[4]

The district screens all CSM candidates to make sure they meet a certain minimum threshold—much of which is required by Human Resources—and then forwards the top three candidates to the school site for interviewing. The principal ultimately makes the hiring decision. While CSSS is very keen to find a specific match between the CSM and the principal (skills, personality, needs), they also must keep in mind that, due to the role classification, the CSM needs to be someone who can also thrive in another school environment. Given the centrality of the CSM-principal relationship to site-level implementation, the district sometimes looks for complementarity of CSM and principal; sometimes for similarity.

The district's role in screening and hiring candidates helps principals from a logistical and/or time perspective, and also because the district staff have knowledge and experience with what to look for in a CSM. As one relatively new FSCS principal described it, "It's really, really hard to run a school and also recruit for external positions and do the initial screening. So I think one of the benefits of having [the district] do it was [they are] holding the community school model in mind and then creating job descriptions and screening for people that are going to be well fit with their prior experience and their attitude."

District staff also sit with principals to discuss how they may distribute work and think about the role of CSMs. While the district has made a point to inform school principals and CSMs that the CSM role should be adapted based on school needs, there remain certain core responsibilities that a CSM should assume. Especially for principals new to FSCS, district guidance in conceiving and fully leveraging the CSM role is crucial.

The CSM hiring process illustrates a "top-down support for bottom-up change" approach in practice. In this case, the central office holds the collective vision for the CSM role, drawing from the experience of CSMs across the district; yet is responsive to the requests, feedback, and experience of site-level staff. The district can hold the normative space of what a CSM is and should be able to do; yet support sites in a pragmatic way by lessening the administrative load around hiring.

A Professional Learning Community

Building coherence in the role across multiple school and organizational contexts has been a district priority since the early years of the initiative. All CSMs, regardless of funding source, participate in a professional learning community (PLC) facilitated by the CSSS Community Partnerships office. Now in its sixth year, the PLC provides a monthly opportunity for CSMs across the district to step out of the demands of their daily school lives to reflect on practice, share experiences, and engage with district offices. Sometimes the CSMs meet as a whole group; at other times, they meet in smaller groups with their school-level (network) cohort peers. This practice allows participating CSMs to dive more deeply into issues, challenges, systems, and best practices related to school-level priorities. For instance, the middle school cohort of CSMs may focus on high school readiness, while those working in high schools focus on ninth-grade transitions, college and career readiness, and school climate. The Community Partnerships group manages the PLC meeting agendas, and designs them to reflect CSMs' interests and priorities. In the 2019–2020 academic year, the PLC will be led by a small group of

CSM "peer leaders" who have been offered an additional stipend to plan and organize the PLC.

The PLC also enables CSMs to stay connected to district developments, priorities, and practices related to their work. District staff from other department or groups often attend the PLC to share emerging priorities, developments, and new systems. For example, staff from the Research, Assessment, and Data (RAD) office attended multiple PLCs to seek CSM input while refining a new data system to track student use of support services. The PLC provides a feedback loop to improve and refine district systems.

Ongoing Supervision and Support to CSMs

The central office staff support the CSMs to develop their work plan at the beginning of the year. Throughout the year, the staff meet monthly with each CSM. Typically, these meetings are on-site, and also involve check-ins with the site leader. The specifics of district support and supervision vary by school, often relating to how long the CSM has been in the role. For example, one CSM who transitioned from a different role at the school described receiving support from his district supervisor in clarifying and negotiating his new role with the principal. More experienced CSMs underscored both the importance of having someone to listen to and support them generally, as well as more explicit efforts at aligning partners and resources toward school and district goals. For instance, one CSM reported that monthly check-ins with her district supervisor helped her develop and adapt a process to assess whether partners were meeting school needs (this assessment process now informs the partnership tools available to all CSMs, school staff, and district partners).

Coaching meetings can also help CSMs learn about relevant district resources to bring to their sites. For example, after one CSM shared about extremely low reading proficiency levels among black boys at her school, her district supervisor told her about the district's African American Male Achievement (AAMA) initiative, whose aims include (among other things) increasing reading proficiency for black youth in the district. The CSM worked successfully with other central office staff to bring AAMA to her campus. Subsequently, parents expressed an interest in supporting black girls, so the CSM reached out to learn about a number of different relevant initiatives and programs. As the CSM stated, it was "really helpful to give us the district-level view of things and help get us connected to resources."

The central office can also be a resource when a CSM comes up against a wall. For example, one CSM was struggling to get time with her principal. The principal was new to the school and new to FSCSs. Central office staff reached out to the principal and arranged time to sit down and discuss the FSCS model, including the CSM's role and opportunities available through working with the CSM. The central office can also help CSMs identify peers to connect with; for example, other CSMs who might have addressed similar issues and might have insight into problem solving.

One of the primary district contributions has been developing clear expectations and a shared understanding of the CSM role. The expectations and definition of the CSM role has evolved over time and has been deeply shaped by ongoing reflection by, feedback from, and experience of CSMs themselves. Especially for newer principals, this coaching and guidance from central office is essential. When the initiative started, there was a much less clear and shared understanding of the role. CSMs who started in the first years remember being introduced at the school site and having to explain their role to their site leadership. In one CSM's words, "I think we were charged from the gate, 'You go and explain to people your work. You go and champion community schools.'" As the FSCS initiative has matured, the onus for explaining and negotiating the CSM role has shifted to not be as fully on the shoulders of the CSMs themselves. The CSSS Community Partnerships office has increasingly gained traction communicating with principals, as well as district network superintendents, to clarify expectations for the CSM role and help school leaders effectively leverage the role.

Community school managers are a critical conduit for FSCS implementation. The district's creative adaptation of the CSM role facilitates both coherence and flexibility. CSMs have been the primary
drivers for many of the new structures, practices, and processes that
facilitate site-level culture change. In chapter 12, we discuss one final
element of site-level implementation: expanding the school community to include families.

Appendix 11a

Community School Manager Job Description

PROGRAM MANAGER, COMMUNITY SCHOOLS: COMMUNITY SCHOOLS AND STUDENT SERVICES (CSSS)

Basic Function

Work in partnership under the direction of the Site Administrator and assigned Family, Schools, and Community Partnerships Supervisor to manage and lead the development of the full service community school, including assessment of the school community's needs and assets, coordination of all student and family support services and development of resources and partnerships.

Representative Duties

Incumbent may perform any combination of the essential functions shown below. This position description is not intended to be an exhaustive list of all duties, knowledge, or abilities associated with this classification, but are intended to accurately reflect the principal job elements.

Essential Functions

- Work in partnership under the direction of the Site Administrator and assigned Family, Schools, and Community Partnerships Supervisor.
- Manage and lead the development, in partnership with the Site Administrator, of a seamless system of support services for students and families.
- Facilitate and/or provide technical assistance to the various school leadership teams, including School Site Council, Coordination of Services Team (COST), Student Success Team, and site-based providers.

- Develop, manage, and oversee the implementation of an effective referral process including facilitating the Coordination of Services Team (COST).
- Conduct outreach to students and families about available resources and how to refer, and regularly assess effectiveness of outreach efforts.
- Train and support service providers to understand and align programs with school structures, systems, curriculum and goals.
- Work with school staff and administration to integrate academic and non-academic supports.
- Establish systems to manage and maintain quality partnerships, including, but not limited to: development of MOUs, facilitation of regular meetings, planning sessions, joint work plans and collaborative problem-solving/conflict resolution.
- Provide support and guidance for school staff and partners in resolving issues related to service delivery, access, and coordination.
- Develop, manage, and sustain partnerships with city, county, and non-profit agencies to provide supports and opportunities to students and families that meet their identified needs.
- Act as point person for agencies and programs interested in partnering with school and help to broker new partnerships that are aligned with school goals and needs.
- Facilitate integration and coordination of site-based services with other District programs and services including mental health, family and community support, and school nursing.
- Support the integration of youth leadership, parent engagement, and family support throughout all Full Service Community School efforts.
- Design programs to support student transitions, including but not limited to transition between grades, re-entry from juvenile justice system or prolonged illness.

- Manage and lead the development of new programs, including service provider selection and program implementation and monitoring.
- Provide training and technical assistance to ensure cultural and linguistic appropriateness of services, programs, and communication efforts.
- Assist school and partner agencies with resource management and development, including fund development and grant maintenance.
- Facilitate data and information sharing between school and agencies, in accordance with state and federal law.
- Assist with program evaluation, including data collection, analysis, and reporting.
- Coordinate the allocation of space for student and family support services, and for special events.
- Participate in professional development opportunities around development of Full Service Community Schools provided by the Family, Schools, and Community Partnerships Department and other partners.
- Provide cross training to other staff members within the department.
- Perform related duties as assigned.

Minimum Qualifications

- Bachelor's degree required and three years of relevant experience in one or more major student and/or family support areas, and the ability to meet the Essential Functions stated above.
- Experience working in an urban school setting preferred.

Licenses and Other Requirements

- Valid California driver's license
- Employment eligibility will include fingerprints, tuberculosis and/or other employment clearance.

Knowledge and Abilities

Knowledge of:

- Applicable laws, codes, regulations, policies, and procedures governing work scope
- Strategic direction of the District
- Social, emotional, health, and economic issues faced by Oakland youth and their families
- Diverse groups across race, ethnicity, religion, gender, class, and sexuality
- Local community-based organizations providing mental health services
- Research methods, report writing, and record-keeping techniques
- Correct English usage, grammar, spelling, and punctuation
- Principles and practices of effective leadership
- Telephone techniques, systems, and etiquette
- Interpersonal skills using tact, patience, and courtesy
- Principles and practices of supervision and evaluation

Ability to:

- Interpret and implement applicable laws, codes, policies, procedures, and District regulations governing work scope
- Maintain current knowledge of applicable laws, codes, regulations, policies, procedures, and District regulations related to work scope
- Establish and maintain effective working relationships with multi-faced public and private agencies and District departments
- Work successfully with diverse groups across race, ethnicity, religion, gender, class, and sexuality
- Identify and resolve school site health and safety issues in a timely manner
- Communicate effectively in English orally and in writing
- Plan and organize work

- Work confidentially and with discretion
- Work independently
- Meet schedules and timelines
- Manage multiple projects simultaneously
- Complete work as directed despite frequent interruptions
- Prepare and deliver clear and concise presentations to a variety of audiences
- Develop and implement training and evaluation programs
- Supervise and evaluate assigned staff
- Operate personal computer, related software, and other office equipment
- Cross-train department personnel

Working conditions

Environment

- Office environment, school sites, and off-site locations; driving a vehicle to conduct work; face-paced work; constant interruptions.

Physical demands

- Consistent mental alertness; sitting or standing for extended periods of time; lifting, carrying, pushing, and pulling light to moderate weight objects; bending and twisting at the waist, reaching overhead, above the shoulders and horizontally; dexterity of both hands and fingers while performing duties; seeing to read, write, and use the computer; hearing and speaking to exchange information, in person or on the telephone, and make presentations.

CHAPTER 12

Family Engagement

You're always going to need that voice that pushes the school to be the best possible version of itself and not make excuses. Parents need a seat at that table. They might not always know how to do it, which is why that cycle of action is so important. Doing research, going and visiting other schools, helps parents both see what's possible—especially if they had lower expectations—and challenge the school to say: "Why can't we do what they're doing?" And once parents see something like that, they get stuck on that: "Why can't we do that?" And you find yourself not making excuses and trying to be more solutions-oriented.

—OUSD principal

OUSD's emphasis on family engagement reflects a central commitment to broaden the stakeholder base of *who* is included in community schools. The district's family engagement efforts rest on the fundamental assumption that families want their students to succeed and need to have information about how the system works, as well as agency.[1] While, like many districts across the country, OUSD schools aim to build positive school-family relationships and provide families with strengthening resources, Oakland's efforts are unique in their grassroots organizing approach to building parent power.[2] Over time, this approach has garnered widespread support and adoption across the district, despite initial skepticism or capacity of school leaders. Supports from the district's Office of Student,

Family, and Community Engagement (OSFCE) and a wide array of community partners working to bolster parent voice in educational equity undergird school-site efforts.

Community Schools, Thriving Students features family engagement at its center. In fact, the district's work around family engagement predates the FSCS initiative, and has been strengthened, deepened, and extended as they've been incorporated into the district's FSCS approach.[3] Additionally, OUSD's family engagement work is a central tenet of the district's equity strategy and targeted universalism. For example, district and school efforts set explicit targets to increase opportunities for participation for families from underrepresented backgrounds to become leaders and advocates in their children's schools. The OSFCE was originally housed in CSSS, but in 2017–2018, moved to the newly created Office of Equity. This new location, under Instruction, links OFSCE's family engagement strategies even more tightly to learning. The district's family engagement theory of action (see figure 12.1), outlines four central and interrelated strategies.

SUPPORTING STUDENTS' ACADEMIC SUCCESS

The OSFCE aims to "To expand [family] participation in learning, leadership, and advocacy through community organizing and building OUSD capacity, resulting in high levels of academic achievement and life opportunities for students and school communities." This framework values parents for their diversity of experience and inspires, engages, and supports them to be co-owners of their children's education. Parental roles in their children's education look different across the developmental spectrum. Family engagement activities vary by school level, such as home supports for literacy, afterschool program participation, and student attendance for elementary school students; high school readiness, summer learning, and enrichment at the middle school level; and linked learning and internship opportunities, college readiness, and youth leadership in high school.

Figure 12.1 *OUSD Family Engagement Pyramid*

OUSD Engagement Goals
- Increase representation from school sites on district engagement bodies.
- At school sites, increase representation and participation of students and families from under-represented and underserved communities.
- At school sites, establish shared governances bodies in compliance with LCFF, MSFE Standards, Core Waiver.
- At school sites, engage more students and families from under-represented/underserved communities in school improvement efforts.
- Align school-led and CBO-led engagement efforts at school sites, towards mutual school improvement goals.

Engagement Pyramid

Level 4: Get involved in DISTRICT-level engagement

District Engagement Activities	
- LCAP Parent Advisory, LCAP ELL Parent Advisory	- Shared decision making
	- Advise LCAP priorities and implementation in the district
- Student Directors on Boad of Education (advisory vote)	- Provide representative leadership for your site and constituency and bring info back to respective school sites
- LCAP Student Advisory	
- ACC Governing Board	*Students/parents move to Level 4*

Level 3: Get involved in SCHOOL governance

District Engagement Activities		Site Engagement Activities
- PR the BAR monthly trainings for school governance teams (prep for SGT/SSC summits)	- Shared decision making	- School Governance Team (SGT)
	- Ensure stakeholder priorities are implemented	- LCAP Committees: African-American Parent Council, ELL Parent Committee, SPED Parent Advisory
	- Set budget priorities	
- SPED parent summit	- Evaluate impact	- MSFE Committee
	Students/parents move to Level 3	- Classroom observations

Level 2: Get involved to help your SCHOOL improve

District Engagement Activities		Site Engagement Activities
- ACC Middle and High School meetings/trainings	- Understand school data	- RJ Peer Leaders
	- Help set and implement school improvement policies	- CBO engagement events
	- Provide input on school policy and practice, and feedback for school staff	- Elections for SGT and LCAP committees
- Middle and high school peer resources/Eth Studies Conferences	- Opportunities for all families to engage with learning and volunteering	- MSFE student/family forums
		- Elections of student officers
- Youth Leadership Summit	- Leadership development programs for students	- Parent volunteers with attendance, culture, reading
	- Leadership development programs for parents/families	- Academic parent-teacher teams
	Students/parents move to Level 2	- Peer mentors/educators

Level 1: Get informed to help your CHILD succeed

District Engagement Activities		Site Engagement Activities
- Common Core workshops	- Learn about academies, internships, and other opportunities	- Back-to-School Night
	- Learn to navitate school	- Parent orientations
- LCAP input events	- Learn about Common Core	- Family resource centers
	- Parent-teacher communication	- Parent skills trainings
	- Address student/parent complaints	- Mailings/calls
	- Parent support programs	
	- Inf translated and accessible meeting locations/times	
	- Welcoming school environment	
	- Student leadership and civic engagement classes	
	- Student support service programs	

Point of entry—for parents/families and students to get involved

At the school-site level, family engagement efforts focus on preparing families to support their students' academic success. (See Appendix 12a for the district's standards for family engagement.) Many FSCSs have family resource centers (FRCs), which become a locus of family engagement and support. FRCs provide direct service and basic supports for families—for example, ESL classes, legal aid, food assistance, and computer access. They also become hubs for engaging with families around their students' learning. For example, at the elementary school level, that may mean facilitating monthly literacy or science nights. In the older grades, involving families in their students' college preparation, helping to navigate Free Application for Federal Student Aid (FAFSA) forms, keeping on track with the application process, identifying and applying for scholarships and loans, communicating with their child's teachers, and ensuring they understand (and can access) what their child needs to be "college ready."

At one FSCS's FRC, staff work to ensure that all students are enrolled in meaningful summer learning opportunities and internships that match student interests, skill level, and aspirations. The staff are constantly building relationships with new partner organizations reflective of student interests, and correspondingly, support families overcome the multiple barriers that might exist to access. Bureaucratic misunderstandings, linguistic barriers, and inadequate transportation can all limit families' ability to access resources for their children. Coming from a place of recognizing families' desire to support their children succeed means addressing these barriers pragmatically and systematically through ongoing supports. As one CSM noted: "From the outside, you might be like, 'Oh, like, the kids don't care, the families don't care. They don't have any follow-through.' But then from the inside, you see all these little things that can become big things or can make the difference between a student accessing something amazing or not."

Strong parent-school communication at one OUSD full-service community school played a central role successfully implementing an important school policy change designed to provide students with more targeted academic support. For the last several years, students with a GPA of less than 3.0 are required to stay after school until 3:30 or 5:00 p.m. to participate in afterschool enrichment and academic support. Initially, parents resisted this practice. However, the school's administration worked with the families to help them understand the value and importance of the extra time, and eventually, the parents got on board. As the principal describes it, "We have a relationship with the students and their family that, well, we can really [be blunt] with the kids and the parents and say, 'We need this,' and they will respond."

Another FSCS adopted Academic Parent-Teacher Teams (APTT) as a powerful approach to engage families in student learning. APTT reimagines the structures of a traditional parent-teacher conference and offers a yearlong set of structured class and parent-teacher conversations focused on specific grade-level goals.[4] It builds the capacity of teachers to gain a better understanding of families and their unique circumstances, and the capacity of parents to provide targeted support for student learning at home. In the APTT model, teachers facilitate three seventy-five-minute team meetings each year, consisting of teachers meeting with the families of each of their students. The team meetings give families opportunities to learn and contribute in a collaborative environment. They also allow teachers and families to exchange important grade-level information and effective home practices with all families at once. Once per year for each student, the teacher holds a thirty-minute individual session with the student and the student's family to provide individualized, personal support. These sessions allow families and teachers to deepen their relationship as partners, discuss each student's progress at home and at school, and collaboratively create a course of action to support student growth and improvement.

The Parent-Teacher Home Visit model is another innovative practice used across OUSD FSCSs.[5] Teachers are trained (and paid) to conduct twice-yearly home visits with families—once in the fall and again in the spring. The first visit focuses on the families' hopes and dreams for their children; the second on students' academics. Teachers conduct visits in pairs, and the visits are voluntary for both teachers and families. Visits are offered to all students in the class (as opposed to a targeted group). The model has been shown to increase trust and positive communication between families and school staff, as well as provide teachers with helpful context to better connect with and support their students during the course of the year.[6] After successfully piloting the program at several schools, the district's OFSCE staff worked with the Parent Teacher Home Visit Project national office to become certified trainers, so they can now provide their own in-house training to teachers wishing to participate in the program. By engaging with families as well as the partner organizations, OUSD FSCSs work to ensure that families are informed and capable of navigating the nuances of the US education system to help their students succeed. In turn, this work helps minimize barriers to opportunities and maximize access for students. It is supported by myriad community partners—such as Oakland Community Organizations (OCO)—as well as the district itself. The district provides an eight-week leadership training, Parents Raising the BAR (behavioral expectation, attendance, reading), facilitated by parents, to build parents' knowledge around important topics critical to student success, and strengthen their capacity as problem-solvers and school leaders.[7]

HELPING SCHOOLS IMPROVE

Some studies show that when parents are involved at school, the performance of *all* children at the school tends to improve.[8] Many schools early on in the FSCS initiative developed parent-advisory groups organized around a "cycle of action" for school improvement. With the introduction of LCAP, many of these advisory groups were folded into the SSC process, as the SSC itself, or English Language Advisory Council (ELAC), or one of their subcommittees. Partner organizations often facilitate the groups, and sometimes the CSM or parent liaison acts as facilitator. In cycles of action, parents look at data regarding issues at the school (e.g., student achievement gap); then form a plan to learn more (e.g., by visiting other schools that have developed best practices in response to a similar issue), and propose action in response. As these efforts have become part of SSC, the proposed action inevitably involves fiscal resource allocation as part of the school's site plan.

FSCS principals strongly endorse the importance of family engagement for fostering school improvement. As one principal stated, "Parents can hold the highest vision for their children," and harnessing that vision can unleash tremendous potential. In one elementary school, early on in FSCS implementation, a school quality review showed they were weak in in the area of family engagement. So the principal worked with a community consultant, identified by the school's partner organization, to conduct in a yearlong listening campaign with families, staff, and partners. School leaders focused on what families wanted for their students. The results clearly showed that families aspired for their children to attend college (this contrasted with a more jaded view among some teachers that "success" for students would mean graduating from high school). The listening campaigned kicked off a schoolwide focus on a college-going culture that continues six years later.

Meaningful family engagement requires principal support, which may not happen overnight. Often, principals come to perceive only slowly the value and power of family engagement. As one principal reflected: "So . . . what does it mean to be in partnership with parents around a change process and improvement in the school[?] . . . I don't think when I came in, I saw the value of that. And now we've set up systems, and I'm seeing that everything that is dramatically improving at this school at a fast rate is not because it's just me and the teachers, it's usually because it's me and the parents setting the expectation that this is now something that [our school] will do."

While principal support can strengthen family engagement efforts, leadership turnover and a history of contentious school-community relationships can make for a difficult start. It can take time to re-build relationships and create trust between school leadership and the school community. One family advocate describes the conten-tious environment she and her colleagues worked to overcome when starting at their school several year ago. Before the new principal started, there had been a big "disconnect" between the principal and parent community. The parents had been circulating petitions to get rid of the principal, in fact. "It was a total communication break-down . . . especially between the principal and the bilingual parents." Now, five years later, the new principal has been intentional about "making sure that he's keeping our families informed about what's going on around the school. Data is shown everywhere. They have nothing to hide."

While principals are often hesitant or skeptical of this approach at first, they come to find parent advocates to be powerful catalysts for positive school change. At one site, the principal credits her school's parent advisory council for advocating at the district and state levels for the passage of district Measure N in 2014 and state Proposition 30 in 2012, both of which brought significant new funding to the school.[9] At one school, these measures added up to three quarters of a million dollars in the annual budget. At another school, staff attri-bute parents' tenacity in demanding district attention to the poorly equipped science labs for the creation of its new science center. Whereas in many wealthy schools, parents play a role in fundraising for the school through the PTA, this can be more of a challenge in lower-income communities. The focus on political action leverages parents' political power to bring money and real resources to their schools and to the district.

PARENTS GET INVOLVED IN SCHOOL GOVERNANCE

The 2013–2014 academic year, with the implementation of the LCFF and LCAP, saw a dramatic shift toward local control in California (see chapter 3 for more details on LCAP and school governance). LCAP established as a state priority that parents be afforded meaningful opportunities to become involved in the design of school plans and to partner with schools in efforts to improve the academic achievement of children and youth in their communities. OFSCE efforts leveraged this important legislation, and for the last five years have been building schools' capacity to engage families in their SSCs, the legal entity responsible for determining school spending (and legally required for all schools receiving federal Title I funds). As budget cuts have further reduced site-level staff, sometimes including parent liaisons, the district-level supports for parent involvement in SSCs have become even more critical.

Much of the district's family engagement work was spearheaded by Raquel Jimenez, currently Executive Director of the Office of Equity and an OUSD alumna, teacher, and long-time student and family advocate. Currently (2019–2020), there are five district-level family engagement staff, one assigned to each network (three elementary networks; one middle; one high). Within each network, district family engagement liaisons have three to five schools at any one time where they are focusing on building up capacity; however, they are always available to respond to requests that come up. In addition, OFSCE includes a school governance specialist (SGS), funded by Title I dollars, charged with educating families, schools, and district staff to support parent involvement in school site governance.[10] As school governance specialist Sara Nuno said, "It really comes down to seeing the school site council as a shared decision-making space. Seeing parents at the table as partners. And really looking at data. I'm shocked when I'm at a SSC and there are decision-making conversations happening absent of data." The OFSCE team leads five trainings throughout the year that follow the funding cycle and are grounded in the five standards for SSCs. Since beginning nearly five years ago, the work has gained much more traction at school sites. Nuno recalled, "When I first started, I remember practically having to beg principals to focus on family engagement. Now, we're getting way more requests from principals at the beginning of the year, asking us to help them with recruitment, with setting agendas. It shows me that we're starting to shift culture."

As school funding priorities and decision making have increasingly become tied to LCAP, the SSC has become an instrumental body in building parents' abilities to contribute to meaningful discussions and decision making in school governance. Additionally, the OSFCE runs a districtwide parent advisory committee, which has helped inform implementation of LCAP, the creation of site-level standards and tools around family engagement, and many other district-level policies.

In many US schools, staff often struggle to connect with families. Especially in high-poverty contexts, demanding schedules, language barriers, unfamiliarity with the US school system, limited transportation, and competing family responsibilities can all limit the extent to which parents are visibly involved at school sites. Teachers seldom receive training on how to effectively engage with families around their children's learning; linguistic and cultural differences between staff and families can further the divide. The many ways parents support their children's learning at home—for example, instilling the importance of education, sacrificing so their children can study—may not always be visible to school staff, leading to the misperception that families are uninterested, or not invested in their children's education. Further, even when schools attempt to engage with families, these efforts are often piecemeal—more "random acts" of engagement than systematic, sustained, and integrated shifts in practice.

While schools and families both bear responsibility for strong partnerships, schools and districts are best positioned to support conditions to create key organizational and process conditions for meaningful family engagement.[11] OUSD's family engagement strategy explicitly aims to empower families as leaders, advocates, and first teachers in their children's education. But an essential component of any district's family engagement efforts is not directed only toward families, but also toward school staff. OUSD has created a pervasive culture and expectation of all staff that families are partners in students' learning. This is expressed in teacher responses to a 2017–2018 Gardner Center survey. OUSD community school teachers report that they communicate with families in support of student learning, including calling families at home to share positive news about their child, texting families, holding classroom parent meetings, looking at data with families, and communicating with families about their hopes and dreams for their child.[12] These data suggest far-reaching norms and expectations around school-family partnerships.[13]

Results of a 2017–2018 LCAP parent survey corroborate these positive trends—showing that roughly nine in ten parents feel welcome to participate in their child's school, encouraged to be an active partner with the school in educating their child, and encouraged to participate in organized parent groups (school site councils, committees, parent organizations, LCAP Parent Student Advisory Committee, etc.).[14] While family engagement efforts look different at different schools, the district's family engagement work has taken hold on a broad scale. The standards and expectations around meaningful family engagement have permeated schools across the district, as each one navigates shifting its policies and practices to include families.

At its inception, *Community Schools, Thriving Students* aimed to create system change, marshaling the resources of the community to create more equitable educational opportunities for students. This included targeting resources where they were most needed, and ensuring that groups most impacted by an issue had a presence at the table. Additionally, the FSCS strategic plan aimed to "assemble a broad-based set of community actors" who had the collective capacity to "design and implement educational reform." Concrete stakeholder involvement in the planning process foreshadowed what would become far-reaching practices to see parents as central to the business of their children's education. OUSD's family engagement work underscores once again what it means to be a district "in service of" schools, students, and families. In part 4, we move to discussing key accomplishments, challenges, and lessons learned from OUSD's FSCS initiative.

Appendix 12a

OUSD Standards for Meaningful Family Engagement

Standards

Standard 1: Parent/Caregiver Education Program

Families are supported with parenting and child-rearing skills, understanding child and adolescent development, and setting home conditions that support children as students at each age and grade level. Assist schools in understanding families.

Standard 2: Communication with Parent/Caregiver

Families and school staff engage in regular, two-way, meaningful communication about student learning.

Standard 3: Parent Volunteering Program

Families are actively involved as volunteers and audiences at the school or in other locations to support students and school programs.

Standard 4: Learning at Home

Families are involved with their children in learning activities at home, including homework and other curriculum-linked activities and decisions.

Standard 5: Shared Power and Decision Making

Families and school staff are equal partners in decisions that affect children and families and together inform, influence, and create policies, practices, and programs.

Standard 6: Community Collaboration and Resources

Coordinate resources and services for families, students, and the school with businesses, agencies, and other groups, and provide services to the community.

Vision

Through meaningful family engagement, we envision a transformed school system that has directly confronted and actively addressed inequity and injustice so that every OUSD student graduates and becomes a fully engaged member of our community.

Mission

The mission of meaningful family engagement is to inspire, engage, and support the students, families, and communities of OUSD to become authentic co-owners of our schools who share responsibility for every student becoming college and career ready. Through community organizing, and by building OUSD capacity, we will expand participation in learning, leadership, and advocacy that results in high levels of academic achievement and life opportunities for individual students, and for entire school communities.

Values

- We value the unique and diverse experiences of families in our community.
- We value engaging with students and families with love, care, compassion, and respect.
- We value students as leaders and agents of change. We value family members as leaders and agents of change.
- We value authentic democratic decision-making where students, families, and communities are equal partners.
- We value self-determination with community and family empowerment.
- We value bridging OUSD staff with students, families, and communities to engage in healthy struggle for positive change.

PART IV

ACCOMPLISHMENTS, CHALLENGES, AND LESSONS

CHAPTER 13

Accomplishments and Challenges

OUSD's full-service community school work has deepened and expanded since 2011, despite considerable and ongoing challenges, including multiple leadership changes and budget crises. Early efforts to engage a range of stakeholders in an in-depth planning process, implement new board policies, and reorganize district departments to remove silos and facilitate a whole-child approach have helped FSCSs weather a multitude of organizational and fiscal challenges. The district has also put in place structures to support schools on their FSCS journeys, such as processes for building and evaluating relationships with partner organizations and a professional learning community for community school managers. OUSD full-service community schools have developed long-term partnerships with CBOs that enable them to dramatically expand their efforts to serve the whole child. Community school managers serve as high-level administrators, aligning efforts of school and partner staff, and often freeing up principals' time to focus on instruction. High-functioning community schools have increased parental voice and participation in school governance, enriched the school day through an array of learning opportunities, and integrated and normalized health services in their schools. At the student level, graduation rates have increased substantially, access to services has increased, and suspensions have decreased, although, performance on standardized tests continues to lag for Oakland students and an achievement gap persists between white students and students of color. This chapter synthesizes key accomplishments of Oakland's full-service community schools and the challenges they face going forward at system and school levels.

SYSTEM-LEVEL ACCOMPLISHMENTS

District leaders employed a variety of tools—culture shifts, policy levers, and structural modifications—to bring about substantial change in the OUSD system operations. Shifts in district and community culture around K-12 education accompanied Superintendent Tony Smith's passionate advocacy for a focus on equity and social justice. The district's comprehensive and stakeholder-based nine-month planning process to develop *Community Schools, Thriving Students* brought participants' deep involvement in the initiative's whole-child comprehensive vision—a commitment that continues today across the district and within the community.

Board policies enacted after the 2011 strategic plan created the African American Male Achievement program,required new school governance procedures that increased family involvement in core site-level decisions (curricula, budgeting, discipline), made social-emotional learning (SEL) a district priority for all schools, and shifted OUSD budgeting guidelines in ways that enhanced resource equity between sites. The finding that OUSD was in violation of the federal Title IV of the Civil Rights Act brought a mandated Voluntary Resolution Plan that required OUSD to put new discipline policies (restorative justice) in place, develop a plan to reduce suspensions, provide positive behavioral intervention and support (PBIS) strategies, review the district's climate surveys, and improve its data collection.

A new department, Community Supports and Student Services (CSSS), brought together programs and resources previously scattered across the central office (PBIS, afterschool, family and youth engagement) and enabled the district-level development of three fundamental FSCS elements—community school managers, Health and Wellness, and Partnerships. Every OUSD school now has a Wellness Champion and health connections, even those without school-based health clinics. The district's Partnership staff support community partnerships, relationships that grow site-level opportunities and services. The CSSS department's interconnected work and collaborative cross-boundary culture embodies the strategic plan's goal of a coherent central office operating "in service of" the work of each school. One observer dubbed the CSSS department an "oasis" in an otherwise often chaotic central office.

All OUSD schools became community schools with the 2011 passage of *Community Schools, Thriving Students*. "All means all," Tony Smith was fond of saying. Fruitful FSCS implementation affirmed the value of the model and spurred expansion across the district, supported by school-level and district funds, state and federal program monies, and philanthropic grants.

SCHOOL SITES

OUSD developed systems and supports within individual schools that prioritize and sustain the FSCS work. Arguably, schools have changed more in ways allied with the FSCS vision than has the central office. Initially, only eight schools functioned as FSCSs supported by full-time CSMs; by the start of the 2019–2020, forty-two CSMs work to support FSCSs in Oakland. Nearly all OUSD schools have family engagement in school site councils, youth leadership councils, Wellness Champions, COST supports, SEL training and supports for teachers and families, afterschool programs, and restorative justice practices. The CSMs have been sustained and their numbers have grown despite district budget cuts, in part because of continued private support for their work and because of schools' own prioritization and underwriting of the CSM positions.

All schools have developed a system of long-term community partnerships that increase the range of resources and opportunities available to students and families. They are, as one FSCS principal said, the "legs of the school. We can't move without them." Although partnerships differ depending on a school's needs, resources, and context, partner management and relationships proceed similarly across schools because of CSSS partnership tools and support. Increasingly, structured district practices are in place to identify needs, evaluate partners, and make adjustments as necessary.

As relationships between partners and educators develop, partners and their services (e.g., health services, expanded learning) become integrated as part of the school. In some well-developed FSCSs, for instance, principals and teachers make little distinction between in-school and out-of-school activities. Adults at the school—principal, teachers, CBO staff, CSM, COST, families—work together toward shared goals for students. Schools and health partners find ways to increase student access to services and normalize participation in counseling.

In most OUSD schools, family engagement practices have changed from the old PTA model, which generally failed to interest parents—especially low-income flatlands parents—to school governance procedures that ask parents to take part in important decisions about the school's curricula, budgets, and partnerships. Parents also review site-level student data to consider accomplishments and shortfalls. In most—if not all—Oakland schools, board-mandated family engagement strategies provide parents voice, power, and an authentic role in school governance.

In many FSCS, CSMs have come to function in a senior school management role, operating as a partner and becoming a priority for principals who see the value of collaborative leadership. The district defines the CSM's general job description, but the role varies by school, depending on the CSM's background and school needs.

SCHOOL AND STUDENT OUTCOMES, 2011–2019

The preceding sections of this chapter summarize the ways in which FSCSs changed the way that systems and schools operate to serve the whole child. What ultimately matters is the difference that community schools make for the students and families they serve. *Community Schools, Thriving Students* set out academic goals for students and expressed commitment to providing the opportunities, supports, and resources students need to graduate college-, career-, and community-ready. Those resources include extended learning time, tutoring, and other academic supports as well as opportunities to promote their health, well-being, and personal growth. Thus, important FSCS school and student outcomes include both academic and wellness measures.

Data collected by the district about student characteristics, services, and outcomes provide important information about how OUSD students are doing and how this has or has not changed since FSCSs took hold in Oakland. This discussion is not an assessment of the causal impact of FSCSs on student outcomes. Indeed, assessing the impact of such a complex, multifaceted approach as FSCS entails a host of challenges (see the appendix, "Lessons for Community School Research and Evaluation."). Rather, these data shed light on the students that FSCS reach, their access to programs and services, the culture of their schools, and trends in educational outcomes across OUSD schools over time.

The most striking and positive change on student outcomes since FSCS began is a substantial increase in graduation rates, both overall and for specific student subgroups. In addition, there have been moderate decreases in suspension rates, consistent with OUSD's emphasis on restorative justice. Other important outcomes, including chronic absence and standardized tests scores, did not improve and remain a concern. In viewing these results, it may be important to remember that many FSCS activities are not explicitly academic in nature, focusing more on reducing barriers to learning and increasing engagement in school.

Expanded Access to Services

Students Served The full-service community school is an equity-driven initiative aimed at increasing resources and capacity at the schools that have less of these things. Though all OUSD schools serve some number of high-poverty students (over 90 percent receive ESSA Title I funds), consistent with the FSCS equity agenda, the majority of the district's ELLs, students eligible for free and reduced-price lunches (FRPL), students of color, and students in foster care attended a FSCS.[1]

FSCS achievements are especially noteworthy given the many obstacles that their students face. The FRPL rate is well over 75 percent, and for many schools it is over 90 percent. For instance, the FRPL rate for high-achieving Coliseum College Preparatory Academy is 97 percent; and 95 percent of Roosevelt Middle School students, a school honored by CORE for "high-impact growth," qualify for FRPL. The positive outcomes for these schools show that several of Oakland's FSCS have significantly mediated the consequences of concentrated poverty that neuroscientists consistently demonstrate can lead to academic deficits and poor life outcomes.[2]

Health and Wellness OUSD addresses health and wellness goals through three program areas: Health Access, Healthy School Environment, and Health Education. School health centers, part of the Health Access program, provide the most comprehensive physical and mental health care; in 2016–2017, forty-seven OUSD schools had linkages to one of sixteen school health centers. The clinics offer medical and behavioral health, dental services, and first-aid; since 2011–2012, they have provided more than 250,000 student visits.

The California Healthy Kid Survey (CHKS) found that high-frequency clinic users (ten or more visits a year) were more likely to report academic, social, emotional, and sexual health issues than other users, indicating that the clinics were reaching higher-need students. Such students also reported that they knew where to go for help when feeling depressed, stressed, or anxious, and that they always got mental health care when they needed it:

- 96 percent said that they feel like they had an adult to turn to if they needed help.

- 96 percent said they felt safe talking about their problems.
- 90 percent said the clinic helped them deal with stress or anxiety better.

The CHKS also reports that School Health Center positively enhanced academic success for all users. Clients said the health center helped them: have goals and plans for the future (92 percent); stay in school (88 percent); do better in school (85 percent); and have better attendance (79 percent).

Expanded Learning Time Chapter 10 describes how afterschool programming is integrated with the school day in mature FSCSs; quantitative data also indicate high levels of student afterschool participation. An analysis of data from the 2014–2015 school year shows that in OUSD middle schools, FSCS students attended afterschool programming at more than twice the rate of other district middle schools (73 percent versus 31 percent). Further, participation in FSCS afterschool programming was associated with small decreases in the likelihood of being chronically absent from school.[3]

School Culture and Discipline

Consistent with OUSD's changes in disciplinary practices and focus on restorative justice, suspension rates have decreased slightly over time, including meaningful reductions for some student subgroups. In high school, overall suspension rates have gone from 6.3 percent in 2015–2016 to 4.8 percent in 2018–2019, and in middle school from 8.4 percent to 7.5 percent over the same time frame. Suspension rates for African American students specifically have decreased, although remain at considerably higher levels than for the student body overall.[4]

Academic Outcomes

Graduation OUSD graduation rates have risen significantly since 2011 from 59.3 percent to 73.5 percent in 2019, and dropout rates have fallen. Not only are more students graduating in four years, but also fewer students are dropping out, and more students continue toward graduation beyond four years of high school. Since 2010, when California moved to a four-year cohort model, OUSD has for the first time achieved both a graduation rate over 70 percent and its lowest cohort dropout rate—now 15.3 percent, down from 20.0 percent in 2016.

Oakland's community schools also show progress in addressing the equity goals that motivated the initiative. Since 2011–2012, the first year of *Community Schools, Thriving Students* implementation, the cohort graduation rate for groups of students who have traditionally been the furthest from completing high school have shown substantial growth:

- Black cohort graduation rates have increased from 53.5 percent to 70.8 percent.
- Latinx cohort graduation rates have increased from 52.7 percent to 64.0 percent.
- ELL graduation rates have increased from 45.6 percent to 57.7 percent.

While cohort graduation rates went up across almost all OUSD high schools, several FSCS schools have made remarkable progress. In 2018, seven of the eleven traditional FSCS high schools graduated students above the California graduation rate of 83.5 percent, and six of them posted graduation rates above 90 percent.

Academic Achievement and Growth

Academic achievement as measured by standardized test scores continues to lag in OUSD (as it does around the state). However, despite low proficiency rates overall, there has been improvement. For instance, reading at grade level has increased significantly. Since the baseline year of 2012–2013, Scholastic Reading Index assessment rates have increased by 12.2 percent for third grade, 8.9 percent for sixth grade, and 11.3 percent for ninth grade. In 2011–2012, overall rates of students reading at or above grade level were only 22.4

---

percent. In 2017–2018, nearly 37 percent of students are reading at or above grade level. These data show both progress and considerable room for continued growth.

Further, several OUSD schools recently received recognition for their academic accomplishment. CORE's 2019 Academic Growth Awards honored twenty-five OUSD schools for their significant impact on student achievement. In schools with high academic growth, students consistently make academic gains faster than do students at similar schools. The awards recognize the growth in student achievement by considering how much a student is learning over time, rather than just comparing test scores from one year to the next, and consider high academic growth as a reflection of school effectiveness.[5] Of the twenty-five OUSD schools recognized for academic growth, thirteen operate as full-service community schools serving the highest concentration of the district's low-income students. Further, all but one of the seven schools honored in the middle school network, and both of the high schools receiving "high-impact" awards, are FSCSs.

OUSD also highlighted school success with its first cohort of ten "Schools to Learn From" (2018–2019). This program aims to celebrate impact and collaborative efforts, grow expectations for OUSD students, and share promising practices. Multiple data sets informed honorees' selection that reflected sustained improvement over time and closure of opportunity gaps for disadvantaged, ELL, black, and Latinx students. Three of the ten schools recognized as "Schools to Learn From" are FSCSs.

CHALLENGES AT SYSTEM AND SITE LEVELS

OUSD faces challenges similar to those of many high-need urban districts in the country, as well as some issues particular to Oakland and California. Many factors frustrate Oakland's mission to "build a Full Service Community District focused on high academic achievement while serving the whole child, eliminating inequity, and providing each child with excellent teachers, every day." While FSCS goals and vision are embedded throughout the district and in school board policies, Oakland faces substantial fiscal, organizational and, political challenges to its operation as a FSCS system.

Fiscal Instability and Deficit

Budget crises have been building for more than twenty years, a consequence of pervasive OUSD fiscal mismanagement and instability. In 2019, an Alameda County grand jury concluded that the district wastes millions of dollars pointing to "lax competitive bidding practices" and poor contract management.[6] The grand jury also concluded that the spring 2019 settlement of the teacher's strike "will certainly add" to OUSD's financial millstone. However, even in light of the newly negotiated pay raises, OUSD teachers' salaries remain the lowest in the Bay Area, a factor associated with high rates of teacher turnover. Sixty-seven percent of teachers responding to the OUSD Retention Survey say that their salary makes them want to leave the district. Teacher churn undercuts district efforts to improve instructional quality through professional development in content areas, pedagogy, or professional collaboration. Furthermore, teacher turnover was highest in schools with a majority black student body (38.3 percent); majority Latinx schools were second-highest in teacher turnover (34.5 percent).[7] Moreover, new teachers—those most in need of professional support—generally teach in the flatlands schools most requiring experienced teachers and high-quality instruction. OUSD schools with predominately black and Latinx student bodies had the highest percentage of teachers in their first five years of teaching.

A House Divided

The district's 2011 strategic plan highlighted the need to bring coherence to central office operations: "We need to organize our central district structures so that the financial operations, human resource efforts, and overall culture of OUSD fosters Full Service Community Schools and thriving students."[8] Although district leaders proposed a number of strategies to change the siloed central office culture, they were unsuccessful. The operations side of the house—finance, human resources, and facilities—remains largely disconnected from the district's FSCS mission and from each other. As one long-time central office leader said, "Ops have always been our Achilles' heel. There's recognition that something is broken between how the business services are aligned to the academic program." Several key staff positions have changed under Superintendent Johnson-Trammell's tenure, and central office leaders hope the new staffing and procedures can foster cross-boundary connections aligned to the mission of a FSCS district.

Political Confrontations

OUSD's goal to "right-size" the district has fueled bitter disagreements and protests that continue to rock the district's political context. District leaders agree with the grand jury that Oakland operates too many schools; across district-run schools, eleven thousand seats sit empty. The proposed *Citywide Plan* aims to close under-enrolled schools, merge others, and expand a few, moves that would affect more than twenty schools and free up resources to invest in school quality.[9] The process of downsizing has proved exceedingly contentious. Community members and some teachers have confronted the board and superintendent in response to the closure or merger of affected schools. Community members' September and October disruption of board meetings prompted the board to bring in extra security.[10] Former OUSD superintendent and three-term board member Gary Yee, who rejoined the OUSD board this school year after an absence of six years, provides important perspective on the current context. He regards "this board work [involving school closures and mergers] as easily the most difficult of my life . . . so much rancor and suspicion has crept into my relationships with the teachers and parents at the schools."[11]

NEXT STEPS FOR OUSD

Under extraordinarily difficult conditions, *Community Schools, Thriving Students* spurred system change at both system and school levels—changes associated with positive outcomes for students and for schools. Moreover, elements of Oakland's FSCS work have been recognized nationally as best practices: the African American Male Achievement program, district CSSS partnership work, restorative justice, and social-emotional learning practices.

Yet OUSD's future as a FSCS district remains uncertain. Academic, health, and behavioral indicators are up, but OUSD's equity gap in achievement remains unclosed. For example, the on the state's standardized tests (SBAC) proficiency rates for OUSD students of color are below state averages and drastic disparities persist between racial groups. While all racial groups have made positive gains on California's SBAC proficiency exams over the past five years, white and Asian students are two to three times more likely to be proficient than are black and Latinx students, especially in ELA and math. These concerning and enduring racial gaps between OUSD students track similar patterns across the state and the nation.[12]

The existing academic equity gap as well as questions about the quality of instruction may suggest a need for a closer connection between FSCS whole-child goals, opportunities, classroom teaching, and student-centered instruction. OUSD's current *Instructional Focus Plan* for 2019–2022 addresses this challenge head on: "Our #1 job is effective instruction . . . While we have made some progress, our work is far from done. Now, we can be even more intentional and more effective about how we allocate our limited resources."[13]

The district's ability to focus on instructional improvement in this difficult fiscal and political context remains an unknown. FSCS site-level work aimed to strengthen integration of whole-child resources and academics. However, while FSCS initiatives raised significant out-of-school resources, OUSD budget cuts and fiscal shortfalls, together with high rates of teacher turnover, squeezed the district's instructional capacity, shortchanged investments in school quality, and eroded morale across the district. While much of OUSD's full-service community schools' primary work was funded largely outside the core education budget through other public funds (e.g., health and mental health, out-of-school time), leveraging partner resources, philanthropy, and private donors, this reality suggests that for OUSD schools to become the "quality schools" envisioned in the strategic plan, more effort and resources are needed. Oakland leaders agree. David Kakishiba, while supportive of the FSCS vision and goals, said "We can and must do a whole lot better" toward improving instructional practice and student learning.

"GETTING TO OUR NORTH STAR"

Superintendent Kyla Johnson-Trammell recognized that in order for OUSD to achieve its North Star vision of all students being prepared for college, community, and career success and its mission of having a quality school in every neighborhood, "We need to make some important shifts in how we operate . . . Our biggest hurdle by far is consistently delivering a high quality education to every student in our district, in a sustainable manner than is within our fiscal means."[14] The Superintendent's three priorities for 2018–2023—organizational resilience, fiscal vitality, and quality community schools—capture that lesson and provide direction for next steps.[15] In her letter announcing the district's 2019–2020 priorities, she acknowledges the challenges and opportunities that lie ahead:

> I know we have work to do before every student across the district reaches their full potential. As an Oakland native, I have seen firsthand the strength of this community and the dedication of our educators. The time is now to turn our good intentions into strong results. Together, we can transform OUSD from a school district showing areas of improvement and pockets of success to one that is known for consistent excellence and equity, transparent and honest communication, and quality schools in every neighborhood.

Chief of Staff Curtiss Sarikey reflects on OUSD's unswerving subscription to the goals embodied in *Community Schools, Thriving*

Students: "We remain committed to the vision of a full-service community school district; it remains our north star." But the work of *Community Schools, Thriving Students* remains unfinished.

The process of system change is a long-term undertaking, at least ten years in the best of circumstances. Districts and schools on their own likely do not have the resources to build and sustain quality FSCSs. Oakland benefited substantially from philanthropy, partnerships, and funding from other government agencies. This array of resources made it possible to sustain the programming in the face of budget crises. Oakland's experience underscores the significance of these non-district supports, and the need for patience and a willingness to stay the course—acceptance that it will take years to see results.

CHAPTER 14

Lessons from Oakland for Community Schools

The almost ten-year operation of Oakland's Full Service Community School initiative and its remarkable stability over that time provide many lessons for the community school field, and most especially for policy makers and practitioners interested in launching a district-led FSCS system. Whether practitioners and policy makers approach a community school initiative in terms of individual schools or as a district-led system change effort, Oakland's experience features the following broad lessons.

AN APPROACH TO EDUCATION, NOT A PROGRAM

Oakland's experience drives home the lesson that a FSCS initiative is not a "program" to be merely adopted. Community schools embody an approach to education for students and their families, one that extends beyond traditional academics to address the needs of the whole child. Community schools are not programs but rather a philosophy that guides the design and implementation of school activities. While all community schools embrace this conception of education, on the ground, community school practices and policies fall along a spectrum of development. Being a community school is not a binary condition (i.e., "either you are or you aren't a community school"). Many schools include components of community school work such as expanded learning, parent engagement, or restorative justice, whether they identify as community schools or not. Community schools aim to integrate and align these multiple programs and stakeholders, considering them part of the school. For instance, Oakland teachers do not always speak of their school as a "full-service community school"; it is just their school and how it operates with children, families, and partners. Indeed, many elements of community schools overlap with those of quality schools more broadly.[1]

Community Schools and Rigorous Instruction Can Be a "Both/And" Choice

In under-resourced urban districts such as Oakland, deliberations about whether or not to introduce a community school approach often prompt the critique that it will drain supports from academics and compromise efforts to enhance instructional rigor. These discussions frequently frame the policy choice in "either/or" terms; based on an assumption that schools can either focus on improving instructional quality or supporting a whole-child, community school approach, but can't do both. Oakland shows how a whole-child approach represents a both/and enterprise, not an either/or option. OUSD's full-service community school system and site-level work aimed to strengthen the interconnectedness between whole-child resources and academics, as a both/and undertaking. Curtiss Sarikey points to the interconnections essential to a whole-child model: "You wouldn't separate cognition from emotion, you wouldn't separate their home from their school, and you wouldn't separate the neighborhood they walk through to get to school. If you understand 'whole child,' then you understand community school. Community school is not just about closing achievement gaps."

DEVELOPING AND SUPPORTING A COMMUNITY SCHOOL

As we heard often from Oakland educators, a community school initiative involves a fundamentally different way of "doing school." Three elements of policy and practice stood out as especially fundamental to an effective FSCS.

Site-Level Autonomy and Decision Making

OUSD intentionally adopted the stance of "top-down support for bottom-up change" as opposed to top-down directives to schools; in other words, as the strategic plan described, a district office "in service of" schools and students. This stance embodied a direct response to educators' distrust of the central office at the end of state receivership and distaste for top-down mandates. More importantly, core assumptions about FSCS implementation and effectiveness required this central office position. As expressed in *Community Schools, Thriving Students*, all FSCSs must be tailored to the needs of their students, families, and neighborhood, and so schools necessarily will differ from one another. A central goal of the 2018–2023 Citywide Plan reflects this lesson: "Increase the opportunities of those closest to the school site to make decisions about improving outcomes for students." The central office role involves supporting that site-level learning, adjustment, and implementation. As one CSM said, "No cookie-cutters here! We're all different in some important ways. One size does not fit all!" While the central office (particularly the CSSS) functions "in service of . . . ", it also oversees the coherence of FSCS implementation across the district at both the delivery and receiving ends and between tactics chosen and core FSCS values. Coherence does not mean tight alignment. Likewise, not all partners fit all schools. Partnerships need to suit the needs and character of partner schools. This "matching" between schools and partners benefits from central office oversight and support; otherwise, partnerships can become ad hoc and vary in quality. Taking on the role of "top-down support for bottom-up change" requires clear, consistent communication between central office and school sites.

Attention to Teachers' Role

Community schools design reflects Maslow's hierarchy of needs—a belief that students' basic physical and mental health needs must be met in order for them to take on higher-order learning activities and to thrive academically. Community schools partner with CBOs and other public agencies to provide health services, expanded time for learning, and countless other opportunities. Community schools engage parents in school decision making and in their own child's education. Serving the whole child with a focus on equity is foundational to community schools' work. At the same time, although ensuring that students' basic needs are met is crucial, it does not necessarily guarantee that they will then thrive academically—learning algebra or US history, for instance. Not only must community school activities be comprehensive and sufficient to address barriers to learning that students living in poverty may experience, but they must also fundamentally ensure that teachers are supported to provide rigorous and culturally responsive instruction. Increasingly, educators and researchers are considering what it means to be a teacher in a community school.[2] This focus on where teachers fit in the community school model and how the community school philosophy and associated supports can create classrooms where all student learn and achieve is another important step for the continuing evolution and strengthening of community schools as a mechanism for equitable access to learning.

Engaged Families Make a Difference

Schools serving low-income families of color typically fall short in parent engagement efforts. Parents have little interest in the usual PTA-type agenda, do not see a consequential role for themselves, and often feel disrespected by administrators and teachers. Oakland deliberately set about changing that school-level reality through mandates that created new parent engagement requirements (mandated School Site Councils; see chapter 12), and through supports: coaching from CSSS/OFSCE staff for site-level educators, educational sessions for parents, and oversight from network superintendents. As a result of this focus and investment in family engagement, parents across the district play an active and significant role in supporting students' learning and school success. Organized parents helped bring millions of dollars into the schools through support for new ballot measures and help shape site budgets to respond to students' highest needs and priorities. Teachers and principals point to parent voice in setting expectations for students' experiences and outcomes at school and the value of their participation in the site-level Cycle of Action discussions about data, what is working well at the school, and what needs to change. OUSD's parent involvement strategies and supports also have changed many teachers' and administrators' minds about parents' goals for students and how they could support students' learning. Parents, teachers, and administrators all point to powerful parent-school partnerships at FSCSs.

BUILDING A COMMUNITY SCHOOL DISTRICT

Oakland shows the value of framing the building of a community school district in terms of system change. Community schools represent responses to structural, systemic problems, most particularly inequitable resources and performance for low-income students. These problems require structural, system solutions, not short-term, programmatic one-off fixes. Further, Oakland's experience highlights the value of starting with the system, not with individual schools dependent on the commitment and tenure of their leaders. Oakland shows how system change at the district level leads to system change at the school level—and to site-level practices that vary by need and neighborhood context but adhere to common district-level design principles. In addition, starting with the system requires strategic, not tactical, thinking about system change. That strategic thinking focuses on what matters to *kids*, not on program elements. It involves backward mapping from purpose to policy and practice—what former Superintendent Tony Smith called the three Ps.

Community schools operating as part of a district community school *system* profit in many ways from this implementation stance. Teachers, principals, and partners report sharing effective practices across sites and collaborating in shared problem solving. Community school managers comment on how other CSMs helped them articulate and approach their new roles (see chapter 11). Focusing on full-service community schools as a system goal—rather than an effort of individual schools—also brings stability in the face of school leadership change since the vision animating school practices reflects the commitment not only of an individual school leader but of the entire system.

An Inclusive, Extensive Planning Process

The planning process Oakland put in place to develop the district's strategic plan proved critical in both the near and long terms. A methodical, inclusive planning process engaged the community, established a common moral purpose, and led to buy-in that has allowed the mission and vision of *Community Schools, Thriving Students* to sustain and deepen. This extensive, nine-month comprehensive, inclusive planning process yielded many positive payoffs. It built deep commitment to the strategic plan within the district and community. It made *Community Schools, Thriving Students* a community-owned plan for system change—not one pushed down from the top or devised by consultants. The planning process spurred important changes in OUSD's culture and expectations around education, in a way that is sometimes lacking from the planning associated with other community school initiatives. As Perry Chen reflected, "Nationally, there's not much 'community' in community schools."

The planning process shaped policy goals and implementation. Because the district asked task force participants to think not only about the question *What do we want for students?* but to also consider implementation issues of *What must change? What do we need to build?* With this direction, planning discussions moved beyond the aspirational to tackle practical "what to do" and "how to do it" concerns. Consequently, actors throughout the district shared common language, vision, and ideas about the plan's rollout priorities as district leaders moved to roll out the *Community Schools, Thriving Students* strategic plan. The broad stakeholder commitment to the strategic plan developed through the 2010–2011 planning process continues today among educators, board members, community partners, and many funders and contributes significantly to its long-term stability in Oakland. An OUSD central office administrator who had been part of the planning process put it this way: "Tony's strategic plan provided a coherent model, enabled us to look at the big picture, weave everything together, and integrate it into the educational setting. [My staff] still uses *Community Schools, Thriving Students* . . . it enables us as staff to really continue to build." Almost a decade after this planning process ended, many educators involved in developing the strategic plan are now district leaders—principals, central office administrators, network superintendents—and so can provide continued support for the FSCS vision. As a network superintendent described it, "The FSCS model is baked into our DNA."

All District Schools Are Community Schools

In a community school district, all schools are community schools, although district support and resources vary by the needs and context of each school. Superintendent Tony Smith's decision that *all* OUSD schools would become community schools—rather than starting out with a few pilots, or involving only a a few schools at a time—flowed from his commitment that OUSD become a FSCS *district.* He drove central office system changes to support a spectrum of schools' transformation. It was not an "opt in or opt out" choice for OUSD schools—*all* schools would carry out elements of a FSCS approach. Although this policy stance was not initially well received by all OUSD school leaders, over time it has changed OUSD's school culture and thinking about "doing school." Smith's commitment to a targeted universalism perspective refined the district's "all means all" stance. Not all students or schools need the same thing; equity means more resources allocated to schools and communities that have the fewest. For instance, the district's approach to allocating FSCS resources, such as having a community school manager, prioritized schools with fewer resources to start with.

Multiple Levers to Promote and Sustain System Change

OUSD demonstrates the importance of using multiple tools to bring about change at central office and school levels: create processes that can change culture, use levers to require or invite change, and change structures to disrupt the *status quo*. Systems change requires all of them—a mix of hard and soft accountability measures and internal and external levers.

Mandates pushed the district and the community to deal with race-based equity issues in ways they previously had not, and to hold themselves to internal accountability standards. "Soft" policies featuring learning opportunities, mentoring, and coaching enabled practitioners and others to enact and endorse the whole-child, wraparound model underlying *Community Schools, Thriving Students*. OUSD's experience demonstrates the need to require action that otherwise would not be forthcoming, coupling mandated changes with supports for normative change in thinking about purpose and practice of school. Oakland's embrace of a FSCS model now is deeply held across the district. OUSD's experience suggests that these normative shifts about "the way we do school," once embedded, likely will endure within schools even in the face of fiscal or operational struggles.

Align the Two Sides of the District House

Accounts of typical district central office procedures often refer to "the two sides of the house": the academic side and the operational functions—finance, business, and human resources. FSCS implementation experiences since 2011 underscore the importance of aligning the two sides of the district house more closely to include operations departments in reform planning, responsibility, and accountability. Failure to do that successfully in Oakland created major problems in central office implementation overall, for site-level implementation, and for the FSCS initiative generally. One long-time OUSD observer reflected that disconnections and lack of capacity in operations departments "could bring down the whole full-service community schools house of cards." A principal noted that the "number-one reason principals leave the district is frustration with ops." As Curtiss Sarikey, Perry Chen, and others advise, the operations side of the central office needs to be as responsible and accountable to the strategic plan as are instructional departments. One Oakland administrator asked rhetorically, "What kind of student outcomes would we have, what type if teacher retention would we have, if our business stuff was just working?"

Strong Partnerships Are Imperative

To conclude that Oakland's experience demonstrates that FSCSs "don't work" to close the achievement equity gap would not be correct. Rather, the FSCS experience does show that improved student outcomes—behavioral and academic—entail a long journey of learning, system change and culture shifts in under-resourced, diverse urban settings such as Oakland. A main lesson is that by themselves, FSCS district resources are and will always be insufficient to support a whole-child approach to education.

Community schools and community school districts rely fundamentally on partnerships for their definition, broad capacity, and stability. As chapter 9 details, *site-level* partnerships enable individual schools to respond to the needs of their students and families. *System-level* partnerships play a substantively different, crucial role in Oakland's *Community Schools, Thriving Students* initiative's longevity and effectiveness. District (system) partners allowed FSCS to develop and grow across OUSD, but even more critically, these partners subsidized the initiative's sustainability through the staffing, resources, and—in many cases—deep connection to local communities that they bring to schools. An OUSD principal called partners the school's "legs"; Oakland leaders refer to their system partners as the initiative's "backbone." Oakland education and community leaders stress the importance of OUSD's long-term partners' support "through thick and thin." Despite the district's economic, social, and political turmoil since *Community Schools, Thriving Students* launched, key partners such as Kaiser-Permanente, La Clínica, Alameda County Public Health Department, East Bay Asian Youth Center, and the YMCA stood with the district and its comprehensive, youth-centered mission.

Significantly, long-term partners' investments evolved not from particular program implementation checklists, but from strategic questions of "How can we help?" "What's needed?" These committed partners understood they were investing in Oakland, in an educational approach, not a program, and that the journey would be a bumpy one given Oakland's realities.

Furthermore, the majority of the partner dollars supporting FSCS are public health and mental health dollars, followed by public out-of-school time funds, raising not 'either/or' questions, but providing opportunities for enlarging schools' reach and influence. Since 2011, around $461 million in public funds have supported FSCS activities (~$300 million for health centers, mental health, and nutrition, and ~$140 million for afterschool), funds that augment the core educational budget.

Community Schools, Thriving Students teaches that it would be impossible to carry out and sustain a FSCS initiative in an urban setting like Oakland absent these dedicated partners. As OUSD's fiscal crises devastated the district's budget and undercut institutional capacity, partners' resources kept the FSCS work going. Partners funded health services, afterschool activities, and restorative justice procedures and contributed to CSM positions, among other FSCS elements. Although the fiscal value of these partner contributions to district efforts has not been tallied, more than one partner commented on the "innovative" and successful work underwritten with their funds—such as AAMA, COST, wellness providers—and grantees' ability to take a risk, try an idea, do something new.

Some criticize Oakland's reliance on philanthropic dollars, outside categorical funds, or private donors to finance core FSCS elements and point to this funding reality as evidence that OUSD has not really bought into community schools: "It has not been institutionalized." As one community leader observed, "I don't see a hard through line [for FSCS] in the core district budget." Long-term community partners generally think about budget realities differently, however. One counseled, "You have to have a realistic perspective. Oakland does not have unlimited funds—they constantly are digging their way out. They are constantly dealing with things beyond their control. You have to be committed for the long haul." Another emphasized "how important it is to a city like Oakland to invest in its youth—they are the pipeline to the future." In "a city like Oakland," partners' steadfast support over the years has spurred the innovations that energize the initiative at both system and site levels as well as the "both/and" investments essential to vibrant community schools. These long-term, youth-focused, and equity-driven relationships present a unique approach to school-community partnerships, and offer a different way of "doing school."

Afterword

by Tony Smith

> *We want to do more than survive.*
>
> —Bettina Love

Bettina Love's proclamation is at the heart of *Community Schools, Thriving Students.* The purpose guiding the work in Oakland is for all students to *thrive*; it has never been to simply endure and survive the oppression and inequity. The questions about what conditions are necessary for thriving to occur and how it can be responsive to the intersectionality of both the individual and the collective aren't answered yet. As Pam King at the Fuller Theological Seminary says, "Thriving is a process. It is change over time." The now nearly ten-year journey of Oakland's systemic full-service community schools effort is certainly a process of change over time.

In this book, you've read about some joyful advances to celebrate for students, as well as some painful setbacks that undermine progress. There is a perpetual power struggle that puts caring people in public conflict about the best possible future for Oakland's children. The first and clearest thing I can say after reading the events chronicled in *The Way We Do School* is that the work is unfinished. Creating a coherent system where the whole child, the whole school, and the whole community thrive is aspirational work. However, if being whole and healthy isn't the goal, then it certainly will not happen— and worse, without explicit efforts to interrupt current patterns of purposeful exclusion, then children will not have opportunities be- cause those opportunities are unfairly kept from them. It seems that the larger purpose of thriving that's in the plan and deep commu- nity engagement in writing it are key aspects that have sustained the effort over time.

I have come to believe that the common good requires *uncom- monly* good public systems and that healthy community requires daily effort. Individuals and communities are susceptible to differ- ent pressures at different moments. Health is not a static state, and the common good is not a "common" experience. We have to cre- ate forms of political, economic, and social networks that may in practice be in conflict with each other across the broader context of a city. Our public schools, when conceived of and operated as com- munity schools, can foster community well-being in ways that al- most no other institution can. While I believe this is true, our school districts sit in complex social ecologies. The Oakland FSCS effort is an expression of our national need to learn how to create healthy prosocial public school systems that are built to enhance, heal, and expand equitable human relationships so that every neighborhood, US postal code, and census tract is made up of thriving communi- ties. We need strong families, strong schools, strong neighborhoods, and strong communities that enhance our entire social fabric. Our public schools are situated in political, economic, and social con- texts that they did not create and that are mostly hostile to the no- tion that everyone truly belongs. Talent is broadly distributed in the US; opportunity is not. The underlying foundational inequity in our communities is framed by federal, state, and local policy that pub- lic schools operate within. School boards and communities have the choice to exacerbate or interrupt those systems of privilege and op- pression. There is no neutral position. As detailed in the research reported in these pages, the community school approach in Oakland is an important strategy to pursue as a means of fostering thriving in diverse settings and is a potential mechanism for transforming the broader civic landscape as well.

A public school system can interrupt the political practice of *opportunity hoarding*—the practice of using policy to restrict access to public assets (such as parks, housing infrastructure, employment opportunities, transportation) by explicitly distributing resources where they have been stripped away through laws and policies enacted by other political agencies. City planning and zoning organize the neighborhoods surrounding our schools. Too often, the response of the public school system is to simply mirror the surrounding inequity. Making that choice reinforces structural inequity and harms communities. The FSCS attempts in OUSD are an example of becoming an opportunity infrastructure that mitigates the broader structural inequity in the city. Building new partnerships that have health clinics and farmers markets in places where those important basic assets have been stripped away is one example of using a school district to increase community well-being. Deepening partnerships with both for- and nonprofit agencies so that young people have access to mentors who can help prepare them for social, civic, and economic participation is another example of the district using its resources in ways that individual schools are less able to do. Creating the Office of African American Male Achievement is a public system example of how purpose, policy, and practice are always connected. If the purpose isn't to explicitly improve life outcomes for all children, and specifically those who have been least well served, then the policy and practice will ensure that inequity is perpetually reproduced.

Community schools in their best expression are places where all possible assets are intentionally made more available to all students and to everyone in the community. Community schools represent the belief that adults working together across roles, agencies, and personal differences can create places where children thrive. The adults study and seek to understand the lived experience of children and they also understand as adults they have the agency and the power to organize learning experiences that result in students demonstrating academic and social success. Community schools organize themselves around what support all students and families need to thrive. Community school districts organize themselves around what schools need to thrive. The best examples are where public, private, and philanthropic interests of a place cohere to help more members of the community serve children and deeply support those teaching students in classrooms and beyond.

Doing this type of shared work helps forge new ways of knowing, seeing, doing school, and being in community. In-school and out-of-school activities are seen as part of a shared approach to serving the whole child. Partnerships tend to start from a place that says, "That is yours, this is mine, and this is ours" framework. When there is a clear purpose and aspirations are larger than being in a transactional relationship, transformation becomes possible and partnership evolves in what Adrienne Maree Brown calls *emergent ways*. Communicating in ways that honor different lived experience (code switching), empathy, and humility are essential as well as the grace to lead through uncertainty for the benefit of every partner and the whole community. In this way, the Oakland FSCS effort can serve as an example to others wanting to pursue community schools as a mechanism for systemic change. This approach requires a heavy investment in planning, purposeful partnering, and urgent patience. It also requires being committed to struggling through (re)making connections across all levels of relationships in all contexts. Transforming central office design, culture, and orientation from a set of administrative transactions into a dynamic set of interdependent relationships organized to serve every student by becoming what each school needs remains an important aspiration at this point. A systemic approach to FSCS is an ongoing inquiry process that asks people to work beyond their own self-interest. This requires very intense personal and professional work.

One of the hallmarks of the Oakland work is the ongoing commitment to social-emotional learning and development. In the OUSD work, the purpose of social-emotional learning is to foster personal healing and agency in adults and children. Supporting the health and well-being of adults is intended to help create the conditions to deepen care and support for the social and intellectual growth of students. In Oakland, this necessarily includes healing from the impact of racism in ways that foster more authentic belonging. Social and emotional growth is interwoven in every aspect of the FSCS. This practice of radical belonging shows up in the restorative justice practice where some of the most important and raw work of social-emotional learning is happening. Students, families, organizers, and educators came together with a shared purpose to end zero-tolerance discipline policy and replace it with a form of healing and community production that had not ever existed. For anyone reading this who thinks restorative justice is "soft," I encourage you to practice it before you judge it. Take personal responsibility for any harm you cause, listen to those you've harmed, do the work necessary to repair the individual relationship, and then do whatever is required to ensure the broader community is made whole. That's "hard" work. The social-emotional learning system in Oakland is a strand of work that all community schools should consider when they engage their students and families.

Building on that, the family and student engagement work in Oakland is grounded in an approach that grows from focus on knowing the individual, to consideration of the school, and ultimately taking a broader responsibility for the whole system in a way that considers how everyone is connected. Community schools across the country can benefit from this approach. Healthy public schools are the heart of healthy communities when everyone feels and believes they belong. The public school becomes the place where we practice belonging, the place where we learn what belongingness and thriving looks and feels like in relation to people who may be very different. The high-quality full-service community school is always organized around what support students and their families need in order to create their own pathways to success. The strength of the community school strategy is that no pathway is created in isolation. The interdependence and shared purpose of the school is really expressed when all members find meaning and experience success as they build the skills they need to take care of their families. As Angela Glover Blackwell says, "Equity is the superior growth strategy"; or as Eleanor Roosevelt said, "When it's better for everyone, it's better for everyone." This belief is also fundamental to taking a collective systemic approach rather than taking a competitive school-by-school approach.

To close out this afterword, I must say that it feels a bit awkward to reflect on a process I was in, and it feels like I'm too present in the account. So many people have carried, led, and worked hard to bring the Oakland FCSC story to life. There is a very long list of people who were there before me and who are still there now who did, and are still doing, extraordinary work to make the FSCS ideas real. I do understand that it was "my" vision. But I also know that the leader is made by those who follow and already want what the leader is helping them achieve. That is to say, that I believe I acted as an organizer of a larger and already present indigenous hope and as a speaker for the deep hurt and structural injustice in Oakland. I did not discover it, nor did I create a way out. I acted as a servant leader, and I share these reflections with humility. I also agree with the reflection someone shared that I came into leadership in OUSD at the right time. The personal purpose that guides me, the life experiences I had before I arrived, and my willingness to keep the focus on students with whom I feel a very real and lived connection to did set me apart from others. My personal set of dispositions and way of being helped us move toward a larger vision of the school district as a coordinating agency for the benefit of the whole city. I believed OUSD could coordinate, align, and leverage resources in service of students and families in ways it never had before. The brilliance, passion, and craving for fair access to opportunity that communities in Oakland have are what made the process for that shift possible. Many people in district and partner roles built a good vehicle to start the process. The energy that made it move then, and keeps it moving now, is in the people. The students and families in Oakland deserve to thrive, and they all deserve the community schools that will support them to do so.

Lessons for Community School Research and Evaluation

Conceptualizing and Measuring Success for Community Schools

Community schools are a complex endeavor that, when done well, dramatically expands the activities of the school in promoting children's well-being, development, and academic achievement, while expanding the relationships between school staff, families, and community-based organizations. Not surprisingly, assessing the implementation and impact of community schools is similarly complex. In this section, we briefly discuss key considerations in evaluating community schools in general, drawing on the research that we conducted in partnership with OUSD, that forms the basis of this book.

To begin, we draw an important distinction between assessing community school implementation and measuring outcomes/impact. Implementation research provides an opportunity to understand the extent to which community schools are operating as envisioned, what is going well, and where there is room for improvement. This process evaluation plays a key role in informing and supporting ongoing improvements in community schools themselves. In order for community schools to lead to expected outcomes for students, they must be implemented well. Community schools represent a dramatic reconfiguration of what schools are, what they do, and who is included in the endeavor. Quality community school implementation does not happen overnight; it takes time for schools to take on new responsibilities, collaborate with partner organizations, develop relationships, clarify roles, and align activities toward common goals. Understanding this evolutionary, developmental nature of community school implementation is fundamental for designing activities to monitor and assess quality and success.

Much of our work with Oakland focused on assessing community school implementation with an eye toward continuous learning and improvement. OUSD's experience both highlights the importance of meaningful indicators and evaluation and underscores the complexity and challenge of evaluation and research focused on FSCSs. Community schools' theory of action aims to develop the whole child by addressing a broad range of barriers to learning for students, engage an expanded set of organizations and adults at school sites, and fundamentally shift school culture and relationships with families and the broader community. At the same time, although most community school activities aim to create the necessary conditions for high-quality teaching and learning, most activities are not directly focused on pedagogy or instruction.

This reality raises important questions about the extent to which indicators of academic achievement are the best or only measure of whether community schools are "working." For example, California's state-level accountability framework necessarily leans on academic indicators such as math and ELA proficiency and provides little data to inform implementation. Other measures, such as the California Healthy Kids Survey, include several school climate indicators (such as caring relationships, high expectations, and school connectedness) yet are not able to provide information on the important qualitative aspects of these school climate and student well-being indicators. OUSD's experience teaches how important these qualitative accounts are to understanding school as experienced by students and families, and to guiding improvement in practices, school contexts, and partner activities.[1]

Finally, community school evaluation may be especially amenable to a research-practice partnership (RPP) approach such as the multi-year collaboration with OUSD that forms the basis for much of this book.[2] RPPs respond to a call for research that explicitly addresses questions relevant to practitioners and decision makers.[3] RPPs are characterized by a long-term mutualistic collaboration aimed to produce rigorous research that informs educational practice. Further, our research partnership with OUSD has been informed by the principles of design-based implementation research (DBIR), which aims to bring both the researcher and practitioner into collaborative and iterative cycles of inquiry about policy development and implementation "in ways that make it more likely that practitioners can adapt innovations productively to meet the needs of diverse students; and that durable research-practice partnerships can adapt and sustain innovations that make a difference."[4]

STRATEGIES FOR LEARNING TOGETHER

In many respects, our approach to this RPP has been to let the district's learning goals lead the inquiry, and for us as researchers to listen and make sure that the research is addressing their questions while looking for places to bring in broader knowledge and context from research and to address gaps in existing literature. Throughout this research process, we have engaged several strategies to bolster the partnership and drive our shared research agenda. We describe each below.

Iterative Research Process

During the first year of our partnership, we co-developed a set of research questions regarding program implementation and student outcomes that have guided the work broadly. Each year, we determined the next iteration of the shared research questions to drive the subsequent year's research cycle. These iterations were informed both by learning from our previous research as well as conversations with our partners about their work. In meetings with our district partners, we asked open-ended questions like, *"What are you struggling with or striving for in your work right now?" "What do you hope to be able to say about community schools a year from now?"* or *"What do you still want to know?"* We listened, probed, contributed, and reflected, then came to our next meeting with a draft of several specific research questions. Once again, we discussed together, reflected, and modified before finalizing.

We would meet approximately every few months, sharing updates and discussing current challenges in both the research and practice. These ongoing exchanges helped to create a web of collective contextual knowledge that informed our research questions and learning goals. While we, as researchers, ultimately formed the methodological framework and rationale for the study, OUSD staff contributed important information about *where* to learn about what we needed to know. In each cycle of the research, OUSD staff were deeply involved in the process of site selection for our sample schools.

Completing the research, we met to discuss initial findings before publishing any written reports. These meetings gave us a chance to test out the response from the district: *Did these findings make sense? Were we missing anything? Did anything not "sit right" with district staff?* They also gave district leaders a chance to discuss the findings and their implications for practice and together, and to discuss remaining questions and possible next lines of inquiry.

Capacity Building

From the outset, OUSD's interest in this RPP has been in learning about how the community schools initiative is actually being implemented at school sites, and what difference it makes for teaching and learning. Specifically, our partners voiced a desire to have an improved sense of which pieces of this multifaceted model might matter most, and more broadly if the initiative as a whole is working. While our research has aimed to help shed light on these broad questions, we also intentionally undertook efforts to build capacity along the way. Importantly, the research process provided an opportunity for our district partners, who are necessarily very focused on the requirements of the work itself, to take a step back and reflect, and to do so with the benefit of new information and perspectives.

MUTUALISM

Traditional researchers often feel at a loss as to how their research is being interpreted and utilized by practitioners. While we are cautious in tracing a direct line from our research to changes in practice, we can say that our work and our conversations within the RPP have allowed district staff to reflect on their practice, identify challenges, and hear systematic feedback on how their efforts are going (and perceived) at the site level.

As researchers, we have also benefited tremendously from our partnership with the district. In addition to being privy to the inner workings of an innovative initiative, we have had support gaining access to school sites, facilitated by our district partner's request that this research is a priority. We receive regular updates on policy and program developments in the initiative, and insight in interpreting data.

LESSONS FOR COMMUNITY SCHOOL EVALUATION

Our OUSD research partnership suggests some key lessons about community schools evaluation:

- Community schools are not a program that a school either has or does not have, but rather an approach/philosophy to education with many gradations along a spectrum. Being a quality community school and being a quality school are not two different things (which can make traditional comparison group research a challenge).
- Co-constructing a theory of change with practitioners implementing community schools can build shared understanding of key activities and goals and provide an important

framework for designing implementation and outcome evaluation.

- Implementation research conducted in partnership with practitioners can provide important information to drive continuous improvement of community schools. Absent such partnerships (RPPs), practitioners may not have the time, bandwidth, or data to step back and reflect on these ambitious efforts.
- Given the broad scope of community schools, evaluation requires a range of indicators measuring both process and outcomes. Although schools regularly collect and report on academic outcomes, other indicators relevant to community schools (e.g., family engagement, use of health/mental health services, social-emotional learning) may not be easily available.
- Causal research designs are challenging given the multifaceted (and non-binary) nature of community schools, complicating the notion of treatment and control.
- Community schools evaluation needs to be relevant and accessible to practitioners.

Community schools are not a program but rather an approach/ philosophy to education.

As context for a discussion of how to evaluate community schools, it is important to consider what community schools are and are not. As discussed in chapter 14, FSCS is not a "program," and being a community school is not a clean/binary condition (i.e,, either you are or you aren't a community school). Many schools include components of the FSCS work—such as expanded learning, parent engagement, or restorative justice—whether they are community schools or not. Similarly, although a community school manager is a distinguishing feature of community schools, it may not be a requirement.

Related to the challenge of determining what is and is not a community school, many community schools contain elements of "community school–ness" before becoming a community school, making evaluations of student outcomes before and after community school implementation less than clean. For example, in Oakland many schools took on elements of the community school work well before the beginning of the district-led initiative, making a before-and-after, pre-/post-research design difficult. While these issues make community school evaluation complex, a comprehensive approach including a focus on both process and outcomes can provide important information to drive improvement and maximize the effectiveness of community schools.

A theory of change provides a framework for community schools research and evaluation.

The framework for our research and evaluation activities with OUSD comes from a theory of change that we developed in collaboration with OUSD stakeholders early in the partnership, which we refer to as the district's Full-Service Community School System Strategy Map (SSM). This framework lays out the key activities that we expect community schools to implement, as well as the anticipated effects on student outcomes, and points us to the questions that should be the focus of both process and outcomes evaluation. The SSM lays out a path that is necessarily incremental, as short- and intermediate-term outcomes build necessary conditions for strengthening teaching and learning. The SSM provides a framework for assessing success with a focus on continuous improvement. As such, many of the indicators of short- and medium-term success focus on the extent and quality of implementation of community school activities, whereas long-term indicators of success reflect the impact of these efforts on student development and learning.

Importantly, the systems strategy map takes a tri-level approach: laying out key activities and outcomes at the district, school and student/family levels. The tri-level framework points not only to the importance of community school implementation and outcomes at each of these levels, but also the value of evaluation at each—requiring different empirical strategies to achieve different goals.

For example, evaluation at the district level may focus on district systems/procedures/norms and include interviews with district leaders and review of policies at protocols. School-level evaluations may involve interviews, focus groups, and observations with a range of stakeholders including principals, partners, CSMs, teachers, community partners, and families. Student-level evaluation tends to focus more on analysis of individual-level data and ideally interviews/focus groups with students themselves.

District/System The success of a district-led community school initiative, such as OUSD's, requires a clear vision that is effectively communicated and widely understood. Indicators of success at the district level point to creating the necessary conditions and supports for effective implementation. More specifically, important district activities include providing accessible training and responsive programming and tools for community school leaders and staff. District strategy and decision making should lead to equitable—rather than equal—distribution of resources, taking into account varying school and student needs.

School/Setting At the school level, well-implemented community schools provide culturally responsive services; and principals, teachers, and partners understand their roles and align services to meet student needs. Ideally, this results in seamless integration of efforts, with adults working together to foster a positive school culture and the necessary conditions to support teaching and learning. The range of integrated, well-functioning services means that, in the classroom, teachers are able to focus on instruction, resulting in more and better learning time.

Student/Individual Early indicators of success for students and families in community schools include knowing how to access services and families feeling welcome and having the confidence and support to engage in student learning and school improvement. As a result, students feel valued and engage in school every day; students and families access services and participate in school governance; and families are partners in student success, with the ultimate outcome of improved student social-emotional learning and academic success.

Assessing community school implementation can inform and drive continuous improvement.

Implementation research is crucial for answering important questions about how community schools are working, what is going well, and what is not. Before assessing whether community schools are yielding the desired improvements for students, it is imperative to examine the extent to which implementation is happening as hoped and planned, and where changes can be made along the way. Of course, community schools are constantly evolving and developing, implementation necessarily looks different in newer versus more mature schools, and there is always room for improvement. Thus, our research was designed to support OUSD's ongoing efforts to scale FSCS implementation across the district, as well as improve policies and practices that to help schools reach the initiative's goals.

Community schools evaluation requires a range of indicators measuring both process and outcomes.

Given the multifaceted nature of community school implementation, a range of evaluation measures are needed, some related to process and other outcomes. Process indicators can include, for example, increased access to quality health and mental health services and improved health, social-emotional development, family involvement in school, and school climate, among many others.

An important question for community school implementers to answer for themselves is whether these are sufficient indicators of success in their own right, independent of whether or not they ultimately translate into academic gains. To this point, Joy Dryfoos, one of the long-time pillars of community school research, argues that such outcomes focusing on child health, parent/school relationships, and the like "have value in and of themselves" (irrespective of their connection to academic achievement); yet because community schools are an education reform strategy, long-term measures of success must necessarily focus on learning and academic achievement.[5] These academic indicators should be broader than just test scores and should include measures such as academic growth, attendance/chronic absence, discipline/suspensions, graduation, and more. In addition, a wide range of other outcomes can capture the difference that community schools make for students, schools, and families.

At the same time, given how comprehensive this school reform strategy is, and the scope of change in how schools operate, improvements in student academic outcomes may not come for years in even the highest-functioning community schools. A recent piece on "research-based expectations" for community schools from the National Education Policy Center argues that implementation of complex school reforms takes at least five years to gel, and that focusing on student test scores too soon is unrealistic and possibly harmful/counterproductive.[6] Further, McLaughlin's recent longitudinal research suggests that supportive relationships and programming can result in meaningful long-term effects for young people living in poverty, even if immediate academic gains are not apparent or dramatic.[7]

Finally, it is worth noting that many of the elements that community schools add to a more traditional school model are not explicitly academic in nature. To achieve the ultimate outcomes of academic success, such strategies that focus on removing barriers to learning related to poverty must work in collaboration with teachers who are prepared and supported to deliver high-quality academic content.

Causal research designs are challenging given the multifaceted (and non-binary) nature of community schools.

Beyond determining and measuring appropriate indicators of success, there are methodological challenges/considerations in determining whether community schools, as implemented, result in or cause desired outcomes. As noted above, community schools represent an educational philosophy rather than a program. They contain a multitude of elements that, when well implemented, should lead to a school working with partners in a manner that is more than the sum of its individual parts.

Indeed, the multifaceted nature of community schools—elements of which are necessarily at different stages of development and some of which may also be implemented at traditional ("non-community") schools—makes isolating their impact quite challenging. For example, in the context of a random assignment research design, considered by some to be the most rigorous design for estimating impact, what would it mean to randomly assign a school to being a community school, when you think of all that encompasses? This all points to the need for mixed-method evaluations that track qualitative elements of community school implementation and intermediate process-level indicators, as well as trends in student outcomes. Furthermore, the presence of various components of the community school does not say anything about the quality or coherence of their implementation, which suggests that, in a sense, community schools evaluation may always be formative, at least in part.

Community schools evaluation needs to be relevant and accessible to practitioners.

In our work with OUSD, it was quite clear that district and school staff were busy implementing community schools and often lacked the luxury of time or bandwidth to step back and reflect on what they had accomplished or the data and research to inform changes to improve programming. A research practice partnership focused on improving community school implementation and promoting equity can provide an important resource for practitioners. For example, as described above, one of our first activities together was developing a System Strategy Map, or theory of change, for the district-led community schools work. The SSM provided a guide both for implementation and evaluation. Three years later, we revisited and revised

APPENDIX

the map through a collaborative process including district community schools staff focused on family engagement, student health, expanded learning, and more. This process provided an opportunity to
discuss and align activities and goals based on their subsequent experience as well as learning from our research together. In research
that is conducted in partnership with practitioners and driven by
their questions and priorities, some researchers perceive a tension
between relevance and rigor. Alternatively, as Coburn and Penuel
among others would argue, within a research practice partnership
framework, relevance in fact is rigor.[8]

NOTES

PROLOGUE

1. Oakland Unified School District, *Community Schools, Thriving Students: A Five-Year Strategic Plan*, Summary Report, Version 2.0, June 2011, www .thrivingstudents.org.
2. McLaughlin began interviews with district and community respondents in 2011 and has continued conversations with district and community leaders through 2019. Unless otherwise noted, all quotations derive from these interviews. Since 2011, she has attended FSCS-related gatherings (such as meetings of community partners) and collected relevant record data and articles about OUSD performance and student outcomes as well as fiscal, staffing, and administrative challenges.
3. This research/practice partnership focused on school-level implementation of FSCS, and involved a small group of district staff in the Community Schools and Student Services (CSSS) department. The CSSS provides the majority of district-offered student support services, including after-school learning, family and community engagement, school-based health clinics, restorative justice, and other health and behavioral health services. The Gardner Center's interdisciplinary team included quantitative and qualitative researchers, community engagement specialists, a project facilitator, and policy/data analysts.

INTRODUCTION

1. R. Rothstein, *Class and Schools: Using Social, Economic, and Educational Reform to Close the Black-White Achievement Gap* (Washington, DC: Economic Policy Institute, 2004); K.L. Alexander, D.R. Entwisle, and L.S. Olson, "Lasting Consequences of the Summer Learning Gap," *American Sociological Review* 72 (2007); 167–180; S. Reardon, "The Widening Academic Achievement Gap Between the Rich and the Poor: New Evidence and Possible Explanations," in *Whither Opportunity? Rising Inequality, Schools, and Children's Life Chances*, ed. G. Duncan and R. Murnane (New York: Russell Sage Foundation, 2011), 91–116.

2. "The 49th Annual PDK Poll of the Public's Attitudes Toward the Public Schools: Academic Achievement Isn't the Only Mission," *Phi Delta Kappan*, August 29, 2017, https://journals.sagepub.com/doi/pdf/10.1177/00317 21717728274.

3. L. Cuban, "Reforming Again, Again, and Again," *Education Researcher* 19 (1990): 3–13.

4. K. Fehrer and J. Leos-Urbel, "'We're One Team': Examining Community School Implementation Strategies in Oakland," *Education Sciences* 6, no. 3 (2016): 26.

5. Coalition of Community Schools, "What Is a Community School: FAQ" (Washington, DC: Coalition of Community Schools, 2019), 1.

6. Quoted in L. Benson, et al., "The Enduring Appeal of Community Schools," *American Educator* 33, no. 2 (2009): 22–47.

7. R. Jacobson et al., "It Takes a Community: Community Schools Provide Opportunities for All," *Phi Delta Kappan*, January 1, 2018, http://www .kappanonline.org/reuben-jacobson-it-takes-community-schools/.

8. M.C. Johanek and J.L. Puckett, *Leonard Covello and the Making of Benjamin Franklin High School: Education as If Citizenship Mattered* (Philadelphia: Temple University Press, 2007); see also Benson et al., "The Enduring Appeal of Community Schools."

9. Benson, et al., "The Enduring Appeal of Community Schools."

10. National Commission on Excellence in Education, *A Nation at Risk: The Imperative for Educational Reform* (Washington, DC: National Commission on Excellence in Education, April 1983), https://www2.ed.gov/pubs/Nat AtRisk/risk.html.

11. CAS leaders collaborated with Ira Harkavy, the Vice President of the University of Pennsylvania, in the 1992 founding of the Netter Center for Community Partnerships at the University of Pennsylvania. This university-assisted community schools initiative brought faculty into West Philadelphia schools to work with teachers and administrators on cur- riculum, instruction, and structuring partnerships.

12. J. Dryfoos and S. Maguire, *Inside Full-Service Community Schools* (Thousand Oaks, CA: Corwin Press, Inc., 2002), 2.

13. J.G. Dryfoos, J. Quinn, and C. Barkin, *Community Schools in Action: Lessons from a Decade of Practice* (New York: Oxford University Press, 2005), vii.

14. J. Dryfoos, *Full-Service Schools: A Revolution in Health and Social Services for Children, Youth, and Families* (San Francisco: Jossey-Bass, 1994). Despite influential backing for full-service community schools, national uptake of the idea was slow. Joy Dryfoos recalls inviting CAS Vice President Peter Moses and Ira Harkavy, the Vice President of University of Pennsylvania

and creator of the Netter Center's university-assisted schools, to present a workshop at the 1998 Memphis meeting of the New American Schools initiative. Dryfoos was stunned when only four of the six hundred attendees interested in school reform showed up for their workshop. Over dinner that night, she, Moses, and Harkavy decided to form a coalition that would reach out to educators and communities. The Coalition for Community Schools was born.

15. Other programs begun in the 1990s also took a broad approach to meeting the needs of poor children and youth but did not work with schools as active partners. For example, the Beacons initiative offers extensive before- and afterschool programs. In 1991, Geoffrey Canada's Harlem Children's Zone was among the first organizations in New York City to open a Beacon Center. HCZ collaborated with a local public school to keep the building open in the evenings and on weekends. Its Countee Cullen Community Center works with children from kindergarten through high school and serves as a national inspiration and model for programs. The San Francisco Beacon Initiative launched in 1996, inspired by CAS approaches to communities and schools collaborating to extend services for youth.

16. Gunnar Myrdal's classic book contrasts "one-factor theories" and "cumulative causation" approaches to addressing consequences of poverty; see G. Myrdal, *An American Dilemma: The Negro Problem and Modern Democracy* (New York: Harper & Bros., 1944).

17. T. Bundy and S. Butrymowicz, "Linking Home and Classroom, Oakland Bets on Community Schools," *The Atlantic*, June 17, 2013; see also J. Rogers, *Community Schools: Lessons from the Past and Present* (Los Angeles: UCLA IDEA, 1998). Few school leaders took a tougher stance on the question of improving disadvantaged students' academic achievement than did Joel Klein, the former chancellor of New York City's public schools. Klein held that skilled teachers were the key to addressing the achievement gap and that "no single impediment to closing the nation's achievement gap looms larger than the culture of excuse" (quoted in D. L. Kirp, "Invisible Students: Bridging the Widest Achievement Gap," in *Changing Places: How Communities Will Improve the Health of Boys of Color*, ed. C. Edley Jr. and J.R. de Velasco [University of California: Berkeley Law, 2010], 67–96, p. 87).

18. T.J. Payzant, "Extended-Service Schools as a District-Wide Strategy," in Dryfoos, Quinn, and Barkin, *Community Schools in Action*, 215–232.

19. See, for instance, J.R. Henig et al., *Putting Collective Impact In Context: A Review of the Literature on Local Cross-Sector Collaboration to Improve Education* (working paper, Department of Education Policy and Social Analysis, Teachers College, Columbia University, New York, 2015).

20. https://www1.nyc.gov/assets/communityschools/downloads/pdf /community-schools-strategic-plan.pdf.

21. Foundations generally have turned away from *district* reform proposals, especially when they involved initiatives as complex and lacking in proto-cols as community schools. Instead, philanthropies interested in urban education reform funded community school pilots in the expectation that district schools would "learn" from these bright-light models.

22. M.J. Blank, A. Melaville, and B.P. Shah, *Making the Difference: Research and Practice in Community Schools* (Washington, DC: Coalition for Community Schools, 2003).

23. Dryfoos and Maguire, *Inside Full-Service Community Schools*.

24. K. Anderson-Moore and C. Emig, "Integrated Student Supports: A Summary of the Evidence Base for Policymakers," White Paper 2014–05 (Washington, DC: Child Trends, 2014).

25. M. Biag and S. Castrechini, *The Links Between Program Participation and Students' Outcomes: The Redwood City Community Schools Project. Issue Brief* (Stanford, CA:Stanford University, John W. Gardner Center for Youth and Their Communities, 2014).

26. L.S. Olson, *A First Look at Community Schools in Baltimore* (Baltimore: Baltimore Education Research Consortium, 2014).

27. H.A. Lawson and K. Briar-Lawson, *Connecting the Dots: Progress Toward the Integration of School Reform, School-Linked Services; Parent Involvement and Community Schools* (Oxford, OH: Miami University, 1997).

28. S.G. Rao, *Tackling Wicked Problems Through Organizational Hybridity: The Example of Community Schools* (New York: New York University) 2013.

29. J.W. Richardson, *The Full-Service Community School Movement: Lessons from the James Adams Community School* (New York: Palgrave Macmillan, 2009).

30. M. Sanders, "Leadership, Partnerships, and Organizational Development: Exploring Components of Effectiveness in Three Full-Service Community Schools, School Effectiveness and School Improvement," *International Journal* for *Research, Policy* and *Practice* 27 (2015): 157–177.

31. A. Maier et al., *Community Schools as an Effective School Improvement Strategy: A Review of the Evidence* (Palo Alto, CA: Learning Policy Institute, 2017), https://learningpolicyinstitute.org/product/community-schools-effective -school-improvement-report.

32. Important exceptions to the limited attention paid community school implementation include M.G. Sanders, "Leadership, Partnerships, and Organizational Development: Exploring Components of Effectiveness in Three Full-Service Community Schools," *School Effectiveness and School Improvement* 27 (2015): 157–177; M.G. Sanders, "Crossing Boundaries: A

Qualitative Exploration of Relational Leadership in Three Full-Service Community Schools," *Teachers College Record* 120, no. 4 (2018): 1–36; Lawson and Briar-Lawson, *Connecting the Dots*; Rao, *Tackling Wicked Problems*: Richardson, *The Full-Service Community School Movement*.

33. http://www.communityschools.org/aboutschools/national_models.aspx.

CHAPTER 1

1. Insight Center for Community Economic Development, 2015, based on self-sufficiency index calculated for Alameda County, http://www.insight cced.org/tools-metrics/self-sufficiency-standard-tool-for-california/.

2. Alameda County Public Health Department, "Life and Death from Unnatural Causes: Health and Social Inequity in Alameda County," August 2008, http://www.acphd.org/media/53628/unnatcs2008.pdf.

3. Oakland residents and educators prefer the terms *black* to *African American* and *Latinx* to *Hispanic* because students and their families come from many diverse regional backgrounds. However, official OUSD reports use *African American* and *Hispanic* in reference to black and brown students' ethnicity.

4. https://data.oaklandnet.com/stories/s/Equity-Overview/vgam-uuia/.

5. Charters schools account for about one-quarter of total enrollment, with 13,791 students attending one of thirty-four district authorized charter schools (Fast Facts, 2018–2019, Oakland Unified School District, 2019).

6. https://dashboards.ousd.org/views/Enrollment/Snapshot?%3Aembed=y&%3AshowShareOptions=true&%3Adisplay_count=no&%3AshowVizHome=no&%3Arender=false#7.

7. Every Student Succeeds Act of 2015, Pub. L. No. 114-95 § 114 Stat. 1177 (2015–2016).

8. California Longitudinal Pupil Achievement Data System (CALPADS), "Enrollment by Ethnicity for 2015–16," 2016, http://dq.cde.ca.gov/data quest/Enrollment/EthnicEnr.aspx?cChoice=DistEnrEth&cYear=2015-16 &cSelect=0161259--Oakland% 20Unified&TheCounty=&cLevel=District &cTopic=Enrollment&myTimeFrame=S&cType=ALL&cGender=B.

9. D.E. Murphy, "Dream Ends for Oakland School Chief as State Takes Over," *New York Times*, June 8, 2003, http://www.nytimes.com/2003/06 /08/us/dream-ends-for-oakland-school-chief-as-state-takes-over.html?_r=0.

10. Smith wrote his undergraduate thesis on the poetry of Emily Dickinson. When asked why he wrote about Emily Dickinson, he explained that he "encountered the book when I was home alone as a young kid. I fell in love with her."

11. L. Olson et al., *The Unfinished Journey: Restructuring Schools in a Diverse Society* (San Francisco: California Tomorrow, 1994), 133.
12. The MSE Collaborative included the All City Council Governing Board, leadership teachers representing Havenscourt and Castlemont campuses, School Board Director Dobbins, the Oakland Youth Commission, Youth Together, Californians for Justice, Asian/Pacific Islander Youth Promoting Advocacy and Leadership, Oakland Kids First!, and OUSD Parent Engagement Specialist. The MSE standards addressed several student engagement issues: the extent to which student leaders demonstrated self-knowledge, ability to lead, ownership of the school and education, ability to represent constituents, and ability to participate in youth-adult decision making.
13. Subsequently, in a special election in 2009, Measure D replaced Measure K and reauthorized funding for the Oakland Fund for Children and Youth for an additional twelve years (2010–2022); it sets aside 3 percent of the city's unrestricted General Fund and requires a three-year strategic plan to guide the allocation of funds.
14. http://www.youthalive.org/about/.
15. https://www.youthuprising.org/about-us/who-we-are/history.
16. 2018 partners include Alameda County Office of Education; Alameda County Behavioral Health Services; Alameda County Board of Supervisors; Alameda County Health Care Services; Alameda County Office of Education; Alameda County Social Services; Alameda County Probation; Alameda County Public Health; Alameda County Workforce Investment Board; Castlemont Renaissance; Castlemont Community Transformation Schools (CCTS); City of Oakland Department of Human Services; Children's Hospital Oakland; City of Oakland Office of Parks & Recreation; City of Oakland Cultural Funding; Clear Channel; Community Enrichment Organization (CEO); East Bay Asian Youth Center (EBAYC); First 5 Alameda County; First Place for Youth; KMEL 106.1; Oakland Fund for Children and Youth; Oakland Housing Authority; Oakland Police Department; Oakland Unified School District; Oakland Unite (Formerly Measure Y); Social Policy Research Associates; Social Solutions; The Bread Project; Urban Strategies Council; Unity Council; Youth Alive; and Youth Employment Partnership (YEP).
17. https://www.youthventuresjpa.org/partners.
18. 1998 US Representative Barbara Lee (D-Oakland) said that "The Oakland Healthy Start program is, without question, a model community health program"; the *Alameda Times Star* reported that "Oakland's infant mortality rate in 1988 was 18 deaths per 1,000 births; in 1994, the rate had

dropped more than 50 percent to 8.1 per 1,000. Oakland's program is so successful that it recently received a 'high-performance' rating'"; cited in "Healthy Start: Alameda County Receives $2.5 Million Grant," *California Healthline Daily Edition*, October 13, 1998, https://californiahealthline.org /morning-breakout/healthy-start-alameda-county-receives-25-million -grant-endstoryhed/.

CHAPTER 2

1. Alameda County Public Health Department, *Life and Death from Unnatural Causes: Health and Social Inequity in Alameda County*, August 2008.

2. From 2000–2005, Chen served as Executive Director of OASES, a community organization that provided social, emotional, health and education services to more than four hundred youth and families who have limited resources. From 2005 through 2011, he worked as a strategy consultant, was project manager for several Bay Area philanthropic and educational organizations, and was well connected to community stakeholders and acutely knowledgeable about the neighborhood, community, and school contexts FSCS aimed to affect.

3. Perry Chen says that, in retrospect, locating support for his position as consultant and then chief of staff in the East Bay Community Foundation was "a really smart thing because it is not part of the bottom line, never taking resources from the district's public budget. It was private philanthropic money—either you do this work or you don't get this money."

4. S.M. Childress, D.P. Doyle, and D.A. Thomas, *Leading for Equity: The Pursuit of Excellence in Montgomery County Public Schools* (Cambridge, MA: Harvard Education Press, 2009), 24.

5. S. Sinek, *Start with Why: How Great Leaders Inspire Everyone to Take Action* (New York: Penguin, 2009); see also J.F. Johnson, Jr., C.L. Uline, and L.G. Perez, *Leadership in America's Best Public Schools* (New York: Routledge, 2017).

6. M. Fullan, *Change Forces: Probing the Depth of Educational Reform* (London: The Falmer Press, 1993), 31.

7. Smith refers to P.T. Hill, C. Campbell and J. Harvey, *It Takes a City: Getting Serious About Urban School Reform* (Washington, DC: The Brookings Institution: 2000).

8. C.N. Stone et al., *Building Civic Capacity: The Politics of Reforming Urban Schools.* (Lawrence, KN: The University Press of Kansas, 2001), 52.

9. Stone et al., *Building Civic Capacity*, 1.

10. M. Fullan and J. Quinn, *Coherence: The Right Drivers in Action for Schools, Districts and Systems* (Thousand Oaks, CA: Corwin Press, 2016), 133.

11. Johnson, Uline, and Perez, *Leadership in American's Best Urban Schools*, 79.

12. P. Chen, "Community Schools Thriving Students: Strategic Work Update,"
    PowerPoint presentation, OUSD Board of Education, December 11, 2011,
    p. 5, www.ousd.org/... /PUBLIC_FINAL_December_11_Board_Retreat
    _ Presentation_-_Post_Rehearsal_(12-10-2010).ppt.
13. FSCS task force membership (type of agency/organization and number of
    representatives): OUSD (14); community-based organizations (11); county
    (5); educational policy/advocacy (4); foundation/educational funder (3);
    city (2); health (2); educational consultant (2); educational collaborative
    (1); community member (1). The East Bay Community Foundation pro-
    vided funds to support the heavy and concrete involvement of some CBOs
    such as the Urban Strategies Council.
14. P. Chen, "Overview of OUSD Strategic Initiatives and Taskforces," Power-
    Point presentation, October 28, 2010, 14.
15. See, for instance: A.S. Bryk et al., *Charting Chicago School Reform: Democratic
    Localism as a Lever for Change* (Boulder, CO: Westview Press, 1998); C.N.
    Stone (ed.), *Changing Urban Education* (Lawrence, KN: University Press of
    Kansas, 1998).
16. T. Payzant, *Urban School Leadership* (San Francisco: Jossey-Bass, 2011),
    181.
17. D. Tyack and L. Cuban, *Tinkering Toward Utopia: A Century of Public School
    Reform* (Cambridge, MA: Harvard University Press, 1995).
18. J.R. Henig et al., *The Color of School Reform: Race, Politics, and the Challenge of
    Urban Education* (Princeton, NJ: Princeton University Press, 1999), 114.
19. J. Dryfoos and S. Maguire, *Inside Full-Service Community Schools* (Thousand
    Oaks, CA: Corwin Press, 2002), 21.
20. Targeted universalism is "an approach that supports the needs of the par-
    ticular while reminding us that we are all part of the same social fabric"
    (john a. powell, "Targeted Universalism: Equity 2.0," PowerPoint presen-
    tation, October 25, 2016, https://haasinstitute.berkeley.edu/targeted
    -universalism-20).
21. J.A. O'Day and M.S. Smith, *Opportunity for All: A Framework for Quality and
    Equality in Education* (Cambridge, MA: Harvard Education Press, 2019).

CHAPTER 3
 1. Oakland Unified School District, *Community Schools, Thriving Students:
    A Five-Year Strategic Plan*, Summary Report, Version 2.0, June 2011, www
    .thrivingstudnts.org, 2–3.
 2. *Community Schools, Thriving Students*, 5.
 3. Smith hears an echo of assassinated OUSD superintendent Marcus
    Foster's approaches and goals in the way the community came together

to support the FSCS initiative and develop a strategic plan: "Dr. Foster was all about regional governance, about community engagement, about creating quality schools that the community owns. He wanted unique student identifiers so he would be able to track who was getting what."

4. http://leginfo.legislature.ca.gov/faces/codes_displayText.xhtml?lawCode =EDC&division=4.&title=2.&part=28.&chapter=6.1.&article=4.5.

5. P.M. Senge, *The Fifth Discipline: The Art and Practice of the Learning Organization* (New York: Doubleday, 1990), 65.

6. Senge, *The Fifth Discipline*, 126.

7. *Community Schools, Thriving Students*, 39.

8. *Community Schools, Thriving Students*, 38.

9. *Community Schools, Thriving Students*, 34.

10. *Community Schools, Thriving Students*, 34.

11. The framework also had roots in Superintendent Smith's early CORE work and the subsequent CORE NCLB waiver status, which required the development of new teacher and leader evaluation systems. (CORE is described in detail in chapter 4.)

12. https://www.ousd.org/domain/3423.

13. Lynda Tredway now is Senior Associate for Leaders for Today and Tomorrow Project, Institute for Educational Leadership.

14. https://www.ousd.org/Page/13679.

CHAPTER 4

1. j.a. powell, "Targeted Universalism: Equity 2.0" Power Point presentation, Haas Institute for a Fair and Inclusive Society, University of California, Berkeley, October 25, 2016, slides 3, 44.

2. See https://www.cde.ca.gov/re/lc/ for elaboration of the LCAP template and instructions for Local Education Agencies' completion of the template.

3. The CORE districts are: Fresno, Garden Grove, Long Beach, Los Angeles, Oakland, Sacramento, San Francisco, and Santa Ana. The organization was founded in 2010, when cooperative efforts to implement new academic standards and improve training for teachers and administrators in Long Beach and Fresno grew to include other large urban school districts. In 2013, this shared focus on innovation, collaboration, and local control helped the CORE districts secure a NCLB waiver from the federal government that sets aside NCLB school identification requirements for receipt of ESSA Title I funds and to use more than just test scores to measure strengths and weaknesses in schools and to identify those in need of improvement. See https://coredistricts.org/ for more information.

4. For information about LCFF goals and strategies, see https://www.cde.ca
.gov/fg/aa/lc/lcffoverview.asp.
5. US Department of Education, letter to A. Smith, September 27, 2012.
6. Letter to Smith.
7. Letter to Smith.
8. Letter to Smith.
9. https://www.ed.gov/news/press-releases/us-department-education
-announces-voluntary-resolution-oakland-unified-school-di.
10. https://www.ousd.org/Page/12804.
11. https://www.ousd.org/Page/495; see also http://kingmakersofoakland
.org/.
12. AAMA initiated a Student Leadership Council (SLC) in September 2014.
Consisting of African American <<AU: Just confirming—You want "African
American to stand here, and your addition below indicates "black" is used
because it came from a different study"?>> males from middle and high
schools across the district, the SLC create a network of African American
male student leaders who support each other at their school sites, serve
as role models for each other as well as other African American males,
and take part in school council assessments of programming for African
American males. It offers annual Man Up! conferences designed for grades
3–12 around intergenerational mentorship and a full day workshop
focused on academic and social living. AAMA annually organizes the nation's largest K–12 academic achievement celebration of African American
students with the OUSD African American Honor roll. Research conducted in 2019 showed that black boys' participation in AAMA's extra
class substantially cut their dropout rate. See https://chalkbeat.org/posts
/us/2019/10/21/oakland-african-american-male-achievement-research/.
13. Oakland Unified School District, Administrative Regulations Business
and Noninstructional Operations, AR 3625, School Governance, https://
boepublic.ousd.org/Policies.aspx.
14. OUSD Network Superintendents: https://www.ousd.org/Page/968.
15. https://www.ousd.org/cms/lib/CA01001176/Centricity/Domain/3466
/FINAL%20-%20QSD%20POLICY%206005%20ADMIN%20REGS%20
02%2010%2015.pdf.
16. SEL standards: https://drive.google.com/file/d/0B2DcKbJpERRRQmYzV0
NqQUU3MFQ0SnVGbzlWNmhldUxENE5R/view.
17. https://www.ousd.org/Page/15473.
18. Oakland Unified School District, Community Schools, Thriving Students:
A Five-Year Strategic Plan, Summary Report, Version 2.0, June 2011, www
.thrivingstudnts.org, 8.

CHAPTER 5

1. Oakland Unified School District, *Community Schools, Thriving Students: A Five-Year Strategic Plan*, Summary Report, Version 2.0, June 2011, www .thrivingstudnts.org, 20.

2. j.a. powell ,"Targeted Universalism: Equity 2.0" Power Point presentation, Haas Institute for a Fair and Inclusive Society, University of California, Berkeley, October 25, 2016.

3. john powell's tree provided a model for OUSD's tree.

4. https://www.ousd.org/Page/14159.

5. https://www.ousd.org/CommunitySchools.

6. J. Dryfoos and S. Maguire, *Inside Full-Service Community Schools* (Thousand Oaks, CA: Corwin Press, 2002), 100.

7. Concern about these ad hoc arrangements and the resulting variability in partnership quality prompted the formation of Oakland Community After School Alliance (OCASA), which negotiated with the school board and OUSD for an end to informal agreements. OCASA had grants to work with the district After School office on certification, program quality standards, and multi-layered agreements with California Department and Oakland Fund for Children and Youth (OCYF).

8. *Community Schools, Thriving Students*, 6.

9. Partnerships deemed key in 2012 played a significant role in defining the partnership process at both central office and school levels. They included: Alternatives in Action; Collaborative for Academic, Social, and Emotional Learning (CASEL); College Board; ConnectED; Kaiser Permanente; La Clínica; Oakland Freedom Schools; Oakland Literacy Coalition; Partners in School Innovation; Urban Strategies Council; and the Oakland Housing Authority.

10. Oakland Unified School District, *The Annual Partnership Process*, Community Partnership Process White Paper, https://www.ousd.org/domain /3242.

11. School contacts and community partner representatives complete separate evaluations for discussion.

12. These conversation guides were built from the OUSD's original Quality Partnership Rubric, which articulated five content areas of quality partnership and provided a sliding developmental scale of "emerging" to "mature." The Quality Partnership Rubric was developed through the district's Partnership task force, composed largely of long-term partner organizations. The Quality Partnership Rubric continues to influence and inform daily practice through the templates and guides.

13. https://ousd.communitypartnerplatform.org/.

14. According to the home page of OFYC:

> The Oakland Fund for Children and Youth was established in 1996, when Oakland voters passed the Kids First! Initiative (Measure K), an amendment to the City Charter, to support direct services to youth under 21 years of age. In a special election in 2009 Measure D replaced Measure K and reauthorized funding for the Oakland Fund for Children and Youth for an additional twelve years (2010–2022). Measure D (formerly known as Measure K) sets-aside 3% of the City's unrestricted General Fund and requires a three-year strategic plan to guide the allocation of funds (https://www.ofcy.org/).

CHAPTER 6

1. Gary Yee, "Responding to Diversity: The Strategies of Seven Oakland School Superintendents 1962–1990" (paper presented to the Mayor's Commission on Education, Oakland, CA, June 23, 1999), 6. For a full account of the long-term effects of OUSD's seven short-tenured superintendents, see G. Yee, "Miracle Workers Wanted: Executive Succession and Organizational Change in an Urban School District" (PhD diss., Stanford University, January 18, 1996).
2. C. Johnson, "Oakland: Tony Smith's Priorities Straight, *San Francisco Chronicle*, April 8, 2013.
3. The seventeen closed programs/schools include:
   2009–2010: BEST and EXCEL closed on McClymonds HS campus; Robeson School of Visual and Performing Arts closed on Fremont High School campus; Tilden Elementary
   2010–2011: YES (Youth Empowerment School) high school
   2011–2012: Lakeview Elementary, Marshall Elementary, Maxwell Park Elementary, Santa Fe Elementary, Far West Alternative High School, Barack Obama Alternative Middle School, Lazear (closed as district school while under district decision to close); three alternative high schools closed on Fremont campus, becoming one; three alternative high schools closed on Castlemont High School campus, becoming one; and three schools converted to charter (ASCEND and Learning Without Limits).
4. To learn more about Occupy Oakland, see https://ipfs.io/ipfs/QmXoy pizjW3WknFiJnKLwHCnL72vedxjQkDDP1mXWo6uco/wiki/Occupy _Oakland.html.
5. See Oakland Unified School District, "Focus 4B.1 Results-Based Budgeting (RBB)," *Community Schools, Thriving Students: A Five-Year Strategic Plan*, Summary Report, Version 2.0, June 2011, www.thrivingstudnts.org, 42.
6. https://www.ousd.org/cms/lib07/CA01001176/Centricity/Domain/3282 /OUSD%20Superintendent%20Job%20Description.pdf.

7. A. Wilson, *Superintendent Entry Plan*, OUSD, July 2014, https://www.ousd
.org/cms/lib07/CA01001176/Centricity/Domain/10/ousd_supe_entry
_plan2014_ENG_FINAL_web.pdf.

8. Wilson, *Superintendent Entry Plan*. In his conversations with students in
the fall of 2014 about how school was going, Wilson learned that the kids
loved the new electives OUSD had introduced to high schools, but that
huge capacity issues crippled them. There were no cameras in the photog-
raphy class, no books in AP government. Kids also mentioned rats in the
schools and expired food in the lunchroom. Superintendent Wilson was
determined to put forth a plan that focused on quality schools.

9. Oakland Unified School District, *Pathway to Excellence*, 2015–2020: *Every
Student Thrives!*, November 2014.

10. A. Wilson, "Stress-Resilient Schools and Communities," YouTube video,
posted May 14, 2016, www.youtube.com/watch?v=LywQ7mBwmNQ.
Antwan Wilson's term in Oakland was bumpy from the start. Wilson
brought nine Denver educators with him and created new OUSD positions for them, at higher pay. Existing OUSD staff came to call them "the
Denver mafia." As he did in Denver, Superintendent Wilson focused his
attention on the district's worst-performing high schools and moved to
"reconstitute" them. He acted to integrate charters more closely with the
OUSD system and proposed using a common enrollment application parents could use for both public and charter schools. Although this strategy
could keep more students in traditional schools—since charters could not
pick them off as they could under the existing options strategy—Wilson's
proposals caused an uproar among teachers, parents, and community
members. African American parents voiced particular anger at Wilson's
"school improvement" proposals as further segregating African American
students.

11. Antwan Wilson, *Superintendent Work Plan: Year-End Report*, prepared for the
Oakland Board of Education, Oakland Unified School District, May 21,
2015.

12. Wilson, *Superintendent Work Plan*, 4.

13. K.A. Epstein, "Former OUSD Supt. Antwan Wilson Overspent Budget for
Administrators as Much as 100 Percent," *Telling Stories & Taking Pictures*
(blog), November 2, 2017, https://blog.oaklandxings.com/2017/11/former
-ousd-supt-antwan-wilson-overspent-budget-administrators-much-100
-percent/.

14. Oakland Unified School District, *Community of Schools: A Citywide Plan*,
2018–2023, 3.

15. OUSD Board of Education, BP 6006, "Quality School Development:
Community of Schools" June 27, 2018, https://www.ousd.org/cms/lib

/CA01001176/Centricity/Domain/3930/BP%206006%20-%20Quality%20
School%20Development%20Community%20of%20Schools.pdf.
16. *Community of Schools*, 4.
17. Oakland Unified School District, "Toward a Citywide Map," in *Community of Schools: A Citywide Plan*, November 14, 2018.
18. "Toward a Citywide Map."

CHAPTER 7

1. Because our research promised anonymity and confidentiality to subject participants, we are not able to call out (or profile) the specific schools involved in the study. Using these case studies allows us to paint a picture of what community school implementation can look like in three distinct contexts. (See https://www.ousd.org/Page/14029 for complete case studies.)
2. http://www.communityschools.org/the_coalition_for_community_schools_announces_the_2018_leadership_award_winners_/.
3. CASchoolDashboard.org, accessed 8/27/2019.
4. CASchoolDashboard.org.
5. With the "house" system, ninth-grade students take two core classes with students from within their house, guaranteeing that they have at least two classes with the same cohort. Teachers within each house have the same preparation period and meet once a week as a team to discuss lessons, plan common activities, identify struggling students, and strategize together about how best to support them.

CHAPTER 8

1. There are some strengths and challenges with each variation of the CSM role (district, CBO, hybrid). For example, the district-paid CSM might have clearer lines of communication/accountability with the district, but CBO managers might come in with their own organizational resources (e.g., Boys & Girls Club/United Way money).
2. For a more thorough discussion of measuring FSCS success, see chapter 13 and appendix Lessons for Community School Research and Evaluation.
3. These strategies also reflect FSCS elements incubated in the initial strategic planning process—for example, bringing families and the community into the school, cultivating a new kind of principal leadership, and providing high quality integrated student supports.
4. Two other central office entities supported widespread implementation. The network superintendents, who sit in a peer position to the Executive Director of CSSS and directly supervise school site principals,

have been essential to working with FSCS site leaders to support FSCS implementation. Network superintendents reflect intimate knowledge of school needs, strengths, and struggle points and can help CSSS staff understand specific schools' instructional goals, dynamics and priorities. For example, when writing the community schools expansion grants, CSSS staff consulted with network superintendents to help identify the best site-level candidates. Network superintendents have also helped create more CSSS staff access to principals—for example, creating time for CSSS departments during principal leadership days at the start of the year. Central office's Research, Assessment, and Data (RAD) office also made important contributions to school-site implementation. Over the past seven years, RAD has dramatically enhanced its data practices to provide ongoing, accessible, and up-to-date reports to FSCS sites that reflect target priority areas. For example, RAD designed a COST intervention tracker to standardize COST data practices across schools and provide rigorous metrics to use in analyzing student outcomes. The office also created a new data dashboard that provides weekly updates on attendance to school site-attendance teams, so schools can immediately target students at risk of chronic absence.

5. All were schoolwide Title I schools. Of the first cohort of schools, the high school reported 55 percent of their more than two thousand students qualified for free and reduced-price lunches; the other schools reported FRPL rates between 93 percent and 98 percent. Latinx students comprised the ethnic majority at two of the schools. All but the comprehensive high school served a significant number of ELLs. Schools in the second (2015–2016) cohort also enrolled students significantly socio-economically disadvantaged—94 percent to 97 percent; the majority identified as Latinx. The findings reported in the subsequent chapters draw from three years of in-depth interviews with staff at each of the focus schools. Additionally, in Spring 2018, Gardner Center conducted a series of focus groups with CSMs and network superintendents, as well as designed and implemented a teacher survey, administered at thirty-five FSCSs. Together, these data provide a robust picture of FSCS implementation and inform the observations of this book.

6. Seventy-two percent of FSCS teachers surveyed reported they use COST to refer students to needed services and supports. While this suggests high utilization, teachers also expressed concern with COST effectiveness. They did not always hear back or see desired "progress" with students, or they found available programs were insufficient for students' needs. Most FSCS teachers refer students for health supports (100 percent), targeted

academic interventions (80 percent), expanded learning programs (78 percent), and attendance support (74 percent).

7. The most common practices included calling families at home to share positive news about their child (100 percent), texting families (94 percent), holding classroom parent meetings (82 percent), looking at data with families (75 percent), and communicating with families about their hopes and dreams for their child (73 percent).

8. K. Fehrer, *Teacher Perception and Experience in OUSD Community Schools* (Stanford, CA: John W. Gardner Center for Youth and Their Communities, 2019).

9. Building teacher knowledge of and empathy around students' life experience has been an explicit focus in the district over the last several years. For example, student leaders facilitate a "day in the life" exercise as part of all new teacher orientations. Some FSCSs organize "community walks" for faculty and staff in the beginning of the year, to ensure that school staff get to spend time in the neighborhood surrounding the school.

CHAPTER 9

1. CDE Code 64001-65001, https://www.cde.ca.gov/fg/aa/co/ssc.asp.

2. Many of these tools are available at: https://www.ousd.org/Page/15637.

CHAPTER 10

1. The CSSS health and wellness team often helps establish these institutional relationships.

2. In fact, schools are increasingly becoming de facto providers of student mental health supports. Currently, 75 percent of students in the US receiving mental health services obtain those services at their schools.

3. In a 2018 Gardner Center teacher survey, nearly all FSCS teachers indicated that they used PBIS; see K. Fehrer, *Teacher Perception and Experience in OUSD Community Schools* (Stanford, CA: John W. Gardner Center for Youth and Their Communities, 2019).

4. OUSD's Voluntary Resolution Plan included a commitment to addressing "disruptive" student behavior through the education system, rather than the disciplinary system, thus limiting removal of students from class for disciplinary reasons.

5. https://www.ousd.org/cms/lib07/CA01001176/Centricity/Domain/134/OUSD-RJ%20Report%20revised%20Final.pdf.

6. The 2018 Gardner Center survey indicated that nearly all teachers used restorative justice techniques.

7. The behavioral health unit also offers professional development at school sites at the request of leadership or teachers. Professional development

occurs on-site with all staff and focuses on brain science, prevention and de-escalation strategies to develop trauma informed classrooms and conditions for learning.

8. Oakland Unified School District, *Community Schools, Thriving Students: A Five-Year Strategic Plan*, Summary Report, Version 2.0, June 2011, www.thrivingstudnts.org, 6.

9. See findings from OUSD report: https://www.ousd.org/cms/lib/CA0 1001176/Centricity/Domain/79/1718OSB_FindingsReport_v2_STC _09282018.pdf.

10. For a more detailed discussion of linked learning pathways as instructional strategy, see any of the following:

https://www.linkedlearning.org/about/linked-learning-in-california /evidence-of-effectiveness/.

http://www.linkedlearning.org/wp-content/uploads/2016/02/Integrated -Student-Supports-within-LL-Pathways_Jorge-Ruiz-de-Velasco.pdf.

http://www.linkedlearning.org/wp-content/uploads/2018/08/SRI-Year -7-Linked-Learning-Evaluation-Report_revised_2018.pdf.

For a discussion of the nexus of linked learning pathways with community school supports, see: J. Ruiz de Velasco, *Defining Integrated Student Supports for Linked Learning Pathways* (Stanford, CA: John W. Gardner Center for Youth and Their Communities, 2016); and J. Ruiz de Velasco, ed., *A Guide to Integrated Student Supports for College and Career Pathways: Lessons from Linked Learning High Schools* (Stanford, CA: John W. Gardner Center for Youth and Their Communities, 2019).

CHAPTER 11

1. One notable exception to this is L. Gomez, "The Community School Coordinator: Connecting Hearts and Mission," in *Community Schools: People and Places Transforming Education and Communities*, ed. J. Ferrara and R. Jacobson (Lanham, MD: Rowman & Littlefield, 2019).

2. This measurement, utilized by the California Department of Education, defines socioeconomically disadvantaged students as those who qualify for free and reduced-price meals or having parents/guardians who did not receive a high school diploma. *English language learner* refers to students who are learning to communicate effectively in English, typically requiring instruction in both the English language and in their academic courses.

3. In a 2017–2018 Gardner Center survey, half of teachers indicated that CMSs helped them in their use of positive discipline practices, family engagement, and connecting students to support services.

4. During the 2019–2020, an unprecedented four CSMs (with instructional backgrounds) transitioned into roles as principals.

CHAPTER 12

1. In OUSD, FSCS staff start from the assumption that families want their students to succeed, and work to provide the information and support needed to get them there. Families' diverse experiences are valued. Family engagement staff work to build parents' capacity to navigate the education system, access resources, and advocate for their child when needed. A large part of the work of family engagement staff is to clarify expectations, make the process transparent, and provide explicit scaffolding and support where needed—especially for parents who come from different cultural contexts or have limited experience with the US school system.

2. A 2014 Annenberg Institute report, *Family Engagement and Education: A Research Scan and Recommendations,* outlines three distinct approaches to family engagement work (http://www.annenberginstitute.org/sites /default/files/FamilyEngagementEducation.pdf). The first, direct service, includes providing direct services to families—for example, afterschool care, medical care, legal assistance, social services, counseling, childcare, or housing assistance—for free or at cost. A second approach includes advocacy. Advocacy groups work on issues that impact families, but while they often work on behalf of low-income constituencies, the advocacy work is typically carried out by professional staff. A third approach includes community organizing. These groups often have a membership and leadership drawn from the community or constituency being represented. Decisions are made by members/leaders, not by paid staff. Grassroots organizing groups provide members with political education and train them in leadership and organizing skills, and use organizing tactics, including collective action, and put pressure on decision makers and public systems where necessary. Community organizing is focused on systemic solutions and demands for equity (http://www.ousdfamilytoolkit.org/wp-content /uploads/2014/09/PR-the-BAR-Facilitators-Guide_Session-1.pdf).

3. Families were active participants in the strategic planning process. Many of OUSD's FSCSs—especially those that emerged from existing small schools—were developed with systematic parent involvement and input.

4. For more on APTT, see https://www.wested.org/wp-content/uploads/2017 /03/services-appt-brochure.pdf.

5. Parent Teacher Home Visit Project is a national model. More info can be found here: http://www.pthvp.org/.

6. https://parenting.nytimes.com/preschooler/preschool-home-visit?fbclid =IwAR2ZMjAdWUySUyzmxRjbt0KtBxAo3Z_pNew5SCmIBnoapFfAn7C STXWEgqU.

7. http://www.ousdfamilytoolkit.org/wp-content/uploads/2014/09/PR-the
   -BAR-Overview.pdf.
8. When combined with other essential supports, parent and community ties
   can have systematic and sustained effects on school improvement. See A.
   Bryk, et al., *Organizing Schools for Improvement: Lessons from Chicago* (Chicago:
   University of Chicago Press, 2010); and A.T. Henderson and N. Berla, *A
   New Generation of Evidence: The Family Is Critical to Student Achievement*
   (Washington, DC: Center for Law and Education, 1995), 14–16.
9. Measure N authorized the district to impose for ten years an annual parcel
   tax of $120 per unit of property. The measure earmarked the tax revenue
   for adding school programs designed to prepare students for colleges and
   real-world jobs and reduced dropout rates; see http://ballotpedia.org
   /Oakland_Unified_School_District_Parcel_Tax,_Measure_N_(November
   _2014).
10. Title I, Part A, of the Every Student Succeeds Act (ESSA), ensures that
    local educational agencies (LEA) provide parents and families of Title I
    students with the information they need to make well-informed choices
    for their children, including more effectively sharing responsibility for
    their child's success and helping their children's schools develop effective
    and successful programs; see https://www.cde.ca.gov/sp/sw/t1/parent
    familyinvolve.asp.
11. California Department of Education, *Family Engagement Toolkit: Continu-
    ous Improvement Through an Equity Lens* (Sacramento, CA: Author, 2017),
    https://www.cde.ca.gov/fg/aa/lc/documents/family-engagement.pdf.
12. Survey specifics include calling families at home to share positive news
    about their child, (100 percent of teachers indicating they did this),
    texting families (94 percent), holding classroom parent meetings (82 per-
    cent), looking at data with families (75 percent), and communicating with
    families about their hopes and dreams for their child (73 percent).
13. Additionally, OFSCE has its own measures for tracking progress, devel-
    oped around Karen Mapp's Dual-Capacity Framework for Family Engage-
    ment; see http://www.sedl.org/pubs/framework/.
14. The 2017–2018 LCAP survey included a 57.5 percent response rate from
    families (12,855 responses) and, at the recommendation of the LCAP
    Parent Student Advisory Committee, included a modified school con-
    nectedness scale. These findings also indicate that 95.1 percent of parent
    respondents felt the school staff treated them with respect; 90.3 percent
    felt the school staff takes their concerns seriously, 89.7 percent felt that
    the school staff welcomed their suggestions, 89.1 percent felt the school

staff responds to their needs in a timely manner, and 91.7 percent felt their child's background is valued at their school (https://www.caschool dashboard.org/reports/01612590000000/2018/conditions-and-climate).

CHAPTER 13

1. K. Fehrer et al., *Becoming a Community School: A Study of Oakland Unified School District Community School Implementation, 2015–2016* (Stanford, CA: John W. Gardner Center for Youth and Their Communities, 2016).
2. See, for instance, N.L. Hair et al., "Association of Child Poverty, Brain Development, and Academic Achievement," *JAMA Pediatrics* 169, no 9 (2015): 822–829. doi:10.1001/jamapediatrics.2015.1475.
3. K. Fehrer et al., *Becoming a Community School*.
4. Unpublished 2019 Gardner Center analysis.
5. CORE calculates growth by comparing students' test scores while taking into account prior test scores and a set of student demographic factors to calculate more accurately a school's impact on student progress.
6. http://www.ktvu.com/news/ktvu-local-news/grand-jury-report-finds -oakland-unified-school-district-is-failing-its-students.
7. *Oakland Equity Indicators: Measuring Change Toward Greater Equity in Oakland*, 2018, p. 60. https://cao-94612.s3.amazonaws.com/documents/2018 -Equity-Indicators-Full-Report.pdf.
8. Oakland Unified School District, *Community Schools, Thriving Students: A Five-Year Strategic Plan*, Summary Report, Version 2.0, June 2011, www .thrivingstudnts.org, 16.
9. OUSD *Community of Schools Citywide Plan, 2018–2023*, https://www.ousd .org/citywideplan.
10. See "Connecting with Kyla," Superintendent's Letter of October 24, 2019, for a detailed account (superintendent@info.ousd.org).
11. https://edsource.org/2019/oakland-unified-moves-forward-with-school -closures-despite-protests/619166.
12. https://www.educate78.org/crunched-sbac-5-year-trends/.
13. Oakland Unified School District, *Instructional Focus Plan, 2019–2022*, June 2019.
14. OUSD *Instructional Focus Plan, 2019–2022*, 4.
15. OUSD *Instructional Focus Plan, 2019–2022*, 10.

CHAPTER 14

1. *From a Nation at Risk to a Nation at Hope* (Aspen Institute commission report, 2018, https://www.aspeninstitute.org/events/national-commission -final-report-release/) makes recommendations for improving education

that align quite closely to elements of quality community schools we have documented in Oakland, without ever mentioning community schools. These recommendations include:

1. Set a clear vision that broadens the definition of student success to prioritize the whole child.
2. Transform learning settings so they are safe and supportive for all young people.
3. Change instruction to teach students social, emotional, and cognitive skills; embed these skills in academics and schoolwide practices.
4. Build adult expertise in child development.
5. Align resources and leverage partners in the community to address the whole child.
6. Forge closer connections between research and practice by shifting the paradigm for how research gets done.

2. J. Daniel, K. Hunter Quartz, and J. Oakes, "Teaching in Community Schools: Creating Conditions for Deeper Learning," *Review of Research in Education* 43, no. 1 (2019): 453–480.

APPENDIX: LESSONS FOR COMMUNITY SCHOOL RESEARCH AND EVALUATION

1. Although this book draws extensively on conversations with district, school, and CBO staff, there is an important gap that should be acknowledged—the lack of student or parent voices from which to learn firsthand about how they experience community schools.
2. Since 2014, Stanford's Gardner Center has partnered with OUSD to support efforts to assess, enhance, and scale its community schools work. Specifically, our work has been conducted in collaboration with a small group of district staff in the Community Schools and Student Services (CSSS) department, with a focus on school-level implementation of FSCS. As chapter 5 describes, the CSSS encompasses the majority of district-offered student support services, including afterschool learning, family and community engagement, school-based health clinics, restorative justice, and other health and behavioral health services. The Gardner Center's interdisciplinary team included quantitative and qualitative researchers, community engagement specialists, a project facilitator, and policy/data analysts. The research included extensive interviews with district leaders, site visits and conversations with a range of school stakeholders, and statistical analysis of longitudinal district data.

   When this partnership began, the FSCS initiative was only three years out and implementation of community schools was still in development. We worked collaboratively with the district to "map" the community schools initiative both to inform our understanding of the initiative's main goals and strategy and to facilitate a dialogue about research objectives and questions. To these ends, we created a System Strategy Map (SSM) for the full-service community schools initiative. Akin to a theory of change, the SSM operationalizes key goals, strategies, and expected outcomes of the initiative at the district, school, and individual-student levels. To kick off the process, we conducted a document review and a half-dozen interviews with key district and community school site staff, followed by a series of conversations with OUSD staff to hone and further refine our understanding. We drafted an initial SSM, which we shared and garnered feedback on. This mapping process yielded a detailed schematic for our partners in planning and communicating the community schools work, as well as a guide to frame our research questions regarding the initiative's implementation and effectiveness.

Next, in consultation with our district partners, we decided to focus initially on a purposive sample representing a range of grade levels, school sizes, and student populations, with relatively developed instantiations of the model where we hypothesized lessons through this research to inform future implementation and scale-up. To inform our site selection, we conducted an initial analysis of administrative data, including trends in chronic absence, suspensions, and student achievement. We met with the district to review these data, and, combining schools with positive trends and the district's anecdotal evidence of strong implementation gleaned from their day-to-day experience with sites, we chose five mature schools for the study. At each site, we interviewed the principal, CSM, two to three partners, and two to three teachers. Our questions focused on how key elements of community schools identified in the SSM were being implemented in practice, key conditions that help or hinder implementation, challenges to the work, and successes.

Upon entering the second full year of the partnership, the community schools initiative was expanding quickly. The district had been awarded two major grants, from a local private foundation, and from the California Department of Education (DOE). As a result of these new resources, six schools became official community schools in spring of 2015, and twelve additional schools during summer 2015. In contrast to the initial cohort of seasoned community school sites, most of the newly designated sites had little or no prior experience with being a FSCS. These new schools presented the opportunity to examine implementation in newer community schools (including several that overlapped from the first year's research).

As OUSD staff considered how to support the newly emerging sites, they sought to learn more about how new community schools were faring in terms of key organizational capacities (coordination, shared leadership, etc.) and how the district could strengthen and bolster these sites' work. We were also interested in capturing (and sharing with the field more broadly) the role of the district in supporting site-level implementation in one of the nation's only FSCS districts. Ultimately, we conducted interviews with the CSM and principal at six of the newly designated FSCSs, in addition to a half-dozen interviews with district staff.

In 2018, our research focused on understanding how mature community schools may build essential supports to strengthen teaching and learning. Drawing from Bryk's (2010) framework of essential school supports, we revisited our sample schools to speak with teachers, principals, CSMs, and families about their experience in elements critical to instruction such as collaborative leadership, school/community ties, teacher professional capacity, and school learning climate (see A.S. Bryk et al., *Organizing Schools for Improvement: Lessons from Chicago* [Chicago: University of Chicago Press, 2010]). Further, we worked with CSSS leaders to revise the initial SSM based on our enhanced understanding of FSCS—especially the role of the district and how stakeholders collaborate to support coherent school change.

Throughout this RPP, we also conducted statistical analysis of existing and available administrative data to complement the qualitative research, including student-level OUSD education data, out-of-school-time (OST) data, and school-level health data to examine trends in outcomes and in-service participation to the extent possible. In this book, we present quantitative analysis of administrative data to describe the population of students served by FSCSs across the district, compared to traditional schools; and trends over time in key student outcomes. We also discuss the complexities of quantitatively measuring the impact of these multifaceted community schools.

3. C.E. Coburn and W. R. Penuel, "Research–Practice Partnerships in Education: Outcomes, Dynamics, and Open Questions," *Educational Researcher* 45, no. 1 (2016): 48–54.

4. B.J. Fishman, et al. "Design-Based Implementation Research: An Emerging Model for Transforming the Relationship of Research and Practice," *National Society for the Study of Education* 112, no 2 (20i3): 136–156.

5. J.G. Dryfoos, *Evaluation of Community Schools: Findings to Date* (Washington, DC: Coalition for Community Schools, Washington, 2000), https://eric.ed.gov/?id=ED450204.

6. J. Daniel, K.G. Welner, and M.R. Valladares, "Research-Based Expectations for Implementation of the Community Schools Initiative in New York City." (Boulder, CO: National Education Policy Center, 2016).

7. M. W. McLaughlin, *You Can't Be What You Can't See: The Power of Opportunity to Change Young Lives* (Cambridge, MA: Harvard Education Press, 2018).

8. Coburn and Penuel. "Research–Practice Partnerships in Education."

ACKNOWLEDGMENTS

The Way We Do School draws on two complementary projects: one, an almost decade-long documentation of the full-service community school initiative's system-level rollout; and two, a five-year research-practice partnership focused on its site-level implementation.

Milbrey McLaughlin's system-level research involved multiple, extended conversations about *Community Schools, Thriving Students* with district and community leaders over the course of several years. These respondents always were accessible, forthcoming, and helpful, freely sharing their views and experiences. Their interest in and support for the project brought critical depth, background, and perspective to this system-level account of *Community Schools, Thriving Students'* evolution, accomplishments, and challenges. Three individuals provided regular assistance and collaboration over the years. Gary Yee, school-board president, interim superintendent, and now again board member, located the full-service community schools initiative in the historical community context and offered insight into board deliberations, local education politics, and the challenges facing education administrators in urban settings such as Oakland. Perry Chen, key to the initiative's planning and early implementation, and later chief of staff to Tony Smith, shared his trove of planning documents, experience with process design, and insights into early operation. Curtiss Sarikey, now chief of staff to Superintendent Kyla Johnson-Trammell and formerly head of the Community Schools and Student Services department, has been an especially invaluable collaborator and substantive adviser since the project's beginning. His ability to simultaneously see "big picture" and smaller site-level details fostered coherent whole-district implementation of the initiative and enabled the book's multilevel, multiphase account. The many talented, dedicated individuals who took part in this research over the years stand as extraordinary urban educators and community leaders. A traditional "Thank you" falls far short as appreciation for their essential contributions to the project, encouragement, and commitment to a better future for Oakland's young people. We thank the Bechtel Foundation for its early support of McLaughlin's research.

Kendra Fehrer and Jacob Leo-Urbel would like to express their gratitude to the many OUSD collaborators whose voices appear throughout the book. We especially appreciate the teachers, principals, community partners, community school managers, and district leaders who made time to share their experiences. We give special appreciation to the community school managers, who were usually the ones charged with facilitating our many interviews, focus groups, and surveys (on top of their already full loads) and once again proved themselves indispensable. Ali Metzler, Andrea Bustamante, Mara Larsen-Fleming, and Curtiss Sarikey of OUSD have truly been partners in shaping the course of this work. We also thank Jean Wing and the RAD team for their exceptional data work.

We thank the many members of the team at the John W. Gardner Center for Youth and Their Communities who contributed to this research over the years, including Amy Gerstein and Jorge Ruiz de Velasco for their big-picture thinking and counsel; Jamila Henderson, Erica Messner, Nicole Tognozzi, and Maureen Carew for their wide-ranging contributions to data collection, analysis, and communication; and Tie Liang and Efrain Brito for their research support.

Lastly, Kendra would like to thank her husband, Jason, and kids, Myles and Ella, who graciously shared their mom's time with this book. Jake thanks his wife, Johanna, and daughters, Talia and Shira, for their support and inspiration. We hope this book contributes to more equitable opportunities for all young people.

ABOUT THE AUTHORS

Milbrey McLaughlin is the David Jacks Professor Emerita of Education and Public Policy at Stanford University and the founding director of the John W. Gardner Center for Youth and Their Communities, an organization that partners with communities and youth-serving agencies to develop leadership, conduct research, and support policies to improve the lives of youth. She also founded and codirected Stanford's Center for Research on the Context of Teaching, an interdisciplinary research center engaged in analysis of how teaching and learning are shaped by teachers' organizational, institutional, and social cultural contexts. Prior to joining Stanford's Graduate School of Education, she was a policy analyst at the RAND Corporation. McLaughlin is the author or coauthor of books, articles, and chapters on education policy issues, contexts for teaching and learning, productive environments for youth, and community-based organizations. She is a fellow of the National Academy of Education and the American Association of Arts and Sciences.

Kendra Fehrer is Senior Research Associate at the John W. Gardner Center for Youth and Their Communities at Stanford. Her research focuses on the intersection of family, community, culture, and policy in the lives of diverse youth. At the Gardner Center, she leads research in the areas of family engagement, community schools, youth development, student/youth services, and early childhood education. Previously, Fehrer lived and worked in Latin America, where she also served as a Fulbright scholar. Fehrer has taught young people from preschool to college-age. She holds a BA and MA in international development and social change from Clark University, and an MA and PhD in anthropology from Brown University.

Jacob Leos-Urbel currently works at Tipping Point Community, a poverty-fighting organization in the San Francisco Bay area. Previously, he was Associate Director at Stanford's John W. Gardner Center for Youth and Their Communities from 2014–2018. His work focuses on understanding and improving programs and policies that promote opportunities and positive outcomes for children, youth, and families. He has published articles in the Journal of Policy Analysis and Management, Economics of Education Review, Youth and Society, and Children Youth and Services Review. Leos-Urbel also has worked as a public policy professor at Claremont Graduate University, Director of Policy Research and Analysis at The After-School Corporation (TASC) in New York City, and school and community development volunteer with the US Peace Corps in Namibia. He holds a BA in sociology from Oberlin College, a master of public affairs from Princeton University, and a PhD in public administration from New York University.

INDEX

AAMA. *See* African American Male
Achievement
academic achievement and growth,
224–225
academic outcomes, 223–224
Academic Parent-Teacher Teams
(APTT), 132, 205
accomplishments
academic achievement and
growth, 224–225
academic outcomes, 223–224
discipline, 223
school and student outcomes
(2011-2018), 220–225
school culture, 223
school sites, 219–220
system-level accomplishments,
218–219
accountability, 72–73
Addams, Jane, 2, 3
African American Male
Achievement (AAMA), ix,
193–194, 218, 228, 240
Oakland Community Organization (OCO), 120–121
Oakland Technical High School
(Tech), 120–121
African American male students,
promoting success for, 69

African American Parent Advisory
Council, 139
afterschool programs, x, 1, 219, 223
community-based organizations
(CBOs), 177
mentors, 178
partnerships, 176–179
After School Programs Office
(ASPO), 176
Alameda County
Health Care Services Agency, 24,
87, 91
Health Pipeline Partnership,
180
Life and Death by Unnatural Causes,
29
Public Health Department,
13–14, 137, 240
Ali, Russlyn, 68
aligned partners, 145
AmeriCorps, 140
Annual Community Partnership
Evaluation, 90
AP. *See* assistant principal
APTT. *See* Academic Parent-
Teacher Teams
ASPO. *See* After School Programs
Office
assistant principal (AP), 184

partnerships (*continued*)
  community school managers
      (CSMs), 84, 91–92,
      188–189
  continuously assessing, 143–144
  core partners, 145
  East Bay Agency for Children
      (EBAYC), 91
  East Bay Asian Youth Center
      (EBAYC), 90
  formalization of arrangements,
      89
  full-service community schools
      (FSCS), 176–179
  La Clinica, 90
  letter of agreement (LOA), 90,
      146–147, 159–163
  memorandum of understanding
      (MOU), 89
  Oakland Fund for Children and
      Youth, 91
  Oakland Housing Authority, 91
  partnership action plan, 157–158
  partnership assessment rubric,
      148–152
  partnership evaluation, 147,
      152–158, 164–167
  relationships, 143
  Roosevelt Middle School, 114
  Safe Passages, 90
  site-level, 239
  specialized partners, 145
  strategic, 137–167
  strong partnerships are impera-
      tive, 239–241
  supportive community partners,
      88
  supports for students, vii
  varying in focus and scope, 89–90
Pathways to Excellence, 101, 103
  social-emotional learning (SEL),
      74

Payzant, Thomas, 5, 40
PBIS. *See* positive behavioral
      interventions and supports
PG&E, 179
Phi Delta Kappa, 1
PLAN. *See* Parent Leadership
      Action Network
positive behavioral interventions
      and supports (PBIS), 172
poverty, youth growing up in, viii
Powell, John, 41, 80
Principal Leadership Framework,
      57–58, 71
principals
  assessing partnerships, 143–144
  communication and coordina-
      tion between central
      office and schools, 80
  evaluation procedure, 57
  family engagement, 207–208
  focusing on instruction, 131
  policies that might negatively af-
      fect their resources, 65–66
  responsibilities and assessing
      their effectiveness, 57
  role in transitioning to full ser-
      vice community schools,
      57
  school site councils (SSCs) infor-
      mation to carry out it's
      role, 70–71
  shifting school culture, 141–142
  value to students of every dollar
      spent, 126
Principal's Advisory, 99
process to change system culture,
      54
  central office, 56–57
  culture of inclusion and buy-in,
      55–56
  large-scale community process,
      55